JUDGES, JUDGING, AND JUDGMENT

In *Judges, Judging, and Judgment*, Chad M. Oldfather offers an accessible, interdisciplinary account of the constraints and pressures on judges in our polarized world. Drawing on law, political science, psychology, and philosophy, Oldfather examines how these constraints have changed over time and the interpretive methodologies that have gained traction in response. The book emphasizes the inescapable need for judges to exercise judgment and highlights the value of selecting judges who possess good judgment and character. The book builds on prior work that emphasizes the importance of judicial character, specifically practical wisdom, and intellectual humility. The work underscores the need to foster a legal culture that values and rewards judges of character. *Judges, Judging, and Judgment* is a valuable resource for academics, students, lawyers, judges, and anyone else interested in the legal system's inner workings.

Chad M. Oldfather is Professor of Law at Marquette University Law School. He has published widely on topics related to courts, judging, and the judicial process; has lectured to audiences of academics, lawyers, and judges; and was awarded the Howard B. Eisenberg Prize by the American Academy of Appellate Lawyers.

Judges, Judging, and Judgment

CHARACTER, WISDOM, AND HUMILITY IN A POLARIZED WORLD

CHAD M. OLDFATHER
Marquette University Law School

CAMBRIDGE
UNIVERSITY PRESS

CAMBRIDGE
UNIVERSITY PRESS

Shaftesbury Road, Cambridge CB2 8EA, United Kingdom

One Liberty Plaza, 20th Floor, New York, NY 10006, USA

477 Williamstown Road, Port Melbourne, VIC 3207, Australia

314–321, 3rd Floor, Plot 3, Splendor Forum, Jasola District Centre, New Delhi – 110025, India

103 Penang Road, #05–06/07, Visioncrest Commercial, Singapore 238467

Cambridge University Press is part of Cambridge University Press & Assessment, a department of the University of Cambridge.

We share the University's mission to contribute to society through the pursuit of education, learning and research at the highest international levels of excellence.

www.cambridge.org
Information on this title: www.cambridge.org/9781009354585

DOI: 10.1017/9781009354622

When citing this work, please include a reference to the DOI 10.1017/9781009354622

First published 2024

A catalogue record for this publication is available from the British Library

Library of Congress Cataloging-in-Publication Data
NAMES: Oldfather, Chad M., author.
TITLE: Judges, judging, and judgment : character, wisdom, and humility in a polarized world / Chad M. Oldfather, Marquette University Law School.
DESCRIPTION: Cambridge, United Kingdom ; New York, NY : Cambridge University Press, 2024. | Includes bibliographical references and index.
IDENTIFIERS: LCCN 2024022012 | ISBN 9781009354585 (hardback) | ISBN 9781009354622 (ebook)
SUBJECTS: LCSH: Judges. | Judicial process. | Judgment.
CLASSIFICATION: LCC K2300 .O43 2024 | DDC 347/.014–dc23/eng/20240527
LC record available at https://lccn.loc.gov/2024022012

ISBN 978-1-009-35458-5 Hardback
ISBN 978-1-009-35461-5 Paperback

To Judge Jane R. Roth

Contents

Acknowledgments

An old quip, which a quick search reveals has been attributed at least to Mark Twain and H. L. Mencken, begins with a question about belief in infant baptism: "Believe in it?," the reply runs. "I've seen it!" In this book, I make arguments in favor of what seem to me to be some out-of-fashion ideas relating to the importance of character and traits including wisdom and intellectual humility. I believe in them. I have also seen them. I've been fortunate over the course of my career to have worked with many lawyers whose judgment I have long admired and sought to emulate. Judge Jane Roth gave me my first real job as one of her law clerks, and I could not have asked for a better initial role model. I realized in the moment that I had it good, and the passage of time and accumulation of perspective have only strengthened that sense. My colleagues in practice, both at what was then Faegre & Benson (now Faegre Drinker Biddle & Reath LLP) and at the Minnesota State Public Defender, showed me what it meant to be a lawyer in a full sense of the word. I carry their examples with me still, and I measure every lawyer and judge I meet against the standards they set.

This book's origin and, in an important sense, my entire career in legal academia both date back to a seminar entitled "The Judicial Process," taught by Judge H. Robert Mayer of the US Court of Appeals for the Federal Circuit, which I took during my last semester of law school. The paper I wrote for that class, about the use of baseball metaphors in judicial opinions, became my first publication. The seminar spurred a long-standing scholarly interest in judicial behavior, processes, and institutions. It also led me to create my own class, entitled "Judging and the Judicial Process," which I first taught over fifteen years ago. This book is a product of that scholarship and the various iterations of that class, and I am grateful for the students who have taken it over the years and who in doing so pushed me to develop and refine my materials and my thought.

Thanks are due to a great many others. Marquette University Law School has provided me with a supportive environment in which to pursue my scholarly interests, and I am grateful to my colleagues there, especially to Dean Joseph Kearney for his consistent encouragement and support. Nathan Ballantyne, Atiba Ellis, Charlie

Geyh, Neil Hamilton, and Brian Tamanaha were kind enough to field questions from me as this project developed, and a great many other colleagues, only some of whom are cited in the pages that follow, have helped shaped my thought over the years. Lisa Andrewski provided excellent research support and feedback on much of the manuscript. My colleagues Bruce Boyden, Christine Chabot, Nadelle Grossman, Nathan Hammons, Alex Lemann, Matt Mitten, Kali Murray, Michael O'Hear, and Jason Reinecke read and provided valuable feedback on portions of the manuscript. Todd Peppers, who was also a student in Judge Mayer's seminar, answered questions, gave feedback, and provided consistent encouragement. I am fortunate to be his friend and occasional collaborator. My wife Lea and my daughters Ada, Audrey, and Laura provided support, encouragement, and inspiration. I love them each deeply and am grateful to share life's journey with them. Our dogs Mango and Retta kept vigilant watch over the neighborhood as I worked and reliably warned me of approaching mail carriers.

Introduction

At the conclusion of their dissenting opinion in *Dobbs* v. *Jackson Women's Health Organization*, in which a majority of their colleagues overruled *Roe* v. *Wade* and concluded that the Constitution does not protect a right to obtain an abortion, Justices Breyer, Sotomayor, and Kagan reflected on stare decisis and the Supreme Court's legitimacy. They looked back to the joint opinion of Justices O'Connor, Kennedy, and Souter in *Planned Parenthood* v. *Casey*, which thirty years prior had preserved the core holding of *Roe* based in large part on respect for precedent. Those justices, the dissenters observed, might not have joined the opinion in *Roe* if they had been on the Court when the issue first arose. Each of them, in other words, would probably have elected not to recognize an abortion right had they been writing on a blank slate. But they were not, and they all understood the potential consequences, for the Court and for the country, of overruling *Roe*. "[T]hey were judges of wisdom. They would not have won any contests for the kind of ideological purity some court watchers want Justices to deliver." What they did, the dissenters continued, was leave the Court, the country, and the rule of law better than when they arrived.

The dissenters thus placed wisdom and ideology in opposition. In doing so, whether intentionally or not, they echoed a characterization of the *Casey* joint opinion offered in its immediate wake. Professor Anthony Kronman called it "an opinion marked by its judicious search for a middle course and wise balancing of principle and precedent. [I]t was judgment, not expertise, that counted ...."[1] Kronman made these remarks in the opening pages of a book entitled *The Lost Lawyer: Failing Ideals of the Legal Profession*, styled as a requiem for a certain conception of the legal profession. That conception was defined by its devotion to what Kronman labeled "the lawyer-statesman ideal" – "the belief that the outstanding lawyer—the one who serves as a model for the rest—is not simply an accomplished technician but a person of prudence or practical wisdom as well."[2] The ideal was in decline,

1 Anthony T. Kronman, *The Lost Lawyer: Failing Ideals of the Legal Profession* (Cambridge: Harvard University Press, 1993) 3.

2 Kronman, 'The Lost Lawyer', 2.

Kronman contended, and he predicted that its demise would have consequences for our nation. Lawyers would continue to lead, but the profession's failure to cultivate the requisite characteristics would have consequences. "Like ripples on a pond, the crisis of values that has overtaken the legal profession in the last twenty-five years must thus in time spread through the whole of our political life with destructive implications for lawyers and nonlawyers alike."[3]

It is difficult to describe Kronman as anything but prescient. For example, Professor Deborah Pearlstein notes just how many of the key players in the alleged misconduct leading to the indictment of former President Donald Trump were members of the bar.[4] So, too, she concedes, were those instrumental in preventing the various schemes from being carried out. But in the conduct of those who encouraged and facilitated Trump, she finds evidence of a professional crisis. Those lawyers, "whose alleged conduct breached a host of rules of professional ethics, in addition to provisions of criminal law—did not emerge from whole cloth. They are the product of a profession that has changed over the past 40 years …." Pearlstein identifies polarization as the primary culprit. Politically minded lawyers begin to self-segregate in law school, where they join different student organizations. They then clerk for different sets of like-minded judges and from there move into practice in firms with established political identities, transitioning into government service when their party has control. Collectively, this delivers "a clear signal to young lawyers: ideological loyalty is a credential, not a disqualification." That credential is increasingly important in another professional context: becoming a judge.

Political polarization is not the only force at work. Ours is a culture oriented toward the tangible and quantifiable. Precisely why this came to be is unclear. It may be a product of deep social and intellectual trends, the need to deal with the massive quantities of information that surround us, or the emergence of sufficient computational power to enable inquiry at a scale not previously imaginable. Perhaps a combination of these factors and more. The manifestations are everywhere – moneyball in sports, six sigma in business, testing in education, the central role of economics in policymaking, and an accompanying devaluation of those intangible, unquantifiable, and often inarticulable components of good judgment in favor of that which can be counted or otherwise easily measured.

We can likewise see the effects when it comes to the judicial system. One dimension of this involves the academic study of courts, which has seen a significant increase in quantitative empirical research. Much of this work relies on a flattened depiction of judicial behavior that assumes ideology as the primary driving force. Economically minded scholars provide models of judicial decision-making that purport to reduce it to a formula. Meanwhile, psychologists have demonstrated that

3 Id., 4.

4 Deborah Pearlstein, 'Why Are So Many of Trump's Alleged Co-Conspirators Lawyers?,' *New York Times*, August 14, 2023.

judges fall prey to motivated reasoning and cognitive biases the same as the rest of us. Make no mistake: this work is valuable. It provides social-scientific backing to claims made decades ago, first by the Legal Realists and later by members of the Critical Legal Studies movement: law is indeterminate (or at least broadly underdeterminate), leaving judges free (or, in stronger versions, with no choice but) to base their decisions on something else. The something else is often understood to be ideology. Again, this has value. As Professors David Graeber and David Wengrow remind us, "One must simplify the world to learn something new about it."[5] But we must also remember that simplification is merely a tool. "The problem comes when, long after the discovery has been made, people continue to simplify."[6]

A second manifestation involves the processes of judging themselves, where a distinct – but, I believe, related – simplification has also taken hold. In the decades since Kronman wrote, scholars and judges have worked to further develop and refine methodologies that, proponents contend, will constrain judicial behavior. The most prominent of these, typically associated with the political right, are textualist approaches to statutory interpretation and originalist approaches to constitutional interpretation. Neither involves the introduction of something new so much as an amplification of the seemingly tangible ingredients of legal decision-making. Advocates justify these methods on both ontological grounds (claiming that the methods simply call for a process that is inherent in law) and pragmatic grounds (claiming that, while not perfect, they constrain judges by providing objective targets for analysis). Critics dispute the ontological claim by pointing to the long history of judicial decision-making undertaken in ways that do not employ these methods and deny the pragmatic claim, characterizing the methods as no less manipulable than any other and therefore as mere cover for the implementation of conservative ideology.

Not surprisingly, these changes have been accompanied by a fraying of the consensus that underlies the professional norms and acculturation that also work to shape judicial behavior. The forces at work are not just intellectual. These shifts have occurred in a world in which the institutional arrangements and procedures that serve to channel judicial behavior have become less powerful. For example, in intermediate appellate courts, these changes have been largely tied to what scholars a few decades ago called "the crisis of volume" – the massive increase in per-judge caseloads that began in 1960 and led to reforms that fundamentally changed the nature of the relationship between judges and their work. Apex courts avoided the deluge by gaining control over their dockets. The US Supreme Court, for example, hears considerably fewer cases per year than it once did. Another change involves delegation. Most appellate judicial opinions – the ones that shape the content of

5 David Graeber and David Wengrow, *The Dawn of Everything: A New History of Humanity* (London: Macmillan Publishers, 2021) 21.

6 Graeber and Wengrow, 'Dawn of Everything', 21.

the law – are drafted by law clerks, who are typically fresh out of law school, rather than the experienced professionals who hold the appointment. Much of the work at the trial court level – where trials have become an infrequent occurrence – has become bureaucratized. In sum, the nature of judges' engagement with their work has shifted alongside changes in the conception of the nature of that work itself. The effect has been the devaluation of wisdom.

Consider, for an example that will serve to illustrate portions of the discussion throughout, *Rucho* v. *Common Cause*, in which the Supreme Court concluded that challenges to election districting maps based on claims of excessive partisan gerrymandering present "political questions" beyond the power of Article III federal courts to entertain. At issue were congressional maps from North Carolina and Maryland, both of which had been engineered to achieve maximum partisan advantage. Chief Justice Roberts's majority opinion was careful to note that the Court was not condoning excessive partisanship in gerrymandering and acknowledged that such gerrymandering can generate "results that reasonably seem unjust," and even "incompatible with democratic principles." Nonetheless, the majority concluded that it is beyond the federal judiciary's mandate to do anything about it. Article III of the Constitution extends the federal judicial power only to "cases" and "controversies," which in turn means that the power extends only to matters "historically viewed as capable of resolution through the judicial process." One criterion for inclusion in that category is that there be "judicially discoverable and manageable standards for resolving" any such claims.

The crux of the majority's reasoning was that, notwithstanding its efforts over several prior cases to do so, the justices had not settled on "clear, manageable, and politically neutral" criteria by which to evaluate partisanship in gerrymandering. The basic problem, in the majority's estimation, is that claims asserting excessive partisan influence "invariably sound in a desire for proportional representation." But, the Court maintained, that can't serve as the baseline. There has always been gerrymandering designed to gain partisan advantage – the practice takes its name from Elbridge Gerry, a signer of the Declaration of Independence, delegate to the Constitutional Convention, and member of the first Congress – and so the question can't be whether the practice is permissible at all. It must therefore be a matter of degree, not "did partisanship play a role?" but rather "did partisanship play too much of a role?" And a notion such as "fairness" provides insufficient guidance, because there are too many conflicting criteria that might bear on the question. Does fairness turn on the number of competitive districts? Or should proportionality be the dominant consideration? Or adherence to "traditional" districting considerations such as existing political boundaries or the protection of incumbents? None is obviously correct, and selecting from or otherwise navigating among them requires resorting to political rather than legal considerations. Even were it possible to do so, the majority continued, it would then be necessary to formulate some sort of yardstick by which to measure when the departure from the baseline becomes excessive. And that is simply not the sort of question the law is equipped to answer.

The Chief Justice's rhetorical tactic is to focus on the trees rather than the forest, to create the appearance of analytical rigor by breaking the problem down into its component parts. "Resolving the claim presented in this case would require us to answer all these subsidiary questions," the gist of it runs, "and look at how difficult and slippery each of them is. Look at how hard it is to weigh these interests against one another. No one could possibly want judges to be the ones doing so." It's a trick he has used before. In *Caperton* v. *Massey*,[7] in which the Court held that the constitutional due process requirement compelled a state-court justice to recuse himself from a case involving an individual who had made a substantial donation to his campaign, the Chief Justice's dissent criticized the majority for failing "to provide clear, workable guidance for future cases." He emphasized the point by listing forty questions ("only a few uncertainties that quickly come to mind") the majority did not address.[8] For Kronman, as we will see, a core aspect of practical wisdom involves mediating among just the sorts of incommensurable considerations at play in these cases. For Roberts, such an exercise of judgment is precisely what courts should avoid.

But the fact that it can be difficult to tell precisely when a line is crossed does not mean that one can never tell that it has been crossed. Justice Kagan's dissent in *Rucho* claims the same with respect to partisanship in gerrymandering. She asks and answers the question as follows: "How much is too much? At the least, any gerrymanders as bad as these." Kagan does not put it this way, but one can imagine the problem as involving a version of the Sorites paradox, which arises in situations involving categories with vague boundaries.[9] A common example involves the seeming impossibility of determining the point at which an accumulation of grains of sand becomes a "heap" or a "pile." No single grain ever seems significant enough to tip the balance, and maintaining a focus at that level can lead one to conclude that the line separating "not heap" from "heap" can never be crossed. But we do not have to know precisely which grain of sand triggered the leap across the conceptual boundary to know, when we stand before a pile of sand, that that is what it is. We need not even believe that asking which grain was "the" grain is a question that

7 556 US 868 (2009).

8 As I have developed elsewhere, it's a difficulty that the Chief Justice recognizes only selectively. Among the more striking examples is his opinion in *National Federation of Independent Businesses* v. *Sebelius*, 567 US 519 (2012), which among other things required the Court to determine whether the Affordable Care Act's expansion of Medicaid involved an unconstitutionally coercive use of Congress's spending power. That, too, involves questions of baselines, the measuring of degree, and the like. But those questions could be left for another day: "It is enough for today that wherever that line may be, this statute is surely beyond it." 567 US at 585. See Chad M. Oldfather and Sydney Star, 'Roberts, Rules, and Rucho,' (2022) 53 *Connecticut Law Review* 705, 726–27.

9 For an overview, see Hyde, Dominic, and Diana Raffman, 'Sorites Paradox', The Stanford Encyclopedia of Philosophy (Summer 2018 Edition), Edward N. Zalta, ed., available at https://plato.stanford.edu/archives/sum2018/entries/sorites-paradox/.

makes sense. Indeed, for a point that Justice Kagan does not make, even someone as skeptical of judicial intervention in the drawing of electoral boundaries as Justice Felix Frankfurter acknowledged that differences of degree are sometimes so great as to become differences in kind.[10] To shift metaphors, the majority is so focused on the trees that it fails to see that the forest is in trouble: "The practices challenged in these cases imperil our system of government."

This book aims to provide a broad survey and synthesis of the developments that have contributed to the trends Kronman identified. I approach judging both in a narrow sense and more broadly as an activity set within a larger social and institutional ecosystem, and seek to identify and assess how changes within that ecosystem have come to affect an activity that so often appears to be, and is analyzed as, the conduct of individuals. The analysis is thoroughly, and I hope responsibly, interdisciplinary. In addition to legal theory, I draw heavily on work done by philosophers, political scientists, and psychologists. While I sometimes necessarily paint with a broad brush, I try not to outrun the evidence, and to qualify my conclusions appropriately.

Doing so is consistent with the other of the book's major thrusts, which is to underscore the centrality of judgment to the enterprise of judging. The developments noted earlier have led to the continuing diminution of judgment's role and perceived significance, and to a considerable degree, its replacement by what are, at least superficially, more algorithmic-seeming methodologies. I believe these trends to be misguided, at least when contrasted with the appropriately formed and directed exercise of good judgment. Recentering the role of judgment in judging entails building on efforts, many of which have been undertaken under the label of "virtue jurisprudence," to identify the necessary characteristics of good judges. It also involves providing an intellectual framework within which to situate that work, including by expressly connecting it to the basic social function that judging is designed to serve. And some of it is simply contributing to, and thereby shifting the framework of, the discussion about judging as part of an effort to generate a salient professional consensus that recognizes the existence and importance of habits of mind that are independent of ideological and methodological commitments.

The book unfolds as follows: Chapter 1 begins with basic questions about the functions and nature of courts, in an effort to set a rough baseline against which to make assessments. It accordingly outlines and unpacks what I label the "standard model" of judging, an intuitively appealing, idealized depiction – involving independent judges applying preexisting legal standards in the context of adversary proceedings that result in the dichotomous declaration of a winner and loser. Reality necessarily falls short of satisfying the model for several reasons. One is that the standard model's components have no settled meaning but are instead the object of contestation. Judicial independence,

10 *Baker* v. *Carr*, 369 US 186, 283–84 (1962) (Frankfurter, J., dissenting).

for example, can mean different things depending on one's view or who or what it is that judges ought to be independent of. Another is that human institutions are rarely capable of living up to theoretical ideals. As the Legal Realists demonstrated (at least in the typical telling of the story), whether because of the limits of language, the limits of foresight, or the fact that even clear legal rules sometimes come in conflict with one another, disputes often arise in which preexisting rules do not, and could not, exist in any moderately strict sense of the idea. Something else must therefore account for the resolution of those disputes. Finally, there is the fact that courts are ultimately functional institutions. They exist not to comply with some idealized model of government but to serve ends that will differ from one historical era to another, from one government to another, and even within a single system. What unites them is that they exist, in the first instance, to resolve disputes. As Professor Martin Shapiro has argued, this means that the one truly universal feature of judicial institutions is what he calls the logic of the triad – two parties with a dispute turn to a third. But, as Shapiro points out, there is an inherent instability because at the moment of decision, the triad collapses into what the loser is apt to perceive as two against one. Resisting this perception is critical. Indeed, Shapiro opines that "[a] substantial portion of the total behavior of courts in all societies can be analyzed in terms of attempts to prevent the triad from breaking down into two against one."[11] Much of the courts' legitimacy depends on fostering an image of being true neutrals.

Chapter 2 builds on a portion of the discussion from Chapter 1 concerning threats to the perception of neutrality. The Realists demonstrated that factors other than law, narrowly conceived, drive judicial decision-making. The Critical Legal Studies movement pushed this point, claiming, in many of its manifestations, that all of law, including judges' decisions, is political. A subset of political scientists developed the attitudinal model of judicial decision-making out of this understanding of law as politics. Empirical work conducted under the banner of that model has, in fact, revealed a correlation between judges' ideology and the ideological valence of their decisions even using highly reductionist measures of ideology. The chapter also surveys refinements of the attitudinal model as well as critiques. Correlation does not mean causation, for one, and it may be that some other mechanism is at work. Nor is it clear that a relationship between politics and decision-making is entirely improper; the law sometimes leaves space for the incorporation of value judgments.

Chapter 3 continues the work of investigating what, other than law (again, narrowly conceived), might produce judges' decisions by considering various psychological phenomena that can distort thought. It first explores work illustrating judges' susceptibility to motivated reasoning, a tendency to interpret available evidence in a way consistent with reaching one's preferred result. Those results might, but need not, be political in nature, and the chapter also explores recent work positing that a

[11] Martin Shapiro, *Courts: A Comparative and Political Analysis* (Chicago: University of Chicago Press, 1981) 2.

desire to maintain the esteem of their salient audiences – often social, professional, and political peers – may provide a source of motivation distinct from ideology. The chapter also surveys research into the influence of heuristics and biases on judicial decision-making. It concludes by considering work that illustrates our difficulty in recognizing our own biases. Simply put, people find it easy to see the effects of bias in other people's judgments and decisions, while at the same time thinking themselves to be entirely free of such influences. In total, the work surveyed in Chapters 2 and 3 provides social scientific support for and adds depth to the Realist claim that nonlegal factors account for a nontrivial portion of judges' decisions.

Chapters 4 and 5 shift the focus to the legal system, whose architecture reveals implicit recognition of both the influences covered in the Chapters 2 and 3 and the resulting need to provide mechanisms to counteract them. Chapter 4 considers features internal to the system, including the adversarial process, the doctrine of precedent, and the practice of justifying decisions via written opinions. Chapter 5 turns to external constraints, including ethical standards, judicial selection processes, and media coverage. Both chapters examine the ways in which the strength of the constraint provided by these mechanisms has eroded over recent decades. In short, wherever the line between proper and improper determinants of judicial decision-making might lie, the forces channeling judges to the proper side of that line no longer appear to have the same force as they once did.

Chapter 6 considers a final source of constraint. Because, as the Realists demonstrated, law cannot be entirely reduced to verbal formulations, much of it exists as a sort of dark matter. Various observers have affixed different labels – situation sense, craft values, professional norms – to describe the notion that legal thinking, and therefore legal decision-making, is driven as much by shared understandings of how things are done as by rule. The effectiveness of these shared understandings naturally depends on their being shared, and here, too, we see weakening. In part, this is a product of changes internal to the profession. The rise of the Federalist Society and, to a lesser degree, the American Constitution Society have helped foster an increasing divide, which largely reflects the high degree of polarization present in society more generally. Other forces are also at work. Ours is a society that is skeptical of tacit knowledge of the sort that forms the law's dark matter. Cost-benefit analysis and economic-based thinking more generally drive policymaking and crowd out consideration of the nonquantifiable. We prefer metrics-driven assessment to reliance on expertise. And this, in the estimation of Iain McGilchrist, is symptomatic of a society that has habituated itself to dealing with information in an isolated, decontextualized way that emphasizes express, linear, and sequential reasoning rather than in a holistic fashion of the sort that facilitates insight and intuitive problem-solving. The majority opinion in *Rucho* exemplifies this sort of thinking.

Chapter 7 focuses on two additional mechanisms for channeling judicial behavior. The first is specialization, which promises to harness expertise to restore some of what has been lost. Though further specialization may be inevitable, as we will see, there are associated costs. The second is the possibility that methodology provides an effective remedy to the erosion of the constraints explored in the Chapters 4–6. Methodologies – devices for getting decision-makers to focus on certain features of a situation while minimizing or disregarding others – are a familiar and useful tool in law. And so the idea seems compelling: if the system's traditional mechanisms no longer provide an appropriate level of constraint, then the solution is to supply judges with a more precise decisional template. Viewed in that light, it is not surprising that the level of interest in methodological frameworks has risen as the forces that have historically provided constraint have receded. The most salient of these are originalism and textualism, both of which serve as responses to the demise of traditional sources of discipline and as efforts to shift the boundaries of permissible legal argumentation. Both also resonate in a general way with the broader social move toward a preference for the tangible and quantifiable by depicting legal reasoning as a fundamentally algorithmic process that aims to extract a fixed and discernable meaning from legal texts, a move most clearly apparent in efforts to use corpus linguistics (the computerized effort to extract the linguistic meaning of terms from a large database) to guide statutory and constitutional interpretation. As noted earlier, proponents defend these approaches on both ontological and pragmatic grounds, sometimes arguing that a proper conception of law requires resorting to such methodologies, and other times suggesting they are appropriate because they best constrain judicial behavior. Both approaches claim relative certainty, objectivity, and the diminishment of the perceived subjectivity inherent in traditional approaches to judging. Yet there are reasons to believe that methodological frameworks cannot deliver on their promises. To tackle first the pragmatic justification, no methodology can constrain a judge consciously motivated to reach a certain result. And it is but a small step from there to the conclusion that methodology will likewise fully constrain the judge unconsciously motivated to reach a result – a conclusion supported by the seemingly opportunistic use of originalism by justices who claim adherence to the approach. Even if we assume an appropriate lack of conscious or unconscious motivation, most judges lack the time, resources, and cognitive bandwidth to faithfully and consistently implement such an approach in cases of even moderate complexity. There will be errors, but they will likely be skewed in one ideological direction. (Hence the general understanding that textualism and originalism are both conservative methodologies.) The ontological justification also falls short. To regard a theoretical ideal as inherent in the workings of a legal system is to fall prey to a form of utopianism. Institutional designers are not primarily interested in theoretical purity or elegance but rather in creating a system that can accommodate all the inconsistent and incommensurable goals and values that a society holds. Zealous methodological commitments can lead judges to regard fidelity to theory as an end in itself, rather than as a tool to accomplish the goals of government. This in turn can lead to a tendency for adherents to invoke the rhetoric of ontological necessity, claiming that their approach is the only proper approach, such that judges with whom they disagree are not merely wrong but that they are acting illegitimately. Among other things, such accusations work to undermine the triadic logic central to the entire endeavor.

The analysis to this point having established that law, even when accompanied by process and methodology, cannot always reliably take us the entire way to the resolution of specific disputes, it then turns back to the person of the judge. Judging inevitably draws upon judgment. It follows that we should seek to have judges with *good* judgment. Chapter 8 explores what that might mean and what we might look for in identifying judges who have that characteristic. The chapter surveys work developing the idea that judicial character matters and emphasizes two characteristics – practical wisdom and intellectual humility – that I contend should be central to a character-based approach. The latter has received comparatively little attention in past treatments, and I draw upon a growing body of work in psychology and philosophy that investigates the concept of intellectual humility and its contribution to thought and decision-making. The chapter concludes by outlining ways in which a renewed emphasis on judicial character might be implemented. A brief conclusion follows.

1

The Standard Model of Judging

This is a book about judging. But to talk about judging is not to talk about a single, uniform activity or concept. The specific functions of the various institutions called courts, and the particular tasks performed by the array of officers called judges, vary widely. The United States Supreme Court plays a considerably different role in our society than does, say, the district court in Faribault County, Minnesota, and the day-to-day lives of the jurists who occupy the bench in the two courts are hardly similar at all. So, too, with judges on the United States Bankruptcy Court, the federal Court of Appeals for Veterans Claims, or the Maryland Orphans Court, each of whom dons their robe with a distinct set of concerns and priorities in mind, and each of whom presides over proceedings governed by largely distinct bodies of law.

Yet these roles are not entirely disconnected. They are all part of the same larger system. Imagine a Faribault County deputy were to conduct a search and seizure in a manner not clearly governed by existing Fourth Amendment law, which in turn led to criminal charges. The defendant in the resulting case could raise a claim of the sort that would conceivably make its way from the courthouse on Main Street in Blue Earth, Minnesota, through the Minnesota state court system, and to the courthouse across from the Capitol on First Street in Washington, DC, in which the Supreme Court sits. Each judge or justice along the way would have a different view of their job, in part because their court serves a different function in the larger system, and in part because each would have a unique understanding of such things as how the law works, how it ought to work, and what the appropriate role of courts and judges in our system of governance is. All of this suggests, as Professor Helen Hershkoff put the point, "that judicial power is not a fixed or natural category, but rather a socially constructed (if also socially constrained) institutional form …."[1] One must be careful about generalization.

Still, it seems inevitable that there should be threads connecting these roles and that by moving away from particulars and toward abstraction we ought to be

[1] Helen Hershkoff, 'State Courts and the "Passive Virtues": Rethinking the Judicial Function,' (2001) 114 *Harvard Law Review* 1833, 1841.

able to identify, in a general way, the functions courts are designed to serve and the role judges are assigned to play. We ought to be able to establish some form of baseline against which to assess courts' functioning and by reference to which to consider modifications. Much of the rhetoric in *Rucho*, in both Roberts's majority and Kagan's dissent, proceeds from the understanding that there are certain tasks that are outside the scope of judicial competence and therefore there are certain problems the nature of which make them not the kind that courts are suited to solve. Courts are among society's tools, the logic runs, and as with any tool, they are best suited for certain uses and not at all suited for others.

To a degree this will be a moving target. The nature of society's needs, the institutional and procedural architecture of courts, and thus the nature of the functions they are designed to serve all undoubtedly change with time and circumstance. Some, however, remain constant. The most basic, surely, is providing a mechanism for the peaceful resolution of disputes. Another involves the making and refinement of the standards by reference to which that happens. These two functions – often referred to as the dispute-resolution and law-declaration functions – are frequently in tension.[2] The best resolution of a given individual dispute could easily conflict with the best rule covering that general type of dispute. "Hard cases make bad law," as the saying has it. This, too, is part of the disagreement in *Rucho*. The majority does not quite say that the best result would be to strike the maps down, but it expresses its clear distaste and disapproval of them. Its concern is with the next case, and the unending stream of cases it foresees after that, most of which would be more difficult and all of which collectively would threaten to undermine the judiciary's institutional legitimacy. The dissent does not share that fear. It believes that this case can be resolved, and that similarly egregious future cases can be resolved, without encouraging challenges to every set of maps. The dynamic arises in more routine situations as well. There are, for example, good reasons to have clear rules against certain conduct – trespassing or driving above a posted speed limit – even if one knows that in many individual cases no harm will come from the violation of these rules, and indeed there may even be compelling reasons to violate them. The values driving law declaration sometimes outweigh those pressing for an ideally just resolution of each dispute.

As the example that opened the chapter suggests, the relative prominence of these functions varies according to a court's place in the larger system. The judge on the Faribault County District Court will focus on resolving the narrow question of whether *this* search and seizure in *this* case violated the Fourth Amendment. The judge's orientation will be almost exclusively retrospective, focused on making the best sense of existing authorities and determining how they apply to the set of facts at hand. The Supreme Court justice's concerns, by contrast, will be primarily

[2] P. S. Atiyah, 'From Principles to Pragmatism: Changes in the Function of the Judicial Process and the Law,' (1980) 65 *Iowa Law Review* 1249.

forward-looking. The resolution of the specific dispute will matter, but it will serve primarily as a vehicle for considering and deciding more general issues. The focus will be less on this case than on this *type* of case. The fundamental point, again, is this: Courts are functional institutions, and each court and judge plays a different part in advancing the larger purposes of the judicial system. Those purposes are often in tension with one another, and they do not remain fixed from one court system or historical era to the next. Generalization is difficult.

Almost always, however, the invocation of judicial power arises in connection with the call to resolve a dispute of some sort, and it seems inevitable that the origin story of the various institutions we call courts is rooted in that basic social need. Human history has undoubtedly featured a wide variety of mechanisms for resolving conflicts, ranging from duels, feuds, and war to reliance on the wisdom of some trusted elder. But violence has obvious costs, and trusted elders work best within the confines of a small community in which the disputants are both more likely to themselves trust, or at least respect the authority of, such a decision-maker. Thus, at some point in our social evolution, presumably at a stage when interactions – and thus conflicts – between strangers became sufficiently common, we developed the notion of the institutional neutral – the court – as a decision-maker. Party A believes that they have been wronged by Party B. They are not members of the same community, except in some relatively broad sense, so there is no elder or other informal authority figure available whose judgment both will respect. The community has prohibited violence and, in its place, provided a forum for the airing of A's grievances. It has staffed that forum with decision-makers who are neutral by design. And the community stands ready to use its collective power to secure a remedy from B if A's grievances turn out to be legitimate.

Providing a peaceful means of dispute resolution, then, is the first and core function of courts, and it entails a certain institutional logic. Professor Martin Shapiro surveyed the literature on courts and extracted from it "an ideal type, or really a prototype, of courts involving (1) an independent judge applying (2) preexisting legal norms after (3) adversary proceedings in order to achieve (4) a dichotomous decision in which one of the parties was assigned the legal right and the other found wrong."[3] As a rough cut, this captures well enough the typical conception of the American judiciary that we might think of it as the "standard model" of adjudication: An independent, reactive judge resolving a dispute framed by the parties and doing so, via what Professor Paul Carrington called "a simple-minded formalism,"[4] by drawing upon identifiable, preexisting legal standards – which is to say, lest the point pass without emphasis, that courts in this model exist primarily to apply rather than to make law.

3 Martin Shapiro, *Courts: A Comparative and Political Analysis* (Chicago: University of Chicago Press, 1981) 1.

4 Paul D. Carrington, 'The Function of the Civil Appeal: A Late-Century View,' (1987) 38 *South Carolina Law Review* 411, 416.

The standard model has a clear intuitive appeal. Party A will be more inclined to resort to the courts, rather than violence or some other means of self-help, if A feels confident that the judge is subject to no influences that might distort consideration of A's claim and that the dispute will be decided according to law that was known (or at least knowable) to both parties at the time of the conduct in issue. It further helps that this will happen via a proceeding in which A has an opportunity to make their case in an effort to persuade the judge and, in some cases, jury that the law and the facts are on their side.

Discussions of the judicial role in the American system often assume this vision of the role as a baseline and more than that tend to give it normative significance. Chief Justice Roberts's opinion in *Rucho* serves as an example. The problem with judicial attempts to resolve claims of partisan gerrymandering, he repeatedly emphasized, is that there are not (and, in his view, cannot be) sufficiently precise standards to generate resolutions. Because it, therefore, would be impossible to have preexisting norms, any decision in any case would appear to be the product of the judges rather than the law. What's more, given the existence of real and perceived connections between the justices and the political actors who appointed and confirmed them, coupled with the inherently partisan nature of disputes involving election maps, it is nearly impossible for the Court or a justice to appear to be independent. The problems presented by partisan gerrymandering are real, as the Chief Justice acknowledged. But, he reasoned, it is beyond the proper role of the judiciary to try to fix them. The intuitive appeal of this conception of the judicial power is such that most of the state supreme courts that have decided cases involving claims of extreme gerrymandering in the wake of *Rucho* have simply assumed that it also describes the power they possess. They have done so despite there being compelling reasons – among them the fundamentally different natures of the governments brought into being by state constitutions and the fact that in many states the justices of the supreme court are elected – not to blithely make that assumption.[5]

Tempting though it may be to accept the standard model as an appropriate archetype, careful consideration reveals that it captures, at best, only a portion of the entire array of courts and the entire range of judicial functions. Courts in the United States do much more than deciding disputes between individuals. Judges preside over bankruptcy proceedings and class actions, oversee the administration of school systems, counsel drug offenders, and generally find themselves involved in just about every aspect of society. Many of these functions fit uneasily, at best, within the standard model. Indeed, Shapiro concludes, "If we examine what we generally call courts across the full range of contemporary and historical societies, the prototype fits almost none of them." Things are more varied, and nuanced, than the standard model suggests.

[5] I explore this point in further detail in Chad M. Oldfather, '*Rucho* in the States: Districting Cases and the Nature of State Judicial Power,' (2023) 1 *Fordham Law Voting Rights & Democracy Forum* 111.

The standard model's components, which the remainder of this chapter will consider in turn, consistently reveal themselves to be "essentially contested concepts" – ideas as to which there are no generally accepted definitions and no available benchmarks by which to conclude that one definition or another is correct. The core of the judicial role is more elusive than first meets the eye, and judges inevitably – and necessarily – have more decisional space in which to operate than the model suggests. Operating within that space inescapably involves the exercise of judgment.

JUDICIAL INDEPENDENCE

That we want independent judges is axiomatic, what we mean by that considerably less so. As Professor Frank Cross put the point, "Few cows are more sacred than judicial independence. Yet the concept of an independent judiciary is more commonly apotheosized than analyzed."[6] Judges certainly do not, and should not, enjoy complete freedom to do whatever they please. A crucial question thus becomes independence from what or from who? Certainly from the parties themselves, but who else? From elected officials? From voters or from the public more generally? Must independence look and function the same in a small community in which everyone knows everyone else as it does in a large metropolitan area? Can judicial independence be the same thing in Delaware or Wyoming as it is in California or New York? Is judicial independence an end in itself? Or does it serve a purpose?

The answer to the last question seems clear. Judicial independence exists to serve a purpose rather than for its own sake. If, as I have suggested, courts are functional institutions, then it follows that the role of judicial independence is to provide courts and judges with the freedom to best serve those functions. Independence is a component in a larger, complex arrangement of governmental institutions, relationships, and processes that collectively serve to mediate and advance the various overlapping and conflicting ends of society. Its primary function is undoubtedly to give judges the space to follow the law (whatever it might mean to do so) rather than the wishes of some other group or audience except, ideally, insofar as those groups or audiences are able to exert pressures that work to push courts toward greater or more consistent adherence to the law. But it can also serve to enable judges to depart from the letter of the law when doing so is necessary to achieve a just outcome. The key point is that, as with the judiciary itself, judicial independence as a concept does not exist for its own sake but rather as a means to an end or, more accurately, a collection of ends. And the identity and nature of those ends might vary from one context to another, and they might at times be in tension if not outright conflict with one another.

6 Frank Cross, 'Judicial Independence,' in Gregory A. Caldeira, R. Daniel Kelemen, and Keith E. Whittington (eds.) *The Oxford Handbook of Law and Politics* (Oxford: Oxford University Press, 2008) 557.

But providing more space to judges involves tradeoffs. More independence not only enables judges to follow the law wherever it leads but also allows the ability for other factors to influence decision-making – things such as ideology, bias, and other improper considerations of the sort that Chapters 2 and 3 will explore. The underlying dynamic is a version of an agency problem.[7] The principal – in this case, society or a subset of it such as the people of a state – wants the agent – its judges – to faithfully carry out the law and to administer justice, and, in general, to do so despite the fact that it will often be in the short-term interest of powerful groups for judges not to do so. That entails giving judges the freedom to discern what the law and justice require but not so much that they are free simply to do as they please. As Professor Stephen Burbank has highlighted, viewing the matter from this perspective makes it apparent that judicial independence and judicial accountability are not "discrete concepts at war with each other" but rather "complementary concepts that can and should be regarded as allies. ... An accountable judiciary without any independence is weak and feeble. An independent judiciary without any accountability is dangerous."[8] Further, Burbank argues, this means that we cannot regard the contours of judicial independence, or the judicial power more generally, as fixed. The judiciary is "one part of a complex governmental apparatus" that changes over time in response to social, intellectual, and other trends and developments. To conclude that the balance of independence and accountability, and the specific mechanisms for maintaining it, were fixed at the moment the judiciary was created is to unwittingly err in one direction or the other, simply because the balance of forces influencing the judiciary will inevitably have shifted over time. It follows that judicial independence cannot be a monolithic concept. State and federal judiciaries, and governmental structures more generally, differ in ways that have implications for the functions of the judiciary as a whole and thus for the role, nature, and characteristics of judicial independence in serving them.

Not surprisingly, then, we see judicial independence operationalized in a range of ways, which vary in both selection procedures and conditions of service. Article III federal judges enjoy the most robust independence, which is assured by life tenure conferred after appointment by the President and confirmation by the Senate, with the only available mechanism for removal being impeachment under the Constitution. Judges on Article I courts, by contrast, generally serve fixed terms and often may be removed pursuant to statutory provisions that reach a greater range of conduct than what's covered by the Constitution. On some Article I courts, there are limits on the number of judges who may be affiliated with a given political party. Selection methods and terms of service in state courts vary widely. Many judges are

7 For a general discussion of agency issues, see Ward Farnsworth, *The Legal Analyst: A Toolkit for Thinking about the Law* (Chicago: University of Chicago Press, 2007) 87.

8 Stephen B. Burbank, 'What Do We Mean by "Judicial Independence"?', (2003) 64 *Ohio State Law Journal* 323, 323–24.

elected; some are appointed. Most serve fixed terms, typically with the possibility of reelection or reappointment, but a few enjoy something approaching the life tenure of federal judges. As we will see in Chapter5, the selection processes for both federal and state judges have changed over time, sometimes in ways that have implications for judicial independence.

These differences in the conditions under which judges serve – which are to a large extent differences in the degree and nature of their independence – undoubtedly affect their behavior as judges. Federal court judges, with their near-complete insulation from political pressure, are often regarded as better protectors of rights than their state court counterparts.[9] For example, studies have suggested that state court judges behave differently when reelection draws near, such as by being less inclined to cast votes that favor criminal defendants.[10] At the same time, elected state court judges may have a legitimate claim to intervene more aggressively in the workings of government since they draw on a base of democratic legitimacy that federal judges do not have. None of these arrangements is better or worse in some absolute manner. Each must be assessed in a functional sense according to standards set by reference to the nature of the power the courts hold, the nature of the power that courts are responsible for checking, and the ultimate aims of government. To paint with a broad brush, a governmental structure with the preservation of liberty as its primary goal would require a different sort of judiciary than one designed primarily to facilitate majority rule or one intended to advance some vision of the common good.[11] The questions cannot be answered in the abstract.

PREEXISTING LEGAL NORMS

There is likewise more to the prototype's second component – preexisting legal norms – than is first apparent. Standing behind it is the rule of law ideal. The rule of law is, of course, most often contrasted with the "rule of men," and it is meant to encapsulate the idea that, in Professor Richard Fallon's formulation, "the law – and its meaning – must be fixed and publicly known in advance of application, so that those applying the law, as much as those to whom it is applied, can be bound by it."[12] The law should apply alike to everyone, with no prohibitions created in an ad hoc or after-the-fact fashion. So stated, however, the rule of law is an *ideal*, and,

9 The classic statement of this position is Burt Neuborne, 'The Myth of Parity,' (1977) 90 *Harvard Law Review* 1105.

10 See, for example, Michael S. Kang and Joanne M. Shepherd, 'Judging Judicial Elections,' (2016) 114 *Michigan Law Review* 929.

11 For examples of these three visions, see, respectively, Rebecca L. Brown, 'Accountability, Liberty, and the Constitution,' (1998) 98 *Columbia Law Review* 531; John Hart Ely, *Democracy and Distrust: A Theory of Judicial Review* (Cambridge: Harvard University Press, 1981); Adrian Vermeule, *Common Good Constitutionalism* (New York: Polity Press, 2022).

12 Richard H. Fallon, Jr., '"The Rule of Law" as a Concept in Constitutional Discourse,' (1997) 97 *Columbia Law Review* 1, 2–3.

as Fallon observes, "It is strongly arguable that no plausible legal system could avoid departing from it in some respects."[13] Any moderately difficult case illustrates the point. The contours of the law are unclear, and the dispute before the court concerns whether this situation falls inside or outside of the boundary. Did the police violate the Fourth Amendment when they conducted this search or not? Is this a statute that regulates commerce, such that Congress had the power to pass it, or not? Did this defendant's conduct in this unique set of circumstances amount to disorderly conduct? There will often be uncertainty at the edges of the law, and someone will have to decide whether some set of facts fell just within or just outside of the boundary. To the losing side the law will not seem to have preexisted the ruling. Some degree of departure from the fully realized ideal is thus inevitable. The question thus arises: What sorts of departures from the ideal we are willing to tolerate and to what extent?

Once one moves away from broad definitions, it becomes clear that the rule of law is another essentially contested concept. The literature here is vast and Fallon's is hardly the final word on the matter, but his analysis effectively illustrates the concepts. As he suggests, some generalization is possible. A nonexhaustive list of the features of a system that facilitates rule-of-law values includes: (1) generality – the rules governing conduct are uniformly applicable and impartially applied to government officials and ordinary citizens alike; (2) publicity – rules can guide conduct only if they are made available to the public; (3) clarity – rules should be understandable in terms of both their substance and their scope; (4) consistency – rules should not contradict one another; (5) congruence – the rules as applied should match the rules as announced; (6) stability – the law should remain consistent so as to enable people to plan and coordinate action over time; and (7) the existence of impartial mechanisms for the enforcement and application of law. Distilled even further, in the ideal rule-of-law world, any of us ought to be able to know in advance, with certainty, whether our conduct will run afoul of the law and further that our conduct will be assessed against rules and through procedures applied consistently and equally to everyone else.

How best to achieve these in an imperfect world is the subject of further disagreement. Fallon suggests that there are four primary versions of the rule-of-law ideal, each based on a distinct understanding of the nature of law and the preferred nature of its implementation. The "historicist ideal type" emphasizes pedigree, based on the premise that lawmaking is an inherently political process that ought to be undertaken by politically accountable actors, such that law consists primarily of rules created in advance by legitimate lawmaking authorities. The primary goal is thus to figure out what rules those authorities created. Originalism as an approach to constitutional interpretation is an example. It regards the meaning of the Constitution to have been fixed at the moment of ratification, such that the

[13] Fallon, 'The Rule of Law', 2–3.

primary task of satisfying the rule of law in that context is to determine and comply with that original meaning. The "formalist ideal type" emphasizes the need for legal standards that have clear edges allowing for easy application and for those who are subject to them to be able to plan their conduct with relative certainty. On this view, legislatures should avoid imprecise language and courts should prioritize deciding cases in a way that remedies any legislative failures to produce the requisite clarity. The more the endeavor can be made to resemble an algorithmic process, the better. The "Legal Process ideal type," as its name suggests, emphasizes process. The concern is not with the pedigree or clarity of rules, but with whether the means by which those rules are created and applied are fair, governed by reason, and appropriately transparent. A citizen may not be able to know in advance whether their conduct falls within the scope of the rules, but they should at least be confident that their position will receive due consideration. Finally, the "substantive ideal type" looks to whether the law satisfies external criteria of morality. On this view, a rule could meet the demands of the other three types and still be fundamentally unjust. The American legal system when it countenanced slavery stands as an example of a system that could be described as satisfying the first three versions of the ideal while failing the fourth. The four versions Fallon identifies are not mutually exclusive. One could, for example, be an originalist who also favors rule-like legal standards, thereby emphasizing the concerns at the heart of the first and second versions, as was the case with Justice Antonin Scalia.[14] Or one could favor a process-based approach that is also bound by substantive limits. To a point, at least, it is a matter of emphasis.

Among the menu of options Fallon provides, the formalist ideal type is the most intuitive and enduring. The popular, superficial conception of the idea is most famously encapsulated in Chief Justice Roberts's opening statement at his Senate confirmation hearing. There he likened the role of the judge to the role of a baseball umpire: "Judges and justices are servants of the law, not the other way around. Judges are like umpires. Umpires don't make the rules; they apply them. The role of an umpire and judge is critical. They make sure everybody plays by the rules. But it is a limited role. Nobody ever went to a ball game to see the umpire."[15]

Underlying Roberts's characterization is the embrace of what is often referred to as a formalistic approach to judging. Formalism is yet another term that is widely used but often not defined. As Professor Frederick Schauer put it, "Even a cursory look at the literature reveals scant agreement on what it is for decisions

[14] Scalia made the case for originalism and for formalism in a pair of essays published the same year. Antonin Scalia, 'Originalism: The Lesser Evil,' (1989) 57 *University of Cincinnati Law Review* 849; Antonin Scalia, 'The Rule of Law as a Law of Rules,' (1989) 56 *University of Chicago Law Review* 1175. For an exploration of the tension between these two positions, see Steven G. Calabresi and Gary Lawson, 'The Rule of Law as a Law of Law,' (2014) 90 *Notre Dame Law Review* 483.

[15] Confirmation Hearing on the Nomination of John G. Roberts, Jr. to Be Chief Justice of the United States: Hearing before the Senate Committee on the Judiciary (2005), 109th Congress 55 (Statement of John G. Roberts, Jr.).

in law, or perspectives on law, to be formalistic, except that whatever formalism is, it is not good."[16] The most common usage is one that imagines judges as ideally engaged in an essentially mechanical activity, an elaborate paint-by-numbers exercise in which answering legal questions is simply a matter of ascertaining the correct answers without exercising discretion or allowing values or ideology to influence the process.[17] On this view, legal interpretation is often conceived of as a linguistic or semantic exercise involving the identification and definition of the legal concepts that apply to a given situation, whether they are found in a statute or constitution or in the language of past judicial decisions. The goal is to figure out what, for example, a statutory provision says rather than to focus in some more abstract or general sense on the problem it is designed to solve or how it was meant to work. In Professor Adrian Vermeule's formulation, the recipe calls for judges to "stick close to the surface-level or literal meaning of clear and specific texts, resolutely refusing to adjust those texts by reference to the judges' conceptions of statutory purposes, legislators' or framers' intentions or understandings, public values and norms, or general equity."[18] Relatedly, formalists tend as well to prefer legal standards that take the form of rules, which work to limit the number of factors to be accounted for in decision-making and thus to further the appearance of objectivity.[19]

The Supreme Court's reasoning about the scope of the Commerce Clause during what is known as the *Lochner* era provides one example. The clause gives Congress the power "to regulate Commerce … among the several States," and the Lochner Court resisted Congress's reliance on the clause as the source of its authority for broad regulation of the economy. For the majority of justices on that court, much turned on the meaning of the word "commerce," which Congress did have the ability to regulate, as contrasted with things like manufacturing, agriculture, and so on, which it did not. From there, it was just a matter of determining which box the regulated activity in question fell into. Thus, in *United States* v. *E.C. Knight Co.*, the Court held that Congress lacked the power to prevent an acquisition that led to the formation of a monopoly in the sugar refining industry on the grounds that what Congress sought to do was an attempted regulation of manufacturing rather than commerce – even though a monopoly in refining would unquestionably have effects on the market for sugar.[20] Consequences didn't matter, labels did.

16 Frederick Schauer, 'Formalism,' (1988) 97 *Yale Law Journal* 509, 509–10.

17 See, for example, Steven J. Burton, *An Introduction to Law and Legal Reasoning*, (New York: Aspen Publishers, 3rd ed., 2007) 2–3.

18 Adrian Vermeule, *Judging Under Uncertainty: An Institutional Theory of Legal Interpretation* (Cambridge: Harvard University Press, 2006) 4.

19 See Schauer, 'Formalism', 510; Frederick Schauer, 'Formalism: Legal, Constitutional, Judicial', in Gregory A. Caldeira, R. Daniel Keleman, and Keith E. Whittington (eds.) *The Oxford Handbook of Law and Politics* (New York: Oxford University Press, 2008) 428, 433–35.

20 156 US 1 (1895).

A second aspect of formalism relates to the conceptual nature of law. In the formalist view of the world, legal concepts have a necessary and fixed content. They are, in Justice Oliver Wendell Holmes's famous critical characterization of the view, part of "a brooding omnipresence in the sky,"[21] a perfectly integrated, logically consistent, comprehensive, and timeless structure of concepts for the regulation of all aspects of human affairs.[22] This was a crucial idea during the heyday of the common law, when most of the law was found in judicial decisions. The judge's task under this approach is to make the best use of the available evidence – in the form of past decisions and the rules and concepts that can be derived from them – to reason toward the proper result in the present case. Done correctly, according to this logic, the processes of legal reasoning are objective and determinate, and thus neither their workings nor their conclusions depend on the identity of the judge who undertakes them. The job of the judge faced with a novel question is not to make law but instead to discover it.

In the standard story about the development of American law, formalism was the dominant approach until the emergence of the Legal Realist movement in the early decades of the twentieth century. The Realists were, in Professor Lawrence Friedman's characterization, "a variegated bunch" about whom it is easier to identify what they were not than what they were.[23] And what they were not were formalists. Among the Realists' revelations was that legal rules are indeterminate – they do not and cannot provide clear answers to all questions – and that as a result legal reason cannot be the mechanistic, deductive process that formalists desire. Holmes again: "General propositions do not decide concrete cases. The decision will depend on a judgment or intuition more subtle than any articulate major premise."[24] Rules can never be precise enough to provide the guidance that formalism demands across a range of cases. There will be gray areas in which the application of a rule is unclear. A rule pointing toward a decision in one direction will sometimes be accompanied by a different, equally valid, and equally applicable rule pointing in the other direction. Often the law will allow multiple and perhaps even contradictory outcomes.

Take, for example, a case with which I begin the semester with my first-year Criminal Law students. Under Wisconsin law, the penalties for committing a theft are more severe if the property is taken "from the person of another." In *State* v. *Hughes*, the defendant took a purse that was hanging on the handle of a wheelchair. One could argue, as the defendant did, that "from the person of another" requires

21 *Southern Pacific Company* v. *Jensen*, 244 US 205, 222 (1917) (Holmes, J., dissenting).

22 See, for example, Brian Z. Tamanaha, *On the Rule of Law: History, Politics, Theory* (Cambridge: Cambridge University Press, 2004) 77–78. For a brief history of the origins and development of the common law, see Kunal M. Parker, *The Turn to Process: American Legal, Political, and Economic Thought, 1870–1970* (Cambridge: Cambridge University Press, 2024) 39–47.

23 Lawrence M. Friedman, *American Law in the 20th Century* (New Haven: Yale University Press, 2004) 490.

24 *Lochner* v. *New York*, 198 US 45, 75 (1905) (Holmes, J., dissenting).

that the victim actually be touching the property. At first glance, this seems to provide a clear line. But further consideration reveals that clarity to be an illusion. It can't be correct to require that the victim's skin must be touching the stolen item, because that approach would exclude takings of items from pockets, which are separated from their owner by at least one layer of fabric, but which surely fall within the scope of "from the person of another." If we conclude that clothing is an extension of the person, then we could say the same about a wheelchair. But if we accept that logic, then we have to ask whether it extends to things such as bicycles, golf carts, or cars. Other efforts to define the phrase likewise fail to produce a distinct, easy-to-administer line that mechanically and satisfactorily governs all cases. Another approach would be to look behind the language of the provision to seek an understanding of the reasons underlying it. Perhaps takings from the person of another are penalized more severely because they tend to make a situation more dangerous by increasing the likelihood of a confrontation. Or maybe it's that the victim feels more violated by such a taking, as contrasted with a theft of property when the victim is not present. There are, of course, multiple permutations and extensions of all these arguments, and it quickly becomes apparent that no mechanical solution is available. Appropriate "legal" reasoning is available to justify either result in the case, though none of it is as simple as calling a ball or strike. Judgment is necessary, together with resort to something beyond a narrow, formalistic view of law. The words of the statute do not alone provide an answer to the questions. The same is true of concepts extracted from judicial decisions.

That was not the Realists' only insight. Not only are rules indeterminate, but they are often also misleading. A newcomer to an area of law might read the applicable legal materials and conclude that a case involving a given set of facts will be resolved in a particular way, just as one unfamiliar with the customs of the United States might imagine that drivers will be fined for even minor violations of speed limits. But a study of the pattern of results over a range of cases may reveal that something other than the factors expressly identified in the law itself best explains the results. An oft-repeated phrase relating to speeding has it that, from the perspective of a police officer, the true trigger is double-digit speeding: "Nine you're fine, ten you're mine."[25] Professor Karl Llewellyn, among the most prominent of the Realists, captured the idea in the distinction between "paper rules" – the formal legal rules that purport to govern the resolution of dispute – and the "real rules" that actually do.[26] Judges may not even realize the extent to which their decisions depart from what the governing law appears, to an outsider, to require.

25 A pair of newspaper reporters analyzed all the speeding tickets issued in Virginia in 2018. Nearly 98 percent were given to drivers exceeding the limit by more than ten miles per hour. Erica Mokun and Catherine Currier, 'Speed 9mph over the limit and you'll be fine, data shows,' The Gazette-Virginian, December 27, 2019.

26 Llewellyn introduced the distinction in Karl N. Llewellyn, 'A Realistic Jurisprudence – The Next Step,' (1930) 30 *Columbia Law Review* 431–65.

The Realists also attacked the conceptual component of formalism. Law, they asserted, is not some timeless set of fixed and self-contained principles but rather a constantly changing mass of rules connected to and arising out of a shifting collection of social norms and mores. Here, too, Holmes stands as the acknowledged progenitor of the idea:

> The life of the law has not been logic: it has been experience. The felt necessities of the time, the prevalent moral and political theories, intuitions of public policy, avowed or unconscious, even the prejudices which judges share with their fellow-men, have had a good deal more to do than the syllogism in determining the rules by which men should be governed. The law embodies the story of a nation's development through many centuries, and it cannot be dealt with as if it contained only the axioms and corollaries of a book of mathematics … The substance of the law at any given time pretty nearly corresponds, so far as it goes, with what is then understood to be convenient; but its form and machinery, and the degree to which it is able to work out desired result, depend very much upon its past.[27]

The job of the judge (especially the common-law judge) working within this understanding cannot be simply to reason from one abstraction to the next. It instead requires attentiveness to the law as it actually functions and consideration of the social context in which it arose and the nature of the problems it was designed to address. A judge resolving a novel case or issue, then, necessarily makes law insofar as the decision in the present case has binding effect in future cases. To some greater or lesser degree, depending on the case, the standard model's preexisting legal norms do not – and cannot – exist.

There is more. The realism thus far described, which focused on the limits of legal materials and of judges in dealing with them, is that of the "rule skeptics." There was a second strand as well, which consisted of the "fact skeptics." From their perspective, not even perfectly determinate legal rules would necessarily result in completely predictable decision-making. The reason is that the facts of each individual case must be discovered and characterized. They must be assigned significance and weight, and credibility determinations must be made. Legal rules might spell out which facts matter, but they cannot remove the uncertainty and unpredictability from the process through which those facts are determined to be present or not. One judge might conclude a plaintiff has provided enough evidence to survive summary judgment, the next might not. So, too, with key evidentiary rulings. The jury's verdict might turn on the happenstance of its membership, or on the fact that a key witness had a bad day or gave an improbably good performance. None of this can be reliably predicted in advance.[28]

[27] Oliver Wendell Holmes, Jr., *The Common Law* (Boston: Little, Brown and Company, 1881) 1.

[28] See Jerome Frank, *Courts on Trial: Myth and Reality in American Justice* (Princeton: Princeton University Press, 1949) 74.

Finally, there is the obvious fact that courts do make law. The law-declaration function is an acknowledged part of the judicial role, especially but not only for judges on apex courts. Indeed, most of the law that existed at the nation's founding, and through much of its history, was common law generated via case-by-case decision-making. Once one rejects the idea of a brooding omnipresence, it can only be the case that it was the judges who were making, rather than finding, the law. Courts' role as primary authors of the law governing our day-to-day interactions has largely shifted, with legislatures and administrative agencies assuming primary responsibility for that role. But statutes and regulations inevitably leave gaps and include ambiguities that courts must address.

Having laid out the Realist critique, a pair of caveats are in order. The first is to acknowledge, as most Realists did, that there are many easy cases in which the rules can be applied in a determinate fashion to generate clear results. To take an easy example, speed limits present no problems of indeterminacy in their paper format, and the applicable real rule likewise provides no room for manipulation in the case of someone driving 120 miles per hour on a highway. Beyond that, a great many potential disputes do not even appear in the legal system at all given the clarity of the law's application to the situation involved, and compliance with clear legal rules enables people to structure their affairs in such a way as to prevent disputes from arising in the first place. When disputes do arise, a substantial portion are likewise, when viewed from a detached perspective, equally clear in terms of what the law requires. Easy cases abound.[29]

The second caveat is that the traditional story of the transition from formalism to realism is, at best, overdrawn. Professor Brian Tamanaha studied judicial and scholarly commentary concerning the processes of judging during the era in which formalism reputedly dominated and concluded that almost no one in that era actually held the beliefs the Realists ascribed to them.[30] Rather than thinking that judges mechanically applied law to facts, judges "had a realistic awareness of the complexities involved in judging and of the foibles of human judges."[31] They understood "that the law has inconsistencies, runs out, and routinely comes up against unanticipated situations and that judges possess a substantial degree of flexibility when working with legal materials. It was obvious to observers that the law can interpreted differently by judges with different views."[32] The difference between the Realists and the judges of the formalist era, Tamanaha concludes, is not that

[29] Estimates of precisely how many cases are truly easy vary widely. Professor Frank Cross identified observers estimating that as few as 5 percent and as many as 90 percent fall into that category. Frank B. Cross, 'Political Science and the New Legal Realism: A Case of Unfortunate Interdisciplinary Ignorance,' (1997) 92 *Northwestern University Law Review* 251, 286–87.

[30] Brian Z. Tamanaha, *Beyond the Formalist-Realist Divide: The Role of Politics in Judging* (Princeton: Princeton University Press 2010).

[31] Tamanaha, 'Beyond the Formalist-Realist Divide', 51.

[32] Id., 91.

they held different understandings of the way in which law and judging work, but that they held different understandings of the significance of those realities. The Realists were skeptical of judging; their predecessors were not. "While the historical jurists recognized that there are social influences on judicial reasoning, they did not describe this as a flaw in judging, but as an essential – necessary, beneficial – link that keeps law and society on the same plane."[33] The play in law's joints was, in the current lingo, a feature rather than a bug.

ADVERSARIALISM

The standard model's third component – the adversarial process – stands at the heart of popular conceptions of how the American legal system works. Lawyers act as zealous advocates for their clients, and the resulting clash provides the decision-maker, whether judge or jury, with the raw materials it needs to get to the truth. This has consequences for the judicial role. It implies judicial neutrality and passivity – a Sphinx-like judge who acts only after the parties have provided all the input they have to provide.[34] In Professor Lon Fuller's classic development of the idea, adjudication's distinguishing characteristic "lies in the fact that it confers on the affected party a peculiar form of participation in the decision, that of presenting proofs and reasoned arguments for a decision in his favor."[35] It follows that anything that enhances party participation also enhances adjudication, while anything that hinders participation or otherwise renders it less effective thereby undermines adjudication. A judge who assumes anything but a reactive posture thus threatens to undermine the legitimacy of the process. Without realizing it, such a judge may come to favor one side as a result of being proactive. The simple act of asking questions, for example, could lead the judge to unwittingly develop a preference by enticing the judge to view the dispute from one party's perspective or could reveal something about the judge's thought processes that a party could use to their advantage. And such an intervention risks creating a perception of prejudgment, regardless of whether the judge has actually departed from neutrality.[36]

Here, too, matters are not as straightforward as the standard model would lead us to believe. There are both theoretical and practical objections to this conception of the judicial role. Complete passivity seems undesirable, and so does neutrality insofar as it is viewed as requiring that a judge work solely with what the parties have presented. Not all litigants are equally situated. There are often differences in

33 Id.
34 Stephen Landsman, *The Adversary System: A Description and Defense* (Washington, D.C.: American Enterprise Institute for Public Policy Research, 1984) 2–3.
35 Lon L. Fuller, 'The Forms and Limits of Adjudication,' (1978) 92 *Harvard Law Review* 353, 364.
36 For a more complete discussion, see Chad M. Oldfather, 'Defining Judicial Inactivism: Models of Adjudication and the Duty to Decide,' (2005) 94 *Georgetown Law Journal* 121, 140.

wealth, sophistication, and access to counsel.[37] Sometimes this will mean that one of the parties will have misunderstood or failed to recognize the applicability or significance of a legal theory.[38] One side will have been better able to develop the facts. Often such imbalances will be consistently present in cases, such as those that pit sophisticated, repeat players against unsophisticated individuals.[39] Sometimes the litigation will have consequences that fall on people whose interests the parties do not share. To remain passive in the face of an obvious imbalance in power or misalignment of incentives would mean to adhere to the requirements of an idealized conception of judging at the expense of justice as it is generally conceived. A baseline obligation of responsiveness to the parties' claims and arguments remains desirable, lest judges use a perceived freedom to depart from the contours of the dispute as the parties have presented it to skirt claims and arguments they find inconvenient or inexpedient,[40] but meeting that responsibility need not entail comprehensive passivity.

Moving from the abstract to the concrete, there are various ways in which the judicial process has evolved over the course of American history that involve departures from, or at least consequential variations on, the standard model's prescriptions. A striking early innovation in the American system compared to the English system from which it descended was the product of geographical necessity. England long followed the "oral tradition," in which all proceedings take place orally and in open court, with very little reliance on written submissions.[41] But the requirement that parties and judges be in the same location for as long as necessary to work through a case at each stage was impracticable in the United States, with its comparatively sparse and geographically dispersed population and small number of lawyers.[42] The US courts accordingly shifted to the use of written briefs and opinions. And not only do American courts issue written justifications for their decisions (as opposed to delivering them extemporaneously in open court), but they also do so via a single opinion for the court, rather than separate, seriatim opinions setting forth the views of each judge or justice. Writing differs from orality in its influence on thought, and, in the case of multi-member courts, the process of generating a single opinion joined by a majority of judges leverages the collective wisdom of the group in a

37 Owen M. Fiss, 'Foreword: The Forms of Justice,' (1979) 93 *Harvard Law Review* 1, 24.

38 Amanda L. Frost, 'The Limits of Advocacy,' (2009) 59 *Duke Law Journal* 447, 450–51.

39 Marc Galanter, 'Why the "Haves" Come out Ahead: Speculations on the Limits of Legal Change,' (1974) 9 *Law & Society Review* 95–160.

40 Much of the motivation for my own early work on these topics arose out of and was motivated by my experience as a public defender. My perception, which I took to be shared by many if not all of my colleagues, was that the opinions we received from the courts to which we made arguments on our clients' behalf did not always engage with the arguments we had made.

41 Robert J. Martineau, *Appellate Justice in England and the United States: A Comparative Analysis* (Buffalo, NY: William S. Hein & Co., Inc., 1990).

42 Suzanne Ehrenberg, 'Embracing the Writing-Centered Legal Process,' (2004) 89 *Iowa Law Review* 1159–99.

way distinct from a process in which each judge offers their own conclusion. The evolution did not stop there. Law clerks, rather than judges, now serve as the initial authors of nearly all opinions issued by appellate courts, and the once unheard of nonprecedential opinion is now a common thing. Their precise nature is difficult to identify, but such changes surely have subtle but nonetheless real effects on the way in which the adversarial process plays out. We will return to them in Chapter 4.

There are other common things courts do that fall outside the bounds of the standard model's call for adversary proceedings. Probate and family courts, for example, often deal with matters that do not involve parties who are opposed to one another in any real sense. Drug courts and the various problem-solving courts that have developed in their wake feature at their core judges who are actively involved in steering a path forward for defendants. All of these, and more, are precisely what Shapiro observed: entities that we call courts in which judges routinely act in ways that do not fit comfortably within the prototype.

A DICHOTOMOUS DECISION

The preceding two components of the standard model have implications for the types of disputes that are appropriate for resolution by courts and thus bring us to the fourth, the idea of the dichotomous decision declaring a winner and a loser. The resolution of A's claim against B will be that one or the other of them will prevail. Either B wronged A in some legally cognizable sense or did not, and if the wrong occurred, B will be responsible for somehow making it right. Compromise solutions are not on the table. In their influential-though-unpublished materials entitled *The Legal Process*, Professors Henry Hart and Albert Sacks argued that this is a necessary part of the standard model, that it follows from an understanding that adjudication works best in the context of disputes that can be resolved by reference to preexisting general rules, that "an either-or question of the existence *vel non* of any right to a remedy seems ordinarily to be essential to an adjudicable dispute."[43] The exercise of *ad hoc* discretion may be appropriate in the context of fashioning a remedy, they allow, but "only when it is strictly ancillary to a clear-cut determination of right, and pertains only to what is necessary to the due effectuation of the right." On this view, decisions that require a forward-looking management of affairs or that otherwise involve what Fuller called polycentric disputes, which involve consideration of an array of interacting and incommensurable factors, are beyond the reach of judicial competence.[44] These are, of course, the concerns that run through the Chief Justice's analysis in *Rucho*. Though his analysis is unmindful of

43 Henry M. Hart, Jr., and Albert Sacks, *The Legal Process: Basic Problems in the Making and Application of Law* (Westbury, New York: Foundation Press, 1994) (William N. Eskridge and Philip P. Frickey, eds.) 640.

44 Lon L. Fuller, 'The Forms and Limits of Adjudication,' (1978) 92 *Harvard Law Review* 353, 394–404.

the distinction between right and remedy – the ability to identify situations in which partisan gerrymandering has gone too far does not turn on the need for a precise formula by which to make things right – it repeatedly invokes the difficulty for judges of weighing and balancing the various considerations that go into the drawing of district boundaries.

But here, too, consideration reveals that we frequently, and often noncontroversially, ask courts to do things that fall outside the contours of the standard model. In his 1976 article *The Role of the Judge in Public Law Litigation*, Professor Abram Chayes observed that much federal litigation at the time concerned "the vindication of constitutional or statutory policies"[45] and was "recognizable as a lawsuit only because it takes place in a courtroom before an official called a judge."[46] Prominent examples included school desegregation and prison reform litigation. He cataloged eight ways in which such litigation differs from the standard model, including with respect to its "sprawling and amorphous" party structure, the overtly active nature of the judicial role, and the forward-looking nature of its factual inquiry and remedial focus.[47] Three years later, Professor Owen Fiss articulated a justification for the active judicial role in such cases – primarily to account for the representational difficulties and disparities that inhere in such cases due to the fact that not everyone who will be affected by the resolution of the suit will be represented effectively or even at all – and suggested that the classic model's emphasis on courts' dispute resolution function overlooked the crucial fact that courts "exist to give meaning to our public values."[48]

All of this leaves us roughly where it left Shapiro. The standard model has considerable intuitive appeal. At first blush, it seems to describe our judicial system well and to provide a solid baseline against which to assess whether a given innovation is sensible. But examination reveals that the American judicial system does not consistently satisfy any of the standard model's components, and moreover that there is ample room for disagreement about what those components mean in their particulars and how to prioritize the various often-conflicting values the system seeks to advance. Whether and to what extent judges are independent depends on the answer to questions such as "independent from what?" and "toward what end?" Whether they can truly be described as applying preexisting legal norms depends on the clarity of the rule and the facts to which the rule applies that is only sometimes present. Adversary proceedings do not always fit the bill, and even when they do, there are often reasons why it makes sense to expect judges to depart from a purely reactive orientation. In similar fashion, we can conclude that dichotomous decisions are sometimes inappropriate to the nature of the problem at hand.

45 Abram Chayes, 'The Role of the Judge in Public Law Litigation,' (1976) 89 *Harvard Law Review* 1281, 1284.

46 Chayes, 'The Role of the Judge in Public Law Litigation', 1302.

47 Id.

48 Fiss, 'The Forms of Justice', 29.

The key point, again, is this: courts do not exist for their own sake, or to meet the demands of a particular concept of what they are to be. They exist to serve social functions, and Louis Sullivan's phrase "form follows function" serves just as well to capture the reality of courts as it does the design of buildings. The nature of judicial power, and of the ways in which it is used and constrained, will vary across time and contexts.[49] The boundaries between courts and other parts of the political system are not fixed, and the powers and responsibilities of the institutional actors within government will shift and overlap.

For these reasons, Shapiro rejects the standard model as a depiction of the necessary ingredients of courts and offers instead "a root concept of 'courtness'" that better captures the core logic of courts and court-like institutions. At its heart is a triad: disputants who find that they cannot resolve their conflict turn to a third party, a neutral standing in an equivalent relation to both. This triad features "a basic instability, paradox, or dialectic that accounts for a large proportion of the scholarly quarrels over the nature of courts and the political difficulties that courts encounter in the real world."[50] That instability is this: once the third party has reached a decision, what was previously a triadic relationship breaks down and threatens to appear, to the losing party especially, as two-against-one. The neutral has taken a side. "To the loser," Shapiro concludes, "there is no social logic in two against one. There is only the brute fact of being outnumbered." This, in turn, has significant implications for institutional procedures and design: "A substantial portion of the total behavior of courts in all societies can be analyzed in terms of attempts to prevent the triad from breaking down into two against one."[51] The upshot is that much (maybe most) of what matters in establishing and maintaining the real and perceived legitimacy of the judiciary is the perception of the court as a true neutral, not only in the stages that precede the moment of decision, but in those that follow as well.[52]

49 To take an easy but underappreciated example, consider the somewhat obvious idea that judicial power has different dimensions in state versus federal courts. See Adrian Vermeule, 'The Judicial Power in the State (and Federal) Courts,' (2000) *Supreme Court Review* 357–432. Vermeule characterizes the results in state cases as "startling": "Some suggest that state legislatures invade the judicial power merely by altering common-law liability rules or common-law remedies; others suggest that legislative prescription of a standard of review, a rule of evidence, or any other 'procedural' rule encroaches upon judicial authority; in others, judges order state or local legislative bodies to increase appropriations for judicial budgets, on pain of contempt." Vermeule's examples tend to involve situations that can be regarded as presenting reasonably direct conflicts between the legislative and judicial branches, such that what he points out is a tendency on the part of state courts to aggressively protect their turf against legislative encroachments – which is one way, but hardly the only way, that state judicial power is different than its federal counterpart. For a brief consideration of this idea in the context of disputes over election maps, see Oldfather, '*Rucho* in the States.'

50 Shapiro, 'Courts', 1–2.

51 Id.

52 It may be that there is something more basic than and therefore prior to the triad. In a small, close-knit society that relies on a trusted elder, it may be that what provides legitimacy is not the triad but rather the shared notion that the elder's decisions deserve respect because they were the decisions of the elder, whose authority might stem from her specific identity and characteristics, from the

To accept the logic of the triad is not to reject the standard model completely. Indeed, considered in the abstract, the model seems to provide a good mechanism for implementing the triad. An independent judiciary applying preexisting legal norms via a process in which the disputants participate as adversaries can be recharacterized as one in which the judicial role entails the freedom to follow the law wherever it leads, and to do so after allowing the parties an opportunity to make their strongest possible cases. The judge can avoid the breakdown of the triad by pointing to the law, rather than the judge, as the author of the decision. (The dichotomous decision, by contrast, does not seem to be a necessary implication of the desire to maintain triadic integrity.) Indeed, both the majority and the dissent in *Rucho* implicitly accept something akin to this depiction of the standard model as a baseline, and in a manner that also recognizes the value of the triad's logic. Both accounts provide valuable fodder for any analysis of the judicial role in the United States, and we will return to both throughout the remainder of this book.

The analysis thus far has revealed that the bedrock concepts that make up the standard model, ideas that are routinely invoked as if they have a settled definition, are in fact both contestable and contested as to their meanings and are ideals that are in practice impossible to meet. The usual materials of law cannot provide clearly predetermined answers in all cases, and the litigants will not always be well-positioned or incentivized to direct the court's attention to all the pertinent materials. The path from law to decision – or, as it is often called, judgment – requires judgment. We want judges who have the freedom to exercise judgment in appropriate ways – whatever we might mean by that – but not to do whatever they want. Understanding the nature and role of courts and judges, and their various manifestations in our society, requires more than abstract reasoning from idealized conceptions. Such thinking can help with both understanding and setting limits. But we must also consider the incentives, capacities, and pathologies that affect individual judges on the ground as they go about their work, the various processes and other features of institutional design that work to channel judicial behavior in the desired directions, as well as larger questions about jurisprudential and intellectual trends that shape the atmosphere in which this work, and analysis of it, takes place. The remainder of the book takes up that work.

social authority that inheres in the position she holds, or some combination of both. Such an elder's decisions might depart in other ways from what we would consider to be the basic demands of due process – reliance on information about who the disputants are and what their characters and reputations are like, the use of judicial investigation and ex parte communications, and so on.

2

Indeterminacy and Ideology

The standard model of adjudication provides an intuitively appealing vision of how the judicial system should operate. Both the majority and dissenting opinions in *Rucho* accepted it, or something very close to it, as the implicit baseline against which to assess whether the adjudication of disputes over partisan gerrymandering is within the scope of the federal judicial power. Yet, as we have seen, the reality of courts as institutions, and judges as actors within those institutions, often departs from the model's prescriptions – and things cannot be otherwise. In a great many of the matters they face, judges are not automatons applying fixed and precise rules, or even umpires just calling balls and strikes. Nor could they be. The law's commands are not always sufficiently precise, and the demands of justice sometimes may seem counter to even the clearest of those commands. Law, as we typically think of it, runs out. Something else must guide the judge on the remainder of the journey to a result. The questions then become what that something is and what it should be.

The Realists provided a variety of answers to these questions. As to the first, their claim was not (usually) that traditional legal materials hold no sway, but that judges are also influenced by factors such as the institutional setting in which they work, their class background, the substantive and aesthetic quality of the lawyering in a case, and the interaction between the facts of the case and judges' individual psychology.[1] Judges are humans and therefore susceptible to the same forces that shape (and distort) human decision-making in other settings. An extreme version of their position, more often used by critics to caricature the movement, but certainly invoked by some of the Realists themselves, is that the law is mere whim, nothing more than what the judge had for breakfast.[2] As to the second question, the Realists often regarded social science as the appropriate source of guidance.

[1] Brian Z. Tamanaha, *Beyond the Formalist-Realist Divide: The Role of Politics in Judging* (Princeton: Princeton University Press, 2010).

[2] For a fascinating history of the phrase, its use, and its connection to the idea that digestive and overall health are related, see Dan Priel, 'Law Is What the Judge Had for Breakfast: A Brief History of an Unpalatable Idea,' (2020) 68 *Buffalo Law Review* 899.

The Realists' successor was the Legal Process School, which likewise rejected formalism but resisted the suggestion that law could only be simply the product of judicial whim. They also offered a different type of answer to the question concerning what judges should do. The process theorists emphasized "reasoned elaboration," the notion that a thoughtful and comprehensive process of justifying decisions, one that recognizes that there are principles standing behind texts that can be drawn on to guide their application, can provide the discipline necessary to keep judges from falling prey to the concerns identified by the Realists.[3] The key was for judges to rely on "neutral principles," Professor Herbert Wechsler's notion that "the main constituent of the judicial process is precisely that it must be genuinely principled, resting with respect to every step that is involved in reaching judgment on analysis and reasons quite transcending the immediate result that is achieved."[4] Put slightly differently, "A principled decision … is one that rests on reasons that in their generality and their neutrality transcend any immediate result that is involved."[5] This commitment to rationality, coupled with a concern for determining which institution is best-suited to handle an issue, would provide the desired legitimacy. Once again, *Rucho* serves to illustrate the idea. The majority saw no hope of developing neutral principles by which to assess gerrymanders – no rule or set of criteria that could credibly resolve the two cases before it as well as those that would inevitably arise in the future – and consequently concluded that institutional responsibility for the creation and assessment of election maps is best placed elsewhere.

By the 1970s, other trends had emerged.[6] Legal academics prior to that time had largely been political centrists, and these successor movements emerged from both the political right and left.[7] From the right came Law and Economics, which placed economic concepts such as efficiency at the center of its analysis of legal rules and institutions. We will return to it in Chapter 6. Emerging from the left was the Critical Legal Studies movement. As with the Realists, it is easier to say what the Crits rejected than what they shared, except that, in Professor Lawrence Friedman's characterization, "they shared a kind of wild and anarchic irreverence."[8]

3 For an exploration of the tenets of the Legal Process school and the history of their development, see William N. Eskridge, Jr. and Philip P. Frickey, 'The Making of The Legal Process,' (1994) 107 *Harvard Law Review* 2031–55.

4 Herbert Wechsler, 'Toward Neutral Principles of Constitutional Law,' (1959) 73 *Harvard Law Review* 1, 15.

5 Wechsler, 'Neutral Principles', 19.

6 This recounting is, of course, incomplete. It overlooks, for example, H. L. A. Hart's argument that, while some indeterminacy necessarily exists as a product of the inherent imprecision of language, most cases fall clearly within the scope of a rule, such that the problems presented by indeterminacy are less significant than the Realists claimed. H. L. A. Hart, *The Concept of Law* (Oxford: Oxford University Press, 1961) 119–25.

7 Lawrence M. Friedman, *American Law in the Twentieth Century* (New Haven: Yale University Press, 2004) 493–96.

8 Friedman, 'American Law', 493–94.

The movement featured "no uniformly accepted views and no canonical texts."[9] Even so, a common theme among the Crits was that the most important piece of the puzzle was politics. Theirs was not just a claim that judicial decision-making is political, but that all of law is political, meaning, as Professor Mark Tushnet put it, "that when one understands the moral, epistemological, and empirical assumptions embedded in any particular legal claim, one will see that those assumptions operate in the particular setting in which the legal claim is made to advance the interests of some identifiable political grouping."[10] Friedman again: "Law was inherently political; it was never impartial, never mere procedure or process; on the contrary, it was always on the side of the rich and powerful; it always deserved to be trashed, exposed, deconstructed."[11] The Crits "sought to identify and focus public attention on systematic discrimination, exclusion, subordination and oppression in modern Western societies and the complicity of law in these evils. They argued that law makes systematic oppression possible and often enhances it."[12] Wechsler's neutral principles simply do not exist. An invocation of the rule of law "merely cloaks power in the garb of right."[13]

When it came to judicial decision-making, the Crits amplified the Realists' emphasis on the law's indeterminacy. The strong version of the indeterminacy thesis is that "the existing body of legal doctrines – statutes, administrative regulations, and court decisions – permits a judge to justify any result she desires in any particular case."[14] The judge who wishes to be result-oriented can do so. And even those judges who might subjectively experience things otherwise – who do not perceive themselves to be acting in a result-oriented way – have no way of preventing their own political views from influencing them. They are political actors through and through, and every judicial decision reflects this.[15]

As noted, the members of the Critical Legal Studies movement were from the political left. Yet decades later, echoes of their ideas surfaced on the political right. The notion that law is simply the exercise of politics and power suffused the rhetoric of Republican President Donald Trump, who repeatedly attacked judges on the grounds that their political loyalties were with his opponents and that he accordingly could not expect to be treated fairly. For example, in 2018, in response to a

9 Richard W. Bauman, *Critical Legal Studies: A Guide to the Literature* (New York: Routledge, 2021).

10 Mark Tushnet, 'Critical Legal Studies: A Political History,' (1991) 100 *Yale Law Journal* 1515, 1517.

11 Friedman, 'American Law', 494.

12 Gerald J. Postema, *Critical Jurisprudence and the Rule of Law, in A Treatise of Legal Philosophy and General Jurisprudence* (New York: Springer, 2011) 213, 214.

13 David M. Trubek, 'Where the Action Is: Critical Legal Studies and Empiricism,' (1984) 36 *Stanford Law Review* 575, 595.

14 Lawrence B. Solum, 'On the Indeterminacy Crisis: Critiquing Critical Dogma,' (1987) 54 *University of Chicago Law Review* 462, 462.

15 For a concise summary of the CLS position, see Paul Baumgardner and Brian Miller, 'On Commonsense Inferences and Radical Indeterminacies: The Murky Future of Abortion Law After *Whole Women's Health*,' (2017) 67 *Syracuse Law Review* 679, 685–88.

ruling concerning his administration's asylum policy, Trump disparaged US District Court Judge Jon Tigar as "an Obama judge." This prompted Chief Justice Roberts to take the extraordinarily rare step of issuing a responsive statement. "We do not have Obama judges or Trump judges, Bush judges or Clinton judges," Roberts declared. "What we have is an extraordinary group of dedicated judges doing their level best to do equal right to those appearing before them." Trump, predictably, was not content to let the Chief Justice have the last word and responded in a series of tweets. He reasserted that "you do indeed have 'Obama judges,' and they have a much different point of view than the people who are charged with the safety of our country" and asked of the US Court of Appeals for the Ninth Circuit "why … are so many opposing view (on Border and Safety) cases filed there, and why are a vast number of those cases overturned. Please study the numbers, they are shocking." The reaction to all of this, in both the legal profession and the public more generally, was largely that of a collective shrug, a "tepid" response that in the eyes of one commentator was "shocking and demoralizing."[16]

But in a sense, it wasn't shocking at all. The standard model of adjudication holds sway over our collective imagination because it provides an intuitively correct depiction of how courts should function. But at the same time, the considerably more Realist-ic view articulated by President Trump has its own intuitive appeal as a depiction of what courts actually do. Ours is a world, after all, in which the media almost without exception reports on judicial decisions as the products of judges who are either "liberal" or "conservative."[17] At the federal level, judicial appointments increasingly reflect greater concern with ideology.[18] In states where judges are elected, campaigns have come to reflect this, with candidates even in officially nonpartisan races increasingly positioning themselves (or allowing others to position them) as affiliated with one side or the other, and voters' behavior tending to reflect the same nationalization of politics that has come to characterize more traditionally political races.[19] In our more reflective moments, we may collectively recognize

[16] For a recounting of the exchange, and the reactions to it, see Bruce Ledewitz, 'The Obama Judge and the Foundations of the Rule of Law,' *Jurist*, December 2, 2018.

[17] Barry Sullivan and Cristina Carmody Tilley, 'Supreme Court Journalism: From Law to Spectacle?,' (2020) 77 *Washington & Lee Law Review* 343.

[18] "Starting in the 1980s … presidents have sought nominees who share the prevailing ideological positions of their increasingly divergent parties – reliable conservatives for Republican presidents, reliable liberals for Democratic presidents. Moreover, in pursuing this goal, they have been more careful than their predecessors in identifying reliable nominees." Neal Devins and Lawrence Baum, *The Company They Keep: How Partisan Divisions Came to the Supreme Court* (Oxford: Oxford University Press, 2019) 121.

[19] Aaron Weinschenk, Mandi Baker, Zoe Betancourt, Vanessa Depies, Nathan Erck, Quinne Herolt, Amanda Loehrke, Cameron Makurat, Hannah Malmberg, Clarice Martell, Jared Novitzke, Bradley Riddle, Tara Sellen, Leah Tauferner, and Emily Zilliox, 'Have State Supreme Court Elections Nationalized?,' (2021) 41 *Justice System Journal* 313–22. For an overview of trends in state supreme court elections, see Jane S. Schacter, 'Polarization, Nationalization, and the Constitutional Politics of Recent State Supreme Court Elections,' (2022) *Wisconsin Law Review* 1311.

the allure of the disinterested neutral. But in the voting booth, and in our thinking about what judges actually do, we seem to accept as normal the idea that the "is" will fall short of the "ought." In a sense, a phenomenon Professor Robert Dahl identified with respect to the Supreme Court in 1957 remains true today: "As a political institution, the Court is highly unusual, not least because Americans are not quite willing to accept the fact that it *is* a political institution and not quite capable of denying it; so that frequently we take both positions at once."[20]

Little of this is surprising to political scientists, who have led the way in providing systematic support for claims that judging is simply another form of political decision-making. The work arose with the development of the "attitudinal model," which holds, especially with respect to the Supreme Court, that legal materials do not constrain and that instead decisions are a product of the justices' ideological attitudes as applied to the facts of the case before the Court. The model imagines that each justice occupies a point on a spectrum ranging from extremely liberal to extremely conservative, and that a justice's decision on the merits in a given case will reflect the result most consistent with that point. "Simply put," in the words of two of the model's architects, "Rehnquist vote[d] the way he [did] because he [was] extremely conservative; Marshall voted the way he did because he was extremely liberal."[21] Thus, the question the attitudinal model regards justice as asking is something like, "Given the facts of this case, which result do I prefer as a matter of policy?" The model takes it as understood, and not controversial, that the Court is a policymaking institution; its decisions entail "choosing among alternative courses of action, where the choice binds the behavior of those subject to the policy maker's authority."[22] On this view, the Court's opinions serve simply to provide a veneer of justification for decisions reached on grounds that have nothing to do with the reasons the justices provide.

Scholars have conducted a considerable amount of research under the banner of the attitudinal model, and that work, in the form of large-scale empirical studies, consistently confirms the existence of a relationship between ideology and decision-making. Liberal justices are more likely to vote to strike down statutes and overturn precedents that are conservative, and the same holds for conservative justices faced with conservative statutes or precedents. Justices are overwhelmingly likely to vote in favor of their preferred policy position even in the face of contrary precedent.[23] Conservative justices are more likely to favor the government in criminal cases, whether the underlying question is constitutional or statutory, while liberal justices

20 Robert A. Dahl, 'Decision-Making in a Democracy: The Supreme Court as a National Policy-Maker,' (1957) 6 *Journal of Public Law* 279.

21 Jeffrey A. Segal and Harold J. Spaeth, *The Supreme Court and the Attitudinal Model Revisited* (Cambridge: Cambridge University Press, 2002) 86.

22 Segal and Spaeth, 'Supreme Court and the Attitudinal Model Revisited', 6.

23 Jeffrey A. Segal and Harold J. Spaeth, 'The Influence of Stare Decisis on the Votes of United States Supreme Court Justices,' (1996) 40 *American Journal of Political Science* 971–1003.

are more likely to side with the defendant. The effect extends to the decisions about which cases to hear. If the lower court reached a liberal decision, a conservative justice is more likely to want to hear the case, and vice-versa.[24]

Understanding this work requires an appreciation for how it is conducted. Quantitatively assessing the relationship between a judge's ideology and the ideological valence of the judge's decisions requires a way to measure each thing. Good social science practices call for those measures to be reliable; that is, the sort that can be implemented consistently from one observer to the next. What results is often quite reductionist. As a first cut, researchers measured judges' ideology (in the case of federal judges, who are the subject of most of this work) according to a simple binary determined by reference to the political party of the President who appointed them. Judges appointed by Republican presidents are deemed conservative, and any appointed by Democratic presidents are deemed liberal. Later refinements account for factors such as which party controls the Senate at the time of a judge's appointment, with the intuition being that judges appointed in eras of divided government will be more moderate than those appointed when a single party controls both branches.[25] The research takes a similar approach to measuring the judges' behavior. A vote in favor of the government in a criminal case is a conservative vote, while one in favor of the defendant is liberal. In tax cases, by contrast, a vote in favor of the government is liberal and a vote for the taxpayer is conservative. The brush is broad, and the language and reasoning of the courts' opinions factor not at all into the analysis.

Given the assumption that "judges' decisions are a function of what they prefer to do, tempered by what they think they ought to do, but constrained by what they perceive it is feasible to do,"[26] scholars generally agree that the model works best as applied to the Supreme Court, where the justices face few constraints on their ability to act on their ideological inclinations. The justices enjoy life tenure, cannot be reviewed by a higher court, and are unlikely to be interested in seeking another position. Their ability, for the most part, to select which cases they hear results in their being continually faced with difficult questions of the sort that are unlikely to be resolved by reference to existing standards. The cases are often politically charged and thus especially amenable to the influence of ideology. Perhaps unsurprisingly,

[24] For an overview of some of that work, see Lee Epstein, William M. Landes and Richard A. Posner, *The Behavior of Federal Judges: A Theoretical and Empirical Study of Rational Choice* (Cambridge: Harvard University Press, 2013) 77–79.

[25] That the measures have become more nuanced does not necessarily mean they have become more accurate. For example, Jonathan Remy Nash examined a subset of decisions made by federal district judges in New York appointed during a period when the state had one Democrat and one Republican senator and found that consideration of senatorial ideology did not appear to account for differences in the judges' decision-making, while the party of the appointing president did. Jonathan Remy Nash, 'Interparty Judicial Appointments,' (2015) 12 *Journal of Empirical Legal Studies* 664–85.

[26] James Gibson, 'From Simplicity to Complexity: The Development of Theory in the Study of Judicial Behavior,' (1983) 5 *Political Behavior* 7, 9.

the model does not perform as well with respect to the portion of the docket involving cases that are not politically salient.[27]

Judges on lower courts, by contrast, have less opportunity to establish policy and are constrained most immediately by the prospect of reversal. In the federal system, this constraint is greater for district courts, whose decisions are broadly reviewable by appellate courts, than for courts of appeals, whose decisions are effectively final in most instances given that the Supreme Court accepts fewer than a hundred cases each year.[28] Moreover, a large portion of the issues before the lower courts are governed by existing law to some degree of specificity, and those courts lack the Supreme Court's broad ability to modify or depart from existing frameworks. Lower court judges, then, enjoy less freedom to follow their own lights in making decisions.[29] They may also be more interested in seeking promotion to a higher court and thus face an incentive to shape their behavior in ways they believe are likely to catch the attention of the people who have influence in the nomination process.

Even so, researchers have consistently found relationships between ideology and the decisions of the federal circuit courts, with a meta-analysis of a set of studies that collectively evaluated over 79,000 court of appeals decisions concluding that ideology accounted for nearly a quarter of the variance in decisional outcomes.[30] The data suggests more subtle effects as well. Judges sometimes choose not to dissent even when they disagree with the decision of a panel majority, perhaps because they do not feel strongly enough about the issues and also do not want to irritate their colleagues. Panels of judges who all share the same ideology will tend more toward extremes in their outcomes, while ideologically mixed panels tend more toward moderation.[31] Ideology matters, at least in the sense that there is a correlation between a judge's ideology and the pattern of that judge's decisions. But its effects can be amplified, moderated, and otherwise shaped by situational factors.

Recognition of these other influences led to the development of the primary descriptive alternative to the attitudinal model within the political science community, which is the strategic model.[32] It, too, regards judges as ultimately motivated by their policy preferences. But it recognizes that judges are repeat players and allows for

27 David A. Lewis and Roger P. Rose, 'Case Salience and the Attitudinal Model: An Analysis of Ordered and Unanimous Votes on the Rehnquist Court,' (2014) 35 *Justice System Journal* 27–44.

28 For an exploration of whether the prospect of review by the Supreme Court affects the behavior of federal court of appeals judges, see Jennifer Barnes Bowie and Donald S. Songer, 'Assessing the Applicability of Strategic Theory to Explain Decision Making on the Courts of Appeals,' (2009) 62 *Political Research Quarterly* 393.

29 Christopher Zorn and Jennifer Barnes Bowie, 'Ideological Influences on Decision Making in the Federal Judicial Hierarchy: An Empirical Assessment,' (2010) 72 *Journal of Politics* 1212–21.

30 Daniel R. Pinello, 'Linking Party to Judicial Ideology in American Courts: A Meta-analysis,' (1999) 20 *Justice System Journal* 219–54. For an overview briefly discussing this and related studies, see Frank B. Cross, 'Collegial Ideology in the Courts,' (2009) 103 *Northwestern University Law Review*. 1399, 1401.

31 Cass R. Sunstein, David Schkade, Lisa M. Ellman and Andres Sawicki, *Are Judges Political?*, (Washington, DC: Brookings Institution Press, 2006) 148–49.

32 Lee Epstein and Jack Knight, *The Choices Justices Make* (Washington, DC: CQ Press, 1997).

the fact that judges will often understand that simply working to advance their preferences in each case may not be the optimum strategy for advancing their goals over the longer term. A judge might, for example, agree to what they regard as a suboptimal result in a case in order to secure the votes of their colleagues and thereby to avoid what they would regard as the greater evil of a contrary or more extreme result. They might be willing to go along with their colleagues on an issue they don't feel strongly about in the hopes that the colleagues will be willing to reciprocate in future cases. They will account for a broader range of factors as well. Perhaps they will moderate their approach because they anticipate that a result in line with their true preferences would trigger reversal by a higher court, or a legislative response. In its broadest incarnations, the model allows for the fact that judges' motivations can include the desire to enhance their reputations, a felt need to satisfy expectations that decisions be based on legal considerations, and, for judges who are elected, the desire to remain in office.

While most of the work exploring and supporting the strategic model relates to appellate courts, there is evidence supporting its applicability in trial court settings as well. For example, Professor Michael Perino studied a set of over 250 decisions by federal district judges on motions to dismiss under the Private Securities Litigation Reform Act of 1995, all in situations where the applicable circuit court had not yet interpreted the act's heightened pleading requirement.[33] Each judge faced the same issue, and each could choose from among three interpretations of the statute: one that was liberal in that it was the least restrictive of claims under the act, one that was conservative and made it much more difficult for plaintiffs to meet the requirement, and an intermediate interpretation. Perino concluded "that strategic considerations played the largest role in the decision to adopt the intermediate standard. Liberal and conservative judges sitting in ideologically dissimilar circuits were significantly more likely to adopt the intermediate standard than were other judges."[34]

Taken together, all of this provides support for the Realist position. Judges vary in their interpretations of legal materials, and that variance is correlated with crude measures of ideology. It may be a product of intentional efforts to reach the judge's preferred result in cases, or it may be due to influences operating beneath the surface of consciousness. But it is not present to the same degree in all types of cases. Nor is it present to the same degree in all courts or all judges. Whether and to what extent it ought to be regarded as troublesome is also a matter of dispute.

The attitudinal and strategic models, and to a degree, the larger project of the quantitative, empirical study of the judiciary more generally, have been subject to critique. One critique relates to the nature of the data itself. Social science's demand for replicability results in reductionism. To draw general conclusions about a judge's ideology

[33] Michael A. Perino, 'Law, Ideology, and Strategy in Judicial Decision Making: Evidence from Securities Fraud Actions,' (2006) 3 *Journal of Empirical Legal Studies* 497–524.

[34] Perino, 'Law, Ideology, and Strategy', 500–01.

based on the party of the appointing president, even when supplemented with other information, is to leave out a considerable amount of nuance. Neither Republicans nor Democrats, whether they are the appointer or the appointee, hold uniform beliefs to uniform degrees in all parts of the United States and at all times. Likewise when it comes to treating the results in cases as if they were either liberal or conservative.[35] Cases are often more complex than the research design is equipped to handle. Is a vote in favor of a criminal defendant who has been charged with a gun crime or for conduct arising out of an abortion protest liberal or conservative? What about a vote in a case that involves multiple issues? The result is that what the studies measure is imprecise at best.

A second critique concerns the models' basic assumption that judges' primary, if not sole, motivation is ideological, that theirs is a one-track mind devoted solely to the task of reaching decisions that advance their political preferences. The models envision that statutes, regulations, and precedents, as well as legal doctrines, concepts, and methodologies, are mere decoration. The parties' arguments do not matter. The law, as normally conceived, does not matter except insofar as it must be manipulated to provide a post hoc justification for a decision. Professor Larry Baum suggested that the models envision judges as a version of Star Trek's Mr. Spock – they "act without emotion or self-interest in order to advance the general good"[36] as they perceive it through their ideological lens. The strategic model assumes even more, that judges "court exhaustion with their arduous and often futile efforts to advance their conceptions of good policy, efforts they expend only for the personal satisfaction of trying to improve public policy."[37] It's a departure from reality that, he contends, exceeds even the standard assumption in the field of economics that people are rational actors.[38] Instead, as Judge Richard Posner and others have suggested, judges are motivated by all sorts of things beyond ideology – cultivating a good reputation, getting promoted to a higher court, allowing adequate time for leisure, and so forth – and those things are not always connected to a root desire to further policy goals.[39] Judge Patricia Wald attacks the assumption from another direction. It's a mistake, she contends, to imagine that judges have their own strong views, or views at all, on many or perhaps even most of the questions that come before them.[40] In many cases, there simply is no ideological preference to advance.

35 See Carolyn Shapiro, 'Coding Complexity: Bringing Law to the Empirical Analysis of the Supreme Court,' (2009) 60 *Hastings Law Journal* 477; Carolyn Shapiro, 'The Context of Ideology: Law, Politics, and Empirical Legal Scholarship,' (2010) 75 *Missouri Law Review* 79.

36 Lawrence Baum, *Judges and Their Audiences: A Perspective on Judicial Behavior* (Princeton: Princeton University Press, 2006) 18.

37 Baum, 'Judges and Their Audiences', 18.

38 Id., 21.

39 Richard A. Posner, 'What Do Judges Maximize? (The Same Thing Everybody Else Does),' (1994) 3 *Supreme Court Economic Review* 1–41; Frederick Schauer, 'Incentives, Reputation, and the Inglorious Determinants of Judicial Behavior,' (1999) 68 *University of Cincinnati Law Review* 615–36.

40 Patricia M. Wald, 'The Rhetoric of Results and the Results of Rhetoric: Judicial Writings,' (1995) 62 *University of Chicago Law Review* 1371–419.

A third critique points out that the models proceed from the erroneous assumption that a judge's views – whether they involve ideology, values, or some related construct – should play no role at all in decision-making. As Judge Harry Edwards and Professor Michael Livermore have argued, "in cases where the law requires it, judicial decision-making can include a situated and disciplined elaboration of the conventional norms of the American political community."[41] Imprecise concepts such as reasonableness, due process, and so forth provide space for the making of value judgments by design. Thus, "some play for inherently contestable political judgments is simply built into law and strikes us as a normal constituent of good judging."[42] It is, at least often, a feature rather than a bug. The fact that there will be a correlation between how judges act in these cases and their perceived ideologies is unremarkable.

Where does all this leave us? Certainly, this work confirms the Realist belief that the law, narrowly conceived, does not and cannot generate the mechanistic reasoning that the standard model envisions. There is space for other factors to exert influence. Ideology, even when it is measured in a crude and reductionist way, is correlated with decision-making. Whether it is the only factor seems unlikely. Whether it is simply another manifestation of something deeper, some feature of judicial psychology that generates both jurisprudential and political views that are correlated even if they do not bear a causal relationship to one another remains to be seen. Whether it ventures beyond the space the law properly allows for the operation of value judgments – which of course requires answering difficult questions about just where the line between appropriate and inappropriate value judgments lies – is also an open question. There are undoubtedly situations where observers would broadly agree that ideology has no legitimate role to play. But without some sense of where that line is, it is impossible to say how often it is crossed.[43]

41 Harry T. Edwards and Michael A. Livermore, 'Pitfalls of Empirical Studies that Attempt to Understand the Factors Affecting Appellate Decisionmaking,' (2009) 58 *Duke Law Journal* 1895, 1946.

42 Edwards and Livermore, 'Pitfalls of Empirical Studies', 1946.

43 Tamanaha, 'Beyond the Formalist-Realist Divide', 151.

3

The Psychology of Judging

One of Realism's key insights was that, because law is indeterminate, something other than law must account for some or all of judges' behavior. That something could be ideology, it could be personality, it could be what the judge had for breakfast. As we saw in Chapter 2, a considerable amount of work, much of it conducted by political scientists, has explored the role of ideology. Among the critiques of that work is that it assumes ideology to be the sole motivating force behind judges' decisions. Judges are humans, and human motivations are varied and complex.

There is another social science that serves as an obvious source of insight into judges' thought processes, namely psychology. Of course, to consider the role of psychological factors is not so much to shift the inquiry as to broaden it. Even a judge motivated entirely by ideology can fall prey to cognitive errors. What's more, a judge's ideological preferences are undoubtedly a product of psychology, and judgments and beliefs may generally be products of psychological mechanisms that are correlated with but distinct from (and perhaps prior to) ideology. And, of course, most humans act under the influence of a combination of motivations, which are often in tension if not outright conflict with one another and only some of which they may be fully aware of.

None of this is a revelation. More than a century ago, Justice Benjamin Cardozo wrote:

> There is in each of us a stream of tendency, whether you choose to call it a philosophy or not, which gives coherence and direction to thought and action. Judges cannot escape that current any more than other mortals. All their lives, forces which they do not recognize and cannot name, have been tugging at them—inherited instincts, traditional beliefs, acquired convictions; and the resultant is an outlook on life, a conception of social needs, a sense in James's phrase of "the total push and pressure of the cosmos," which, when reasons are nicely balanced, must determine where choice shall fall. In this mental background every problem finds its setting. We may try to see things as objectively as we please. None the less, we can never see them with any eyes except our own.[1]

[1] Benjamin N. Cardozo, *The Nature of the Judicial Process* (New Haven: Yale University Press, 1921) 12–13.

Many of these forces, he noted, are unconscious but close enough to the surface "that their existence and influence are not likely to be disclaimed."[2] But they are not the end of things. "Deep below consciousness are other forces, the likes and the dislikes, the predilections and the prejudices, the complex of instincts and emotions and habits and convictions .... The great tides and currents which engulf the rest of men do not turn aside in their course and pass the judges by."[3]

Just as psychological characteristics differ in the extent to which they manifest themselves from one person to another, so, too, with judges. Judge Henry Friendly, writing about the difficulty judges have in describing how they go about their work, related the story of Professor Karl Llewellyn's effort to get seven new judges, each of whom had been law professors before their appointment, to make and provide him with a written record of their processes of decision-making. All seven agreed to do it. Not one of them actually followed through. As Friendly related it, Llewellyn gave "one clue to the failure of the experiment by a reference to William James' shrewd observation that 'the completed decision wipes off memory's slate most of the process of its attainment.'"[4] Friendly provides another: "the new judge soon learns that each judge judges differently from every other judge and that any one judge judges differently in each case."

What's more, each judge's capacity for informed introspection may vary as well. Thoughtful judges – the Cardozos and Friendlys – acknowledge the forces at work and their own limitations in understanding and responding to them. But, as Judge Richard Posner has noted, most judges maintain that they are uninfluenced by such things as ideology, religion, culture, gender, age, and so on.[5] For some, he contends, this is a "noble lie,"[6] less something they believe about themselves than something they think is necessary to bolster public confidence in the system. For others, it is a lack of self-knowledge. "Actually," Posner opines, "the judge who thinks he isn't influenced by his priors ... is more likely to be influenced by them than a more-self-aware judge would be. He is likely to be excessively self-confident."[7]

Based on all this, one could reasonably ask whether there is such a thing as a psychology of judging. To say that individual judges' decisions are influenced by their psychology does not necessarily entail being able to say meaningful things about the collective psychology of judges. There are also reasons to be cautious about drawing conclusions about judicial behavior from research into human psychology more generally. Some of those reasons inhere in the nature of psychological research itself. As Professor Dan Simon has pointed out, psychology, in contrast to disciplines

2 Cardozo, 'Judicial Process', 167.
3 Id., 167–68.
4 Henry J. Friendly, 'Reactions of a Lawyer – Newly Become Judge,' (1961) 71 *Yale Law Journal* 218, 229.
5 Richard A. Posner, *Divergent Paths: The Academy and the Judiciary* (Cambridge: Harvard University Press, 2016) 165–66.
6 Posner, 'Divergent Paths', 181–87.
7 Id., 166.

such as philosophy or economics, tends not to generate insights "deduced from over-arching concepts or axiomatic characterizations of human behavior."[8] Economics, say, lends itself to the making of top-down prescriptive claims – if efficiency or wealth maximization is the goal, then here are the rules and policies that will best achieve it. Psychology, by contrast, tends to work from the bottom up. The findings of psychological studies are typically narrow, and the phenomena they identify are of uncertain breadth and may be amplified, counteracted, or otherwise modified by other phenomena that were neither studied nor accounted for in the research design. The studies themselves are conducted primarily in controlled environments, and the subjects are often college students, both of which generate some concern about whether the results generalize to broader populations acting in the variety of circumstances presented in real life. What holds in the lab may not hold in the home, workplace, or courtroom.

Consider, for example, research showing that people are generally "loss averse" – they are more reluctant to give up something that they already have than they are eager to get the same thing if they don't have it – say, to demand a higher price to sell an item than they would pay to purchase it or choose a safe investment over riskier alternatives that pair the potential for great gains with the possibility of substantial loss. Research likewise demonstrates that people tend toward overconfidence in the face of uncertain outcomes and to interpret information in self-serving ways. But these experimental outcomes do not always transfer in a clear fashion to reality. For example,[9] commentators have puzzled over the fact that the just-discussed psychological phenomena, coupled with others identified by experimental psychology, seem to suggest that criminal defendants would consistently avoid plea bargaining. Accepting a plea deal entails surrendering one's liberty (such that loss aversion would seemingly kick in) in a situation where going to trial involves uncertainty about whether a jury would convict (which should trigger overconfidence). But the reality is otherwise: nearly 90 percent of criminal cases are resolved via guilty pleas. The research doesn't transfer, and there are a variety of potential reasons why. For one, criminal defendants are an inherently nonrepresentative sample of the general population; they have, if they are guilty, transgressed a significant social norm, which suggests psychological atypicality. For another, the decision whether to take a plea deal is not an instantaneous choice made in a laboratory setting but instead the culmination of a process that unfolds over time, involves consultation with others, and presents itself in a context in which they may have come to believe that they will lose no matter what choice they make. Reality presents variables absent or not accounted for in the

8 Dan Simon, 'In Praise of Pedantic Eclecticism: Pitfalls and Opportunities in the Psychology of Judging,' in David Klain and Gregory Mitchll, eds., *The Psychology of Judicial Decision Making* (Oxford: Oxford University Press, 2010) 131.

9 The discussion in this paragraph is based on Chad M. Oldfather, 'Heuristics, Biases, and Criminal Defendants,' (2007) 91 *Marquette Law Review* 249–62, and the research discussed therein.

experimental setting, such that experimentally observed phenomena will not manifest themselves in the same way as they will in other contexts.

So, too, with the judiciary. Judges as a group are undoubtedly of above-average intelligence and perhaps systematically different from the general population in other ways as well. They have been immersed in the study and practice of law, typically for decades. This training and practice foster a distinctive mode of thought. The decisions they must make have been framed and sharpened through the adversarial process, and the decisions once made must usually be justified via written opinions. None of this ensures that judges are immune from psychological mechanisms that impact others' behavior. But it does suggest that judges' decisional processes are more structured and systematic, and thus that one must be careful not to blithely assume that judges will be susceptible to psychological phenomena to the same degree or in the same ways as the general population.[10]

That said, as we will soon see, research involving judges as subjects provides support for the basic idea that the judiciary does not enjoy complete immunity. The remainder of this chapter surveys some of that work. Some of it overlaps with the research discussed in Chapter 2 and offers alternative accounts of the causes of the apparent influence of ideology in judicial decision-making. Some of it involves effects that seem unlikely to skew decisions in a consistent ideological direction. All of it provides further support for the Realist claim that factors other than law often affect decision-making, and much of it is useful in the larger project of thinking about how to shape judicial behavior in appropriate ways.

MOTIVATED REASONING

Judges typically resist claims that their decisions are the product of ideology or other non-legal motivations. The more thoughtful will acknowledge, as Justice Cardozo did, that their personal experiences, beliefs, and judicial philosophies shape their decision-making. Justice Robert Jackson famously observed that "opinions of judges … often suffer the infirmity of confusing the issue of a power's validity with the cause it is invoked to promote" and noted a strong tendency "to emphasize transient results upon policies … and lose sight of enduring consequences …."[11] But even these admissions will typically be followed by the observation that few cases are truly ideological, and that judges simply do not have preexisting opinions or strong preferences in most of the rest of the cases they must decide. Judges, it seems, do not subjectively experience the process of decision-making as politically driven.[12]

10 Frederick Schauer, 'Is There a Psychology of Judging?,' in David Klain and Gregory Mitchll, eds., *The Psychology of Judicial Decision Making* (Oxford: Oxford University Press, 2010) 103.

11 *Youngstown Sheet & Tube Co. v. Sawyer*, 343 US 579, 634 (1952) (Jackson, J., concurring).

12 See, for example, Patricia M. Wald, 'A Response to Tiller and Cross,' (1999) 99 *Columbia Law Review* 235–61.

As one put it, "it is the law—and not the personal politics of individual judges—that controls judicial decision-making in most cases ...."[13]

This reaction is not limited to judges. Participants in the legal system more generally behave as if the law matters. The first-year curriculum in law school focuses on instilling an understanding of basic legal concepts alongside the development of skills in researching and writing about the law. Lawyers counsel their clients by drawing upon the law. Sometimes the law requires that certain steps be undertaken in order to accomplish a result, as with the transfer of property, dissolution of a marriage, or manufacture and sale of a pharmaceutical. In other situations, it may forbid or penalize specified conduct, such as the sale of securities based on insider information or the hiring of an employee in violation of a covenant not to compete. Lawyers, understanding that the findings of both law and fact can be imprecise, regularly advise clients in terms of probabilities. But often they can be confident, and their advice takes the form of "here's how to make this happen" or "you can't do that." Advocates cite statutes, constitutions, and prior cases in their submissions to courts and devote time to refining their arguments to make them as strong as possible. To be sure, lawyers understand that a strong legal story is better when it accompanies a sympathetic set of facts, but they also behave as if the effect operates at the margins, and that a sufficiently compelling set of legal arguments will carry the day for even the most unsympathetic client. In total, all the participants in the legal system routinely act as if the law matters.[14] Not that it provides definitive answers to every dispute that arises, but that it can and does provide answers to a substantial number of the questions that arise, and that it will end the discussion when it does.

What then might explain the evidence of a correlation between a judge's ideology and the ideology of their decisions? Political scientists, as we saw, tend to regard it as the product of judges' ideology, that judges purposefully decide in ways that further their policy objectives, with law serving only to provide an after-the-fact façade of neutrality. Another possibility is that judges, like humans more generally, are susceptible to motivated reasoning – the "less-than-conscious tendency to reason toward one's preferred result."[15] Just as sports fans will be more inclined to regard an official's call as correct when it favors their team and wrong when it does not, so judges will tend to seek out legal materials that support their preferred result, and be more likely to interpret ambiguous materials in a way that favors that result. That preferred result could, of course, be the product of some

[13] Harry T. Edwards, 'Public Misperceptions Concerning the "Politics" of Judging: Dispelling Some Myths About the D.C. Circuit,' (1985) 56 *University of Colorado Law Review* 619, 620.

[14] For an overview of research illustrating the point, see Eileen Braman, *Law, Politics, and Perception: How Policy Preferences Influence Legal Reasoning* (Charlottesville: University of Virginia Press, 2009) 23–24.

[15] Avani Metha Sood, 'Cognitive Cleansing: Experimental Psychology and the Exclusionary Rule,' (2015) 103 *Georgetown Law Journal* 1543, 1547.

general preference, such as the policy positions favored by a political party. But it could also be specific to the case, such as a sense that one of the litigants is especially sympathetic or unsympathetic. Thus, as Professor Eileen Braman puts it, "an alternative way of explaining findings of policy-oriented decision making is that judges believe they are following the law, but somehow their preferences bias their reasoning processes."[16]

The motivations at work in motivated reasoning are of two primary types, and they work at cross purposes. The first is accuracy, or reaching the "correct" conclusion for the problem at hand. It's natural for those presented with a problem to want to find the right solution and to do so within the constraints provided. One can complete a crossword puzzle by looking up the answers, but the accomplishment lies in following the rules. For lawyers and judges, this means employing the tools of legal reasoning in a dispassionate way and following an analysis to wherever it might lead. It's certainly possible to reason backwards from a conclusion, but the proper form is to reason toward one, and the goal is to have that conclusion best fit the applicable sources of legal authority. The second, and more familiar, motivation is directional. Here, the decision-maker's incentive is to arrive at the conclusion that is most substantively congenial, whether it involves one's favorite sports team, preferred policy goals, or a sense of the more just result in a given case.

Both types of motivation will affect reasoning, but only the latter injects the skew typically associated with motivated cognition.[17] Braman accepts judges' reports that they understand themselves to be engaged in a quest to reach the right answers, but also notes, as we have seen, that law does not provide clearly correct answers in all cases. The desire to be accurate can constrain when the legal materials are sufficiently definite, but space opens up for the unconscious operation of directional motivation when they are not. For easy cases, which in this context would be those in which nearly all lawyers would agree about the proper result, the accuracy motivation pushes judges toward a decision even if it conflicts with their ideological preferences. In difficult cases, by contrast, a judge's policy goals tend to influence them as they gather the materials they regard as pertinent to the decision. Then, within that body of materials, they regard certain features of the situation as more significant because those features happen to be the ones shared with past cases and other authorities supporting the judge's preferred conclusion.[18] A judge inclined to rule against an unsympathetic party, for example, will recognize a smaller (or at least different) universe of authority as bearing on their decision, and within that set of authority will be more apt to distinguish away cases and materials running contrary to the preferred result while emphasizing similarities to that which presents as

16 Braman, 'Law, Politics, and Perception', 29.

17 Ziva Kunda, 'The Case for Motivated Reasoning,' (1990) 108 *Psychological Bulletin* 480–98.

18 Nicholas Epley and Thomas Gilovich, 'The Mechanics of Motivated Reasoning,' (2016) 30 *Journal of Economic Perspectives* 133–40.

helpful. And all of this takes place "under an 'illusion of objectivity,' which protects the integrity of decision makers in their own eyes and in the eyes of others."[19]

Research performed with judges as subjects supports the conclusion that judges can be susceptible to motivated reasoning despite the features of the system, such as the adversarial process, that act as counterweights. Professors Chris Guthrie and Jeff Rachlinski, together with Judge Andrew Wistrich, have conducted a large amount of research using actual judges as subjects to investigate their susceptibility to cognitive phenomena. Among that work is a study in which they tested motivated reasoning by giving over 500 federal and state judges a problem designed to tease out directional motivation. In the scenario, the defendant had entered the country illegally and pasted a false US entry visa into a genuine foreign passport. The question for the judges was whether this violated the prohibition against forging an identification card.[20] For roughly half the judges, the defendant was described as having entered the country to track down someone who had stolen proceeds from a drug cartel. For the others, the defendant was described as having entered the country to earn money to pay for a liver transplant for his nine-year-old daughter. The difference in the defendant's identity is legally irrelevant, though it certainly triggers different sympathies, and it influenced the thinking of some of the judges. Sixty percent of those who encountered the version of the problem with the unsympathetic defendant concluded that his conduct violated the statute, while only 44 percent of those who were provided the other description did.

In another study, Guthrie, Rachlinski, and Wistrich investigated judges' ability to ignore inadmissible information.[21] Their subjects were 265 federal and state trial court judges, all of whom had been appointed (rather than elected) to their positions. They presented the judges with a variety of scenarios. The control set of judges received a set of facts accompanied by a request that they resolve a substantive question regarding the existence of liability or the proper award of damages. The remaining judges received additional information, all of which was clearly inadmissible and therefore not properly available for consideration. That information included evidence of settlement demands, privileged communications, sexual history, a confession obtained after the invocation of the right to counsel, and more. Although the effects were not statistically significant in all the scenarios, the overall takeaway was clear enough. "Taken together," they concluded, "our studies show that judges do not disregard inadmissible information when making substantive decisions in either civil or criminal cases. We think the reason is that they are

19 Avani Mehta Sood, 'Motivated Cognition in Legal Judgments – An Analytic Review,' (2013) 9 *Annual Review of Law and Social Science* 307–25.

20 Andrew J. Wistrich, Jeffrey J. Rachlinski and Chris Guthrie, 'Heart versus Head: Do Judges Follow the Law or Follow Their Feelings,' (2014) 93 *Texas Law Review* 855–923.

21 Andrew J. Wistirch, Chris Guthrie and Jeffrey J. Rachlinski, 'Can Judges Ignore Inadmissible Information? The Difficulty of Deliberately Disregarding,' (2005) 153 *University of Pennsylvania Law Review* 1251.

unwittingly influenced by inadmissible information and that they cannot ignore it much of the time."[22] The judges might have disregarded the law and considered the information directly in their decision-making, or they might have allowed it to provide them with a motivation to decide in a particular way. In either case, it had an effect.

Another line of research into a type of motivated reasoning, undertaken by Professor Dan Kahan and his colleagues, posits that "cultural cognition" drives thinking in ways that produce patterns of decisions that correlate with ideology. The underlying theory emphasizes two dimensions along which individuals differ in their cultural values. Some of us are more communitarian in nature, believing that the good of the collective is important in its own right and also as a means for securing individual well-being. Others are more individualistic, tending to believe that it is best to leave each person responsible for their own destiny. And some of us prefer a world that is hierarchically ordered, while others hold more egalitarian preferences.[23] Differences along these measures correlate with political affiliation. Those who are individualistic and hierarchical tend to hold more conservative views, while those who are communitarian and egalitarian tend to be more liberal, and those with such inclinations can be sorted, and tend to sort themselves, into recognizable groups more generally.

Those group commitments in turn shape members' perceptions of the world. People "tend selectively to credit empirical information in patterns congenial to their cultural values," "impute knowledge and expertise to others with whom they share a cultural affinity," and are "more likely to note, assign significance to, and recall facts supportive of their cultural outlooks than facts subversive of them."[24] All of this manifests itself in strong differences on hot-button issues. For example, egalitarians tend to see industry and guns as destructive to the physical and social environment, while individualists decry regulation and interference with personal choice.

Kahan and his colleagues investigated the connection to legal decision-making through a study involving a problem that required subjects to assess whether the police acted lawfully when they intervened to stop a protest.[25] The intervention's legality depended on whether the protesters' behavior crossed the line separating speech, which is protected by the First Amendment, and conduct, which is not. Subjects viewed a video of a demonstration outside a building, were told that police broke it up under the authority of an ordinance prohibiting people from

[22] Wistrich, Guthrie, and Rachlinski, 'Difficulty of Deliberately Disregarding', 1323.

[23] Dan M. Kahan, David A. Hoffman, and Donald Braman, 'Whose Eyes are You Going to Believe? *Scott v. Harris* and the Perils of Cognitive Illiberalism,' (2009) 122 *Harvard Law Review* 837, 859.

[24] Dan M. Kahan, David A. Hoffman, Donald Braman, Danieli Evans and Jeffrey J. Rachlinski, '"They Saw a Protest": Cognitive Illiberalism and the Speech-Conduct Distinction,' (2012) 64 *Stanford Law Review* 851, 859–60.

[25] Kahan, Hoffman, Braman, Evans, and Rachlinski, 'They Saw a Protest', 859–60.

"obstructing," "intimidating," or "threatening" that type of facility, and were told that the protestors had sued the police for violations of their First Amendment rights. For half the subjects, the facility was described as an abortion clinic, with the protesters being opposed to legalized abortion. The other half were told that it was a military recruiting facility and that the protest was directed at the military's then-existing ban on openly gay and lesbian service members. The results were consistent with culturally motivated cognition. "Our subjects all viewed the same video. But what they saw – earnest voicing of dissent intended only to persuade, or physical intimidation calculated to interfere with the freedom of others – depended on the congruence of the protestors' positions with the subjects' own cultural values."[26]

Based on this and others in a series of studies exploring the workings of cultural cognition, Kahan and his colleagues have critiqued attitudinalist models of judicial behavior on the grounds that they fail to account for the mechanisms that turn judges' values into legal rulings. As with researchers studying motivated reasoning more generally, they argue that the correlation between ideology and decision-making is not a product of self-conscious efforts by judges to implement their policy preferences but rather the product of a subconscious relationship between their values and the way they interpret legally significant facts. On this view, we should regard judges as sincere when they contend that they base their decisions on the law, but also recognize that their understanding of what the law requires, and of how best to achieve what the law requires, is "shaped by their values – operating not as resources for theorizing law, but as subconscious, extralegal influences on their perception of legal consequential facts."[27]

Taken as a whole, it would be wrong to conclude that this research demonstrates that judges are, in effect, if not in intent, political actors whose decisions unwittingly effect their preferences just as if they were intentionally meaning to do so. "The research does not support the view that there are widespread, consistent differences between judges based on their background and beliefs. Judges, however, decide cases in which personal characteristics are salient in a manner consistent with their own personal characteristics."[28] Those, one imagines, are precisely the sorts of situations that are ripe for motivated reasoning to manifest itself.

JUDGES AND THEIR AUDIENCES

Judges perform their roles before a variety of audiences. There are, of course, the parties to and participants in the cases over which they preside. But there are also judicial colleagues, the bar, the general public, and the judge's community of personal

[26] Kahan, Hoffman, Braman, Evans, and Rachlinski, 'They Saw a Protest', 883–84.

[27] Dan M. Kahan, '"Ideology in" or "Cultural Cognition of" Judging: What Difference Does It Make?,' (2009) 92 *Marquette Law Review* 414.

[28] Jeffrey J. Rachlinski and Andrew J. Wistrich, 'Judging the Judiciary by the Numbers: Empirical Research on Judges,' (2017) 13 *Annual Review of Law and Social Science* 203–29.

and professional friends and acquaintances. Each of these audiences has expectations about how judges should behave, and judges' perceptions of those expectations will shape their behavior to at least some degree. As with accuracy-driven motivated reasoning, that can serve as a helpful constraint, because some of these audiences will expect that judges act in an appropriately judicial way, including by rooting their decisions in a dispassionate analysis of what the law requires. But some audiences may be interested primarily in results, which can exert a corrosive effect.

Professor Lawrence Baum has drawn on social psychology to consider how judges' self-presentation – that is, their efforts, both consciously and otherwise, to make a favorable impression on others – might affect their behavior.[29] His work proceeds from the assumption that judges, like people more generally, want to be liked and respected and therefore care about the regard in which they are held by the audiences that are important to them. He contends that judges' social groups and professional peers are likely to have the greatest influence on their behavior. That could, as noted, have a salutary effect insofar as those audiences value the impartial, legalist ideal. But it might also create pressure to act in a manner reflective of the social and policy views that predominate among their social peers.

Here, too, the phenomenon can be conceived of as a species of motivated reasoning, though Baum is less concerned with identifying the mechanism than establishing the existence of the phenomenon. One example is the "Greenhouse effect," named after former *New York Times* Supreme Court reporter Linda Greenhouse, which arises out of the supposition that the justices are not immune to the effects of praise and criticism, and that they will, to varying degrees and not necessarily consciously, shape their behavior to achieve favorable press coverage. The existence of such a relationship is, in a sense, unremarkable. Chief Justice William Rehnquist acknowledged as much, observing not only that the justices are unable to insulate themselves from public opinion but also that "it would probably be unwise to try. We read newspapers and magazines, we watch news on television, we talk to our friends about current events."[30] It is not the case, he maintained, that justices cast their votes based on their perceptions of the public's preferences. "[B]ut that is quite a different thing from saying that no judge is ever influenced by the great tides of public opinion in a country such as ours. Judges are influenced by them …."

As its name and history suggest, the Greenhouse effect was identified in the era of pre-internet, legacy media, and as we will see operated differently than it does now. In its original manifestation, the effect was a source of concern for conservative observers, based on the following logic: since those in the media tend to be liberal, a justice motivated by the desire to get favorable coverage, and to avoid

[29] Lawrence Baum, *Judges and Their Audiences: A Perspective on Judicial Behavior* (Princeton: Princeton University Press, 2006).

[30] William H. Rehnquist, *The Supreme Court: How It Was, How It Is* (New York: Alfred A. Knopf, 1987) 98.

unfavorable coverage, will be drawn toward more liberal results. Put somewhat differently, a justice concerned about cultivating a legacy that lands "on the right side of history" will be mindful of the notion that newspapers are the first draft of history. And the effect is more pervasive. It is not just the media that tends to be liberal, but also elite segments of the legal profession, as well as the Washington, DC, circles in which the justices end up socializing. "The cumulative impact is that conservatives appointed to the Court have strong reasons to move to more liberal positions."[31]

Baum extended the point by presenting evidence that, as of the time he wrote in 2006, Republican-appointed justices who had spent time living in Washington before their appointment to the Court, and who had thus maintained their conservatism despite the counter-pressures that DC exerts, tended to remain faithfully conservative while on the Court. There were at that time nine Republican justices who had moved to Washington after their appointment, and "there were clear and substantial increases in liberalism for four and more limited or ambiguous increases for three others."[32] The small numbers involved caution against drawing firm conclusions, but the evidence is certainly consistent with a Greenhouse effect. "Judges want the approval of individuals and groups that are salient to them, and their interest in approval may affect their judicial behavior. The relative autonomy of Supreme Court justices from concrete pressures leaves a great deal of room for them to respond to their personal audiences."[33]

In a more recent book, Baum partnered with Professor Neal Devins to extend and update the analysis.[34] They emphasize the increasing prevalence and degree of partisan division in both society and Congress. This has changed the nature of the processes by which justices are selected. Until the 1990s, the party of the appointing president was not a consistent indicator of whether a justice would be liberal or conservative. Now, however, the appointment process has become ideologically charged, and new justices come to the Court having been selected in a way that ensures congruence between their views and those dominant in the party of the president who appointed them. Since 2010, and "for the first time in its history, the Court has had liberal and conservative blocs that fall perfectly along party lines."[35] And because the polarization present throughout society exists in its elite segments as well, the justices have an increased opportunity to limit their socialization to groups that share their inclinations, which reinforces the perspectives they brought to the Court. It is these elite communities, Devins and Baum contend, that provide the greatest influence on the justices.

31 Baum, 'Judges and Their Audiences', 140–41.

32 Id., 151.

33 Baum, 'Judges and Their Audiences'.

34 Neal Devins and Lawrence Baum, *The Company They Keep: How Partisan Divisions Came to the Supreme Court* (Oxford: Oxford University Press, 2019).

35 Devins and Baum, 'The Company They Keep', 2.

To unpack the argument a bit, Devins and Baum's claim is that the very nature of judicial appointments tends to lead to the selection of people who will be especially responsive to the esteem of others. Acceptance of a judgeship entails the acceptance of constraints on one's behavior; in both formal and informal senses, judges have less freedom than they did as members of the bar. For many, it also involves giving up the considerably larger financial returns associated with the private practice of law. But the role brings its rewards as well. One of the significant gains, in addition to power, is esteem. "Not everyone would find this tradeoff attractive; it would be most attractive to those who care about the esteem in which they are held."[36] Devins and Baum further posit that it will not be the general public's regard that matters to those who hold judicial office, but rather that of the elite, which tends to be the segment of society that the justices come from (and even those not born into the elite world are likely to have lived in that world for the entirety of their education and professional lives) and the one with which they most frequently interact. These include "federal and foreign judges, Supreme Court practitioners, law schools and lawyer groups, high-ranking government officials, and media elites."[37]

Notably, again, those audiences have become increasingly segmented. As a result, "there is a growing trend of Justices speaking to like-minded elite audience; conservative Justices are often featured speakers before the Federalist Society and liberal Justices are headliners for the American Constitution Society."[38] Significantly, this does not necessarily mean the justices become partisans. Even ideologically active members of the legal profession value the rule of law and the associated norms of legal reasoning and argumentation, and adherence to these norms thus helps explain "why Justices, far more than members of Congress, make use of general principles that transcend the stakes for policy in particular decisions."[39] Nonetheless, the clear implication is that the Greenhouse effect has cleaved into two ideologically opposed forces.

The concerns outlined by Devins and Baum help illuminate a pair of recent debates surrounding the Court and the federal judiciary more generally. The first relates to membership in the Federalist Society and the American Constitution Society (ACS), both of which are nominally nonpartisan organizations that are nonetheless widely understood to be, respectively, a group for conservative lawyers and judges and its later-arriving liberal counterpart, respectively. In January 2020, the Committee on Codes of Conduct of the Judicial Conference of the United States – the members of which are all federal judges – issued a draft opinion concerning the ethical propriety of judges being members of (as contrasted with participating

36 Id., 10–12.
37 Id.
38 Id.
39 Id.

in events sponsored by) the two organizations.[40] The issue, in the committee's view, was that the two organizations have "factional missions." "A reasonable and informed public would view judges holding membership in these organizations to hold, advocate, and serve liberal or conservative interests." Of particular significance to the committee was the fact that both organizations were formed due to "the perceived success of their ideological opposition" – the American Bar Association (ABA), in the case of the Federalist Society, and the Federalist Society, in the case of the ACS. All of this, the committee concluded, was enough to make membership in either organization something that could call a judge's impartiality into question.

The committee received over 300 comments on its draft opinion, including a letter signed by over 200 judges, nearly all of whom would be considered conservative in some sense of the word.[41] The letter disputed the Committee's characterization of the Federalist Society, in particular the claim that the organization takes policy positions or that its activities are political. And it objected to the limitation of the prohibition to the Federalist Society and ACS and not to the ABA, which, as the letter asserted, likewise regards itself as nonpartisan but has taken policy positions on a variety of contentious issues. Relying on the public's perception, the letter contended, simply would not do, because all sorts of organizations take policy positions, and the result might be that membership "in specialty bars, law school communities, and even churches would be called into question."

The committee ultimately decided not to issue the Advisory Opinion, citing the lack of consensus among judges as its primary reason.[42] Instead, it left the matter to each judge. But, it admonished, "prudence dictates that as judges confront a world filled with challenges arising out of emerging technologies, deep ideological disputes, a growing sense of mistrust of individuals and institutions, and an ever-changing landscape of competing political, legal, and societal interests, they need to remain vigilant about problems associated with membership in organizations."

The second controversy relates to the celebrity culture that has come to surround the Supreme Court.[43] The justices have long enjoyed celebrity status within the legal world, regularly serving as honored guests and speakers at law schools,

40 Committee on Codes of Conduct, *Advisory Opinion No. 117: Judges' Involvement With the American Constitution Society, the Federalist Society, and the American Bar Association*, Exposure Draft, January 2020. Available at eppc.org/wp-content/uploads/2020/01/Guide-Vol02B-Ch02-AdvOp11720OGC-ETH-2020-01-20-EXP-1.pdf [perma.cc/9QT7-VPT].

41 Letter from Judge Gregory G. Katsas, et al., to Robert P. Deyling, Assistant General Counsel, Administrative Office of the United States Courts, March 18, 2020. Available at int.nyt.com/data/documenthelper/6928-judges-respond-to-draft-ethics/53eaddfaf39912a26ae7/optimized/full.pdf [perma.cc/C6F7-F2FQ].

42 Memo from James C. Duff, Director, Administrative Office of the United States Courts, to All United States Judges, July 30, 2020. Available at fixthecourt.com/wp-content/uploads/2020/07/Duff-update-on-draft-of-op.-117.pdf [perma.cc/5NNL-4A4P].

43 This discussion draws heavily on Chad M. Oldfather, 'The Inconspicous DHS: The Supreme Court, Celebrity Culture, and Justice David H. Souter,' (2020) 90 *Mississippi Law Journal* 183–227.

bar association conferences, and the like. But for the most part, they have otherwise maintained low public profiles. A few, such as Oliver Wendell Holmes, Jr., and William O. Douglas, achieved a degree of renown among the broader public. Holmes, for example, was well enough known that the occasion and celebration of his ninetieth birthday were front-page items in the *New York Times*, and he was invited to deliver a national radio address on the occasion.[44] But for the most part, the justices have historically worked in relative obscurity, sometimes even when recognized. An often-repeated anecdote concerns the time someone mistook Justice Souter for Justice Breyer and asked him what was the best part about being on the Court, to which the faux Breyer responded, "Working with David Souter."[45]

That has changed. The justices have, and in many cases have cultivated, a higher national profile. Judge Richard Posner identified several factors at work.[46] One is simply that the justices have more time. The Court decides many fewer cases than it once did, and the justices are assisted in their work by a staff of highly talented law clerks. At the same time, the media environment has changed dramatically. The internet and cable news have eased access to public-facing platforms and created a never-ending demand for content, creating space for new characters to emerge. The justices increasingly sign lucrative book deals – most recently, Justice Amy Coney Barrett received a $2 million advance for a book, which *Politico* described as "likely the most since book deals won by Clarence Thomas and Sandra Day O'Connor"[47] – and make more public appearances than their predecessors. While Justice Antonin Scalia may have originated the role of celebrity justice in its modern incarnation, it was Justice Ruth Bader Ginsburg – "The Notorious RBG" – who perfected it. She became an icon, the subject of documentary films, and someone whose face appeared on items available for sale at gift shops across the land. Near the peak of her fame, one commentator captured it as follows: "She's pursued by the media, even tabloids, and can hardly take a step without fans stopping her for a selfie."[48]

Both the fracturing of judicial audiences and the rise of celebrity culture, separately and in combination, appear to create precisely the dynamic that Devins and Baum identified. Justices who are members of a group, whether it is partisan in a political sense or one that instead embraces a school of jurisprudential thought that is merely associated with partisan preferences, will be inclined to assimilate the

[44] Associated Press, 'Holmes to Address Nation on Air at 90,' *New York Times*, March 7, 1931, at 1.

[45] There are multiple versions of the anecdote, one of which appears in Bob Cohn, 'Justice Breyer and the "Stress" of Confirmation,' *The Atlantic*, July 14, 2009, available at www.theatlantic.com/politics/archive/2009/07/justice-breyer-and-the-stress-of-confirmation/21304/.

[46] Richard A. Posner, 'The Supreme Court and Celebrity Culture,' (2013) 88 *Chicago-Kent Law Review* 299.

[47] Daniel Lippman, 'William Barr, Amy Coney Barrett Land Book Deals,' *Politico*, April 19, 2021, at www.politico.com/news/2021/04/19/bill-barr-amy-coney-barrett-book-deals-483028.

[48] Sébastien Blanc, 'At 83, US Supreme Court Judge Ginsburg is Pop Culture Icon,' AFP (October 18, 2016), www.yahoo.com/news/83-us-supreme-court-judge-ginsburg-pop-culture-171844355.html [perma.cc/83LW-9Z2U].

group's perspective. Justices who enjoy their celebrity status will have incentives to please their fan base and be disinclined to act in ways that disappoint, a mindset that might be especially consequential when the fan base and the membership of a jurisprudential affinity group substantially overlap. The effect is not merely one that relates to the substance of the positions the justices take but also to style. Justices eager to burnish their personal brand are more inclined to muddle the Court's work by writing separate opinions so as to maintain an image of consistency in their personal jurisprudence.[49] This, in turn, results in the Court looking less like a court and more like a collection of individuals who each happen to have a vote, which is to say more like a political institution.

HEURISTICS AND BIASES

Human thought operates within the limits of "bounded rationality." Each of us has only so much time, attention, and cognitive bandwidth. Any attempt to be fully rational in making the full array of decisions we must make in even an ordinary day would lead to paralysis. Of necessity, and without realizing that we are doing it, we instead depend on a range of mental shortcuts and strategies that save us from having to think from the ground up, or even much at all, about each of the choices we must make. These heuristics are both time-saving and largely correct. They can also lead us astray.

Much of the research conducted in cognitive psychology over the past several decades proceeds from the supposition that human thought is dominated by two modes.[50] "System 1" thinking involves the making of quick, intuitive judgments that require little or no conscious effort. Examples include detecting which of two objects is closer, determining where a sound came from, detecting anger or hostility in a person's face or voice, reading signs, and so on. System 1 employs heuristics, which can be thought of as mental shortcuts or rules of thumb that involve automatic, and usually accurate, responses to familiar situations. "System 2," by contrast, involves conscious mental effort and is largely devoted to complex tasks. It is what we draw on when we think through a problem. Both systems are active while we are awake, with System 1 running automatically and System 2 typically running in a low-effort, standby mode. System 1 constantly feeds System 2 with the raw material of thought, and when complexities arise, or unfamiliar situations present themselves, System 2 engages. It makes sense of the difficult or unexpected, and it monitors behavior to ensure compliance with social conventions. Most of the time, this arrangement works well. Much of what happens as we make our way through the world takes place with little thought. As Professor Daniel Kahneman, who received a Nobel

49 Craig S. Lerner and Nelson Lund, 'Judicial Duty and the Supreme Court's Cult of Celebrity,' (2010) 78 *George Washington Law Review* 1255, 1268–69.

50 For a survey of this work by one of the pioneers in the field, see Daniel Kahneman, *Thinking, Fast and Slow* (New York: Farrar, Straus and Giroux, 2011).

Prize for his role in pioneering this work, put it: "System 1 is generally very good at what it does: its models of familiar situations are accurate, its short-term predictions are usually accurate as well, and its initial reactions to challenges are swift and generally appropriate."[51] But it has its flaws. It processes information in a way that generates systematic errors, or biases, in certain circumstances, sometimes misses the complexity in a situation, and is deficient in logic and statistical reasoning. It will err, sometimes in ways that are consequential.

An array of studies support the proposition that judges, too, can be susceptible to these effects, which include:[52]

- *Confirmation Bias*. This bias comes into play during the processes of seeking out and evaluating information. Those who hold preexisting beliefs tend to prefer information that supports those beliefs and to disregard or minimize information that runs contrary to them.[53] The interplay with motivated reasoning is clear. A judge whose loyalties, sympathies, or intuitions side with one party will be drawn to information that supports those views and tend to discount information that does not.
- *Hindsight Bias*. Hindsight bias involves allowing one's knowledge of how an event turned out to affect one's judgment of conduct undertaken or decisions made before the event took place. An accident that actually happened will seem to have been more foreseeable than circumstances warranted before it did, or a losing bet will seem to have been riskier than it actually was based on the information available at the time it was made. The potential for hindsight bias is pervasive in the legal system, where the core aspect of many lawsuits is whether and to what extent some bad thing that actually happened should have been accounted for beforehand.[54] Studies suggest that judges are at least sometimes able to resist its effects.[55]
- *Anchoring*. Anchoring involves relying on an initially provided piece of information when making judgments or estimates. The anchor, even if arbitrary or irrelevant, tends to bias subsequent assessments. Judges asked to determine compensation in a hypothetical employment discrimination case tended to

[51] Kahneman, 'Thinking, Fast and Slow', 25.

[52] For a comprehensive review, see Brian M. Berry, *How Judges Judge: Empirical Insights into Judicial Decision-Making* (New York: Routledge, 2021) 13–60.

[53] Susanne M. Schmittat and Birte Englich, 'If you Judge, Investigate! Responsibility Reduces Confirmatory Information Processing in Legal Experts,' (2016) 22 *Psychology, Public Policy, and Law* 386–400; Moa Liden, Minna Grans and Peter Juslin, '"Guilty, No Doubt": Detention Provoking Confirmation Bias in Judges' Guilt Assessments and Debiasing Techniques,' (2019) 25 *Psychology, Crime & Law* 219–47.

[54] Chris Guthrie, Jeffrey J. Rachlinski and Andrew J. Wistrich, 'Inside the Judicial Mind,' (2001), 86 *Cornell Law Review* 780.

[55] Wistrich, Guthrie and Rachlinksi, 'Can Judges Ignore Inadmissible Information'; Jeffrey J. Rachlinski, Chris Guthrie and Andrew J. Wistrich, 'Probable Cause, Probability, and Hindsight,' (2011) 8 *Journal of Empirical Legal Studies* 72.

settle on a higher number if they were told that the plaintiff mentioned hearing about a high damage award in a similar case on a television show. Judges presented with the question of how much to fine a nightclub for violating a noise ordinance settled on a markedly lower number when the establishment was called "Club 58" than when it was called "Club 11,866."[56] Anchoring can manifest itself in a context like sentencing, where calculating sentence length in years rather than months (sentences tend to be longer when the unit is years) or shifting the order in which more- and less-serious crimes get sentenced (the first case sets a comparatively high or low anchor that affects the decision in the second) can have a distorting effect.[57]

- *Representativeness*. The representativeness heuristic is a cognitive shortcut that involves making judgments or decisions based on how well an object, event, or person resembles a particular prototype or category. It often leads individuals to overlook baseline statistical information and instead rely on superficial similarities, potentially leading to biases and errors in reasoning. A study by Guthrie, Rachlinski, and Wistrich provides an illustration.[58] They provided a group of judges with a hypothetical case in which the plaintiff was struck by a falling barrel as he passed by the defendant's warehouse. The barrel fell either because it was negligently secured or because the rope holding it broke. Based on a government inspection, it's understood that "(1) when barrels are negligently secured, there is a 90% chance that they will break loose; (2) when barrels are safely secured, they break loose only 1% of the time; (3) workers negligently secure barrels only 1 in 1,000 times."[59] The researchers asked the judges to estimate how likely it was that the barrel was negligently secured. Most judges answered that it was more than 75 percent likely. The actual probability given these number is 8.3 percent. The reason is that properly secured barrels break loose one time out of a hundred, while barrels are negligently secured only one time out of a thousand, and not all of those break loose.

The list earlier is just a sampling of a large body of work. Research has also demonstrated judicial susceptibility to framing effects, the contrast effect, the availability heuristic, the gambler's fallacy, clustering, and more. The key point is simply this: there are all sorts of ways in which human thought can go astray without our noticing, because errors are the product of automatic processes. Judges may be less susceptible to some of these cognitive errors, but they do not seem to enjoy any sort of blanket immunity.

56 Rachlinski and Wistrich, 'Judging by the Numbers'.

57 Jeffrey J. Rachlinski, Andrew J. Wistrich and Chris Guthrie, 'Can Judges Make Reliable Numeric Judgments: Distorted Damages and Skewed Sentences,' (2015) 90 *Indiana Law Journal* 695.

58 Chris Guthrie, Jeffrey J. Rachlinski and Andrew J. Wistrich, 'Blinking on the Bench: How Judges Decide Cases,' (2007) 93 *Cornell Law Review* 1.

59 Guthrie, Rachlinksi, and Wistrich, 'Blinking on the Bench', 23.

The Bias Blind Spot, Naïve Realism, and the Egocentric Bias

There is another complicating factor. People are generally quite receptive to the idea that cognitive biases exist, and they are ready to recognize their operation – in other people. Professor Emily Pronin describes "a broad and pervasive tendency for people to see the existence and operation of bias much more in others than in themselves."[60] My decisions are the product of thorough and thoughtful deliberation. Yours, by contrast, are the obvious product of bias.

One possible explanation for this phenomenon is that biases are the product of processes operating beneath consciousness. They are products of System 1, and part of how they exert their influence is that we do not notice them. Our self-assessments, by contrast, are typically the product of conscious introspection, which naturally places greater weight on consciously perceived factors such as intent or motivation. And because we regard our own motivations as pure, we have little reason to scrutinize our conduct, which must itself be pure as well. When we judge others, we usually do not have access to their internal thought processes. We must as a result focus on their behavior and supply our own explanations for what must be driving it.

Another mechanism at work is naive realism, a cognitive and perceptual bias that leads individuals to believe that their subjective perception of reality is an accurate representation of the objective truth.[61] It is characterized by the assumption that what one sees, hears, or experiences is a direct reflection of the way things truly are and that anyone else who objectively and rationally evaluates the same information will therefore necessarily come to the same conclusions. Someone who holds a different perspective must accordingly be biased, mistaken, or lacking in understanding. The hallmark of naïve realism is a failure to recognize that one's own interpretations of reality are also influenced by their biases, experiences, and limited perspectives. Since we cannot be wrong, then it must be the case that the problem lies with others.

A related bias is the egocentric bias, which is a tendency to overestimate our own abilities relative to others. The classic example is the commonly invoked statistic that 90 percent of drivers consider themselves to be above average.[62] Judges are

[60] Emily Pronin, 'Perception and Misperception of Bias in Human Judgment,' (2006) 11 *Trends in Cognitive Science* 37.

[61] See Lee Ross and Andrew Ward, 'Naïve Realism in Everyday Life: Implications for Social Conflict and Misunderstanding,' in Edward S. Reed, Elliot Turiel and Terrance Brown, eds., *Values and Knowledge* (Mahwah, NJ: Lawrence Erlbaum Associates, Inc., 1996) 103. For an overview of the literature on naïve realism, see Bryan D. Lammon, 'What We Talk About When We Talk About Ideology: Judicial Politics Scholarship and Naïve Legal Realism,' (2009) 83 *St. John's Law Review* 231, 267–88.

[62] As one commentator has pointed out, it is possible, if the distribution of driving talent is skewed, for 90 percent of drivers to be above average. Will Koehrsen, *How 90% of Drivers Can be "Above Average" or Why You Need to be Careful When Using Statistics: Means, Medians, and Skewed Distributions in the Real World*, available at https://towardsdatascience.com/how-90-of-drivers-can-be-above-average-or-why-you-need-to-be-careful-when-talking-statistics-3df7be5cb116.

susceptible to it, too. Here again, Guthrie, Rachlinski, and Wistrich provide the evidence.[63] Over half of administrative law judges asked about where they stood relative to their colleagues in terms of the frequency with which they are reversed on appeal placed themselves in the bottom quartile. Only 4½ percent placed themselves in the top quartile. Judges likewise tend to imagine that they outperform their colleagues in terms of their abilities to evaluate witness credibility and to avoid racial or gender prejudice. Judges, like everyone else, tend to wear rose-colored glasses when looking in the mirror. We should not be surprised to hear them tell us that their decisions are simply a product of the law, even if it may appear to us that they are a product of something else entirely.

The work covered in this chapter is a small sampling of a much larger body of research into how people generally, and judges specifically, are susceptible to systematic errors in their thinking. And how they, like the rest of us, are primed to notice such errors more readily in others than in themselves. It is, of course, important to be cautious in drawing conclusions from the research outlined in this chapter. To say that some phenomenon manifests itself in most people is not to say that it will do so to the same degree, or at all, in all people. As noted at the outset, all of this research involves data collected under conditions that were artificial to varying degrees, simply because it is difficult at best to study the processes of decision-making in actual cases in a systematic fashion. Still, taken as a whole, it provides general support for the observations of Cardozo and other thoughtful judges. Judges, like the rest of us, are to varying degrees susceptible to biases and to the tendencies of heuristics that lead us astray in predictable types of situations. Some of it even provides tentative support for Judge Posner's suggestion that the more strongly judges claim to be objective, the more biased they are likely to be.[64] Much of this is consistent with intuitions that long predated the work. Thoughtful judges have long recognized that neither the robe nor the role shield them from the forces that afflict human cognition. Moreover, as Chapter 4 explores, the legal system more generally has relied on a variety of procedural and architectural features to combat these tendencies. But, as we will see, those protections may no longer be doing the work they once did.

63 Chris Guthrie, Jeffrey J. Rachlinski and Andrew J. Wistrich, 'The "Hidden Judiciary": An Empirical Examination of Executive Branch Justice,' (2009) 58 *Duke Law Journal* 1477.

64 Pronin, 'Perception and Misperception', 38.

4

Internal Constraints on Judicial Behavior

Many of the Legal Realists believed that social science could provide guidance that the law, because of its indeterminacy, could not. Social science has had mixed results in that role, but it has confirmed the Realist insight that judges are, to at least some degree, susceptible to the same human foibles as the rest of us. Whether we acknowledge it or not, each of us can see the world only through our own eyes. What those eyes notice from the barrage of information and other stimuli they encounter, and what sense any of us makes of it, will be influenced by our individual stories, preferences, and attitudes as filtered through our usually efficient but occasionally misled cognitive machinery. And so it is for judges, too.

But of course, the rule of law and the maintenance of the triad call for something more than ad hoc results generated by a motley assortment of individual decision-makers, each bringing their own personal preferences to the job. It sometimes necessarily provides for the exercise of discretion, to be sure. But the overriding aspiration is for uniformity and equality. No one is above the law, we like to believe, and the law should be the same whether applied to a homeless person, a business executive, or the President of the United States. Election maps, if they are to be scrutinized by judges, should receive the same treatment regardless of whether they are thought to favor Democrats or Republicans. The Realists, and our more thoughtful judges, have recognized their susceptibility to these influences. The justices in *Rucho*, both in the majority and the dissent, did so as well. Their disagreement over whether the federal judicial power extends to the review of partisan gerrymandering claims was in part the product of worries over whether it is possible to reduce the force of these nonlegal influences to an appropriate degree.

This chapter proceeds from the supposition that many features of the procedural and institutional architecture of the legal system reflect an implicit recognition of the need to counter the various forces that can lead thought astray. Here again, we encounter ground that others have broken. Writing in 1960, in response to "the dirge-chanters" of the bar and "generations of law students [who] assume, two thirds of them, as of course and despite all your effort, that *if* the outcome of an appeal is not foredoomed in logic it *therefore* is the product of uncontrolled will which is as good as wayward,"[1] Professor Karl Llewellyn identified fourteen "major steadying factors" that, in his estimation, provided restraint and what he called "reckonability" to the system.[2] Our focus here will fall primarily on three of them. Procedural mechanisms such as the adversarial process, reliance on precedent, and the presumption that decisions will be justified in written opinions serve to channel judges toward the detached, long-view consideration that the rule of law requires. They serve to slow judges' thinking, making it more deliberate and increasing the likelihood that judges will encounter, and contend with, counterarguments to whatever conclusions they ultimately reach. They thus also work to preserve the triad.

But, I contend, there is a catch. Developments that began to take shape at almost precisely the time Llewellyn wrote have undercut many of the key assumptions on which those mechanisms rest. Some of these developments are at least partially quantifiable. Others are atmospheric or otherwise intangible. Though the analysis must therefore be somewhat speculative and appropriately tentative, it seems inevitable that they resulted in a system that operates differently and that in important senses provides constraint that is different, and almost certainly weaker, than in the past.

THE ADVERSARIAL PROCESS

As we saw in Chapter 1, litigation under the standard model pits two opposed parties whose dispute relates solely to a past event. The plaintiff claims that they were injured by the defendant's conduct, that the defendant failed to live up to the terms of a contract, that the defendant interfered with their use and enjoyment of their property, or the like. The crux of the dispute may be largely factual. Was it even the defendant who engaged in the conduct alleged to have harmed the plaintiff? Did the defendant's conduct cause the plaintiff's injury, or was it something else? Or it might be legal. Did the defendant owe any duties of care to the plaintiff under these circumstances? What did the language of the contract actually mean? Or it could be some combination.

For this sort of dispute, it is natural for a judge to assume a largely reactive posture. The parties will have access to the key information, and their desire to prevail provides a natural incentive to develop that information as fully as possible and to present the court with their strongest factual and legal arguments. The consequences of such a lawsuit will fall almost exclusively on the parties. There is accordingly little reason for the judge to be concerned about whether the parties have failed to make their best arguments, or failed to account for the interests of people not involved in the litigation. It is natural to remain neutral, and to refrain from any interventions that would appear to involve preferring one side over the other. To be sure, there

1 Karl N. Llewellyn, *The Common Law Tradition: Deciding Appeals* (Boston: Little, Brown, 1960) 4.

2 Llewellyn, 'Common Law Tradition', 19–51.

will occasionally be cases where the governing law isn't clear, such that the court's decision will to some extent entail making new law. But a court can often sidestep concerns it has about the parties' efforts in such cases by limiting the scope of its ruling, thereby providing future litigants with the ability to distinguish their case.

In federal court, the various justiciability doctrines provide some assurance that a lawsuit will involve a live dispute between parties who are truly adverse, and that the adversarialism of the standard model remains in place. State courts do not all follow the federal model, and their practices diverge from that model to a sometimes considerable degree.[3] But in both contexts, things have changed, and the pertinent changes are not merely procedural. The amount and scope of law have increased substantially over the past hundred years, and as the law has expanded to govern a wider range of an increasingly complex and interconnected society, the nature of the disputes that courts must adjudicate has expanded as well. Bilateral private disputes remain. But today's courts often find themselves faced with disputes the resolution of which affects people and groups who have no formal input into the process. This is true not only in classic public law disputes requiring judicial oversight of the resolution of problems in school or prison systems[4] but also in private law matters such as mass torts. In these cases, the adversarial process does not ensure the court will have the information and perspective necessary to resolve the issues in an ideally authoritative way.

In recognition of this, as Professor Judith Resnik detailed over forty years ago,[5] federal and state trial judges have to a considerable degree abandoned the reactive, dispassionate posture of the standard model in favor of a more active, managerial role. They involve themselves in moving cases through the system at an early stage, such as by negotiating with the parties over the timing and shape of the litigation, and they remain involved to supervise remedies. Judges have greater power as a result, and they are able to exercise it in ways that are not subject to the traditional constraints on judicial behavior. Little of this takes place in the courtroom, but rather through discussions in chambers or otherwise outside of the public eye. Few of the judge's rulings or more subtle efforts to shape the proceedings are justified via written opinions. Appellate review is often unavailable because subsequent developments in the case will effectively nullify the significance of decisions made during earlier stages. All of this involves more work for judges, which in turn generates pressure for judges to encourage settlement and otherwise speed the docket along, which in turn provides even more opportunities and more perceived need to use the tools of management. "In short," Resnik concludes, "managerial judging may be redefining sub silentio our standards of what constitutes rational, fair, and impartial adjudication."

[3] Helen Hershkoff, 'State Courts and the Passive Virtues: Rethinking the Judicial Function,' (2001) 114 *Harvard Law Review* 1833.

[4] Sarah Evans Barker, 'Beyond Decisional Templates: The Role of Imaginative Justice in the Trial Court,' (2009) 92 *Marquette Law Review* 667.

[5] Judith Resnik, 'Managerial Judging,' (1982) 96 *Harvard Law Review* 374.

Appellate courts have likewise been transformed.[6] Under the traditional view of appellate judging, which Professors William Richman and William Reynolds called "the Learned Hand model,"[7] judges and judges alone do the work of resolving cases. The members of an appellate panel each scrutinize the briefs, press the parties at an oral argument that proceeds for as long as necessary to explore the issues, and gather with their colleagues to reach a tentative resolution. Collective deliberation characterizes the process. One judge prepares a draft opinion that the others carefully review. The opinion gets revised, recirculated, and revised again until the panel achieves full consensus, at which point it is released to the public and included in the official reports of the court's decisions. It then serves as precedent, prospectively binding that court and all the courts beneath it. Judge Frank Coffin called it a process of "graduated decision-making" that provided no fewer than seven opportunities for the engaged judge to reconsider things and allowed for the recognition that a conclusion reached at any point "is tentative, fragile, and likely to be modified or set aside as a consequence of deepened insight."[8]

There have, without question, always been elements of fiction and wishful thinking to this depiction. The process may not have unfolded in that way all the time, or even most of the time. But the idealized form of deliberation it imagines was achievable and at least approximated with some regularity. Lighter dockets facilitated contemplation and enabled judges to monitor one another more effectively – a judge truly engaged with each case would be more able to detect when a colleague was not engaged, and would be aware that their colleagues were likewise monitoring them. It was also a world of less law, which meant that the judges were more likely to be deeply familiar with the bodies of law applicable to any given case. This, one imagines, enabled them to appreciate aberrational situations more readily, as well as to identify subterranean connections between the doctrinal questions present in a case and similar strands of authority present in other, apparently distinct, sets of cases. And as explored in greater detail later, the bar, too, was different. Most lawyers were generalists, and the bar placed comparatively greater emphasis on the practice as a profession than as a business. A reduced emphasis on the bottom line, and thus on billable hours, left more time for contemplation. In theory, at least, lawyers were able to themselves keep abreast of the entirety of a court's output, and at the very least to be mindful of trends and significant features of the court's decision-making.[9] Knowledge that a substantial portion of the bar was

6 I first developed much of the discussion here in Chad M. Oldfather, 'Remedying Judicial Inactivism: Opinions as Informational Regulation,' (2006) 58 *Florida Law Review* 743, 764–79.

7 William M. Richman and William L. Reynolds, 'Elitism, Expediency, and the New Certiorari: Requiem for the Learned Hand Tradition,' (1996) 81 *Cornell Law Review* 273.

8 Frank M. Coffin, *The Ways of a Judge: Reflections from the Federal Appellate Bench* (Boston: Houghton, Mifflin, Harcourt, 1980) 63.

9 One place where this manifested itself was in the evolution of the unpublished opinion. The initial advocates for the practice were members of the bar, many of whom found that the increasing flow

regularly reading their work undoubtedly served as a powerful, informal source of discipline. The bar is among the most significant of judges' audiences, and most judges would not want to be held in low esteem by its members.

However realistic the Learned Hand model might be as a depiction of how appellate courts once operated, it utterly fails as a description of contemporary practice. The "crisis of volume" accounts for much of the change. The caseload of the federal courts of appeals in 2003 was more than fifteen times what it was in 1960, and increases in the number of judges over that time did not keep pace. The average judge's caseload in 2003 was 450 percent greater than that of the average judge in 1960.[10] Courts reacted by changing their processes. Some of these changes were formal. Oral arguments are no longer available in all cases and for indefinite length, but are instead time-limited when they are available at all.[11] Opinions are drafted primarily by law clerks and are often deemed unpublished or, more appropriately, non-precedential. Central court staff often conduct a screening process, allowing some cases to receive something akin to the traditional appellate procedure but relegating the rest to the truncated version of the process. All of this renders judges less deeply engaged with their work and less able to monitor their colleagues. Appellate judges, too, have increasingly become managers. And this, Professor Owen Fiss suggested in 1983, threatens a significant source of the judiciary's legitimacy, "the obligation of a judge to engage in a special dialogue-to listen to all grievances, hear from all the interests affected, and give reasons for his decisions."[12] A judge who signs an opinion "assures the parties that he has thoroughly participated in that process and assumes individual responsibility for the decision."[13] But "bureaucratization raises the spectre that the judge's signature is but a sham and that the judge is exercising power without genuinely engaging in the dialogue from which his authority flows."[14]

Changes, once they occur, tend to be sticky. As Professor Merritt McAlister has demonstrated, the volume of cases in the federal appellate system declined by a considerable amount in the early 2000s, but the courts did not adjust their practices back toward the traditional approach.[15] What were initially regarded as extraordinary measures designed to deal with crisis conditions have instead become the baseline. As a descriptive matter, this is understandable. The judges of today were law

of decisions, some of which added nothing of significance to the law, made it difficult for them to keep up with the courts' output. See John P. Borger and Chad M. Oldfather, '*Anastasoff v. United States* and the Debate Over Unpublished Opinions,' (2001) 36 *Tort and Insurance Law Journal* 899, 900–03.

10 Commission on Structural Alternatives for the Federal Courts of Appeals, Final Report 14 (1998).

11 Thomas E. Baker, *Rationing Justice on Appeal: The Problems of the U.S. Courts of Appeals* (St. Paul, MN: West Publishing Co., 1994) 109–10.

12 Owen M. Fiss, 'The Bureaucratization of the Judiciary,' (1983) 92 *Yale Law Journal* 1442, 1443.

13 Fiss, 'Bureaucratization', 1443.

14 Id.

15 Merritt E. McAlister, 'Rebuilding the Federal Circuit Courts,' (2022) 116 *Northwestern University Law Review* 1137.

clerks and lawyers in an era in which clerks routinely drafted opinions, unpublished opinions were commonplace, and what yesterday's judges regarded as innovations have become, for today's judges, simply the way things are. Those who practiced and judged in the Learned Hand era have long since departed. What to them was extraordinary became the new normal, which in turn became simply normal.

It is difficult, and to some extent perhaps even impossible, to demonstrate in concrete ways precisely what the cumulative effects of these changes have been. And they undoubtedly have manifested themselves in different ways and to different degrees in different contexts. What is true in federal courts may not be true in state courts in Iowa, which in turn may not be true for state courts in Florida. That there have been changes as a general matter, and substantial ones, seems undeniable, as does the fact that much of this change has happened so incrementally that little of it has seemed especially noteworthy as it has transpired. And the pace has been slow enough that even those at the end of their careers can appreciate only a portion of it. Because we cannot inhabit the world of our long-departed predecessors, we can only guess at the ways and extent to which our practices, assumptions, and habits of thought differ from theirs. What is certain is that they do, and that those differences to some greater or lesser degree affect fundamental aspects of the judiciary's functioning.

PRECEDENT

Precedential reasoning is not limited to the legal system and is quite familiar and intuitive in a wide range of contexts.[16] Children, for example, are quite adept at making the argument that they should be entitled to do something simply because their older sibling was. Administrators and managers learn that one should not grant a request from a student or employee without thinking through the implications for the future, when someone else shows up with a similar request. Although there is no formal entitlement to equal treatment in the two situations, there is nonetheless an understanding that equality is the baseline. If someone else in my situation was treated a certain way in the past, then I should be treated that way now.

A similar dynamic holds in law. The standard model's call for preexisting standards and the logic of the triad more generally imply the need for consistency across cases. That said, the technical meaning and operation of precedent – also referred to as "stare decisis" – are narrower. A later court is bound by the decisions of earlier courts that relate to the specific question before the later court. Given the existence of *State v. Hughes*, a Wisconsin state trial court judge may not conclude that the theft of a purse hanging on the handle of an occupied wheelchair is not a theft "from the person of another." In situations involving vertical stare decisis, where the later court sits beneath the prior court in the judicial hierarchy, the obligation is

[16] Frederick Schauer, 'Precedent,' (1987) 39 *Stanford Law Review* 571.

categorical. Where the later and earlier courts are both iterations of the same court, separated only by time, the obligation is more in the nature of a strong presumption. Trial courts generally have no formal responsibility to adhere to their past decisions. Appellate courts can overrule their prior decisions, but the general understanding is that they are to exercise that authority only in limited circumstances when certain conditions are met.

A subtle point bears emphasis. Past cases exert force as precedent only where they do not point a present court in a direction it was already inclined to go. Put differently, if the court would come out the same way even in the absence of any past decisions, then the past cases are doing no work in the analysis. A later judge who agrees with the analysis in *Hughes* isn't being pushed to a conclusion out of an obligation to follow precedent. It's only in cases where the second judge disagrees that the constraining force of precedent does any work. That judge would decide the question differently but does not have complete freedom to do so. If that judge is lower in the hierarchy than the court that decided *Hughes*, the court must follow *Hughes* unless the facts of the subsequent case differ in legally significant ways. If the second judge sits on a court at the same level, it will have some work to do in determining whether to overrule its past decision.

When considering whether to depart from precedent and overrule a past case, courts typically consider several factors.[17] First, whether the reasoning and legal principles underlying the precedent remain valid and relevant, including whether societal, technological, or legal developments have rendered the precedent outdated or impractical. Courts also assess the reliance placed on the precedent by the legal community and society at large, weighing the potential disruption, instability, and effects on public confidence in the legal system that may arise from overturning it. Additionally, courts evaluate the practical consequences of maintaining or overruling the precedent, including the impact on legal predictability, uniformity, and the overall administration of justice. The decision to depart from precedent is, at least in theory, a weighty one, requiring a careful balancing of these factors to ensure the integrity and adaptability of the legal system. The force that precedent exerts is therefore scalar rather than binary in nature. It varies by context – because, for example, reliance interests take on greater significance in some areas, such as commercial law – and it varies from one court to the next, and even within the same court.

[17] The Supreme Court's most recent articulations of its standards for overruling a past case are from *Planned Parenthood of Southeastern Pennsylvania* v. *Casey*, 505 US 833 (1992), and *Dobbs* v. *Jackson Women's Health Organization*, 142 S. Ct. 2228 (2022), which overruled *Casey*. "The main differences between Casey's stare decisis framework and Dobbs's are (1) the different conceptions of reliance advanced in the two decisions, and (2) the emphasis on the nature of the error and in particular the notion of "egregious" error that Dobbs relies on." Nina Varsava, 'Precedent, Reliance, and *Dobbs*,' (2023) 136 *Harvard Law Review* 1845. For a more in-depth overview of the justifications for stare decisis and a consideration of its application to methodological approaches, on which this section draws heavily, see Chad M. Oldfather, 'Methodological Pluralism and Constitutional Interpretation,' (2014) 80 *Brooklyn Law Review* 1.

For example, the Supreme Court gives its statutory decisions greater stare decisis effect than its constitutional decisions simply because of the difficulty involved in amending the Constitution. By contrast, Congress can much more easily "correct" what it regards as wrong decisions in interpreting legislation.

The justifications for adhering to precedent fall into two main categories. The first relates to rule-of-law values such as fairness, predictability, and stability. Treating like cases alike has a plain intuitive appeal, as discussed earlier, that can be justified in terms of equal treatment being a good in its own right. It's also justified by the consequences it produces in fostering impartiality, consistency, and the satisfaction of parties' expectations – both in terms of being able to rely on prior decisions and in having the ability to predict with a reasonable degree of confidence what future courts will do. Put differently, in a society where the courts adhere to their past decisions, individuals and entities can know that past applications of law provide a template that will also be applied to them. This enables them to determine what aspects of their conduct they should be especially mindful of and to extrapolate as necessary from those past situations to novel circumstances. These in turn combine to foster a more general sense of and confidence in the stability of the system as a whole.

The second set of justifications relates to decision-making itself. In a world without precedent, a court would have to reason from first principles in each case. The ability to regard past decisions as fixed points of departure, by contrast, serves both as a source of efficiency and a mechanism for minimizing error. There's an inherent humility in the doctrine. The collective wisdom embodied in the decisions of past courts is more likely to be correct and is more likely to have accounted for all the considerations that bear on the appropriate resolution of an issue than is a single court reasoning from the ground up. In addition, stare decisis compels a court deciding a current case to attempt to imagine all the future cases that will come within its scope because its decision will serve as precedent for future decision-makers. That serves as an additional source of discipline.

But precedent is not a straightjacket. Cases will arise in which the current court will justly conclude that past courts got things wrong, and the scalar nature of the doctrine enables overruling in these circumstances. But the more frequent situation will be one in which the current court does not have a strong view about the correctness of past decisions, and in those cases, the default position is to fall in line. (As discussed earlier, in instances where the current court feels that the past decisions were correct, the doctrine does no work at all.) Here, too, the dynamic contributes to the overall integrity and social standing of the judiciary by enabling courts to present as standardized institutions deciding cases by reference to external legal standards rather than the personal preferences of the judges.

None of this is algorithmic. Nor is answering the question of whether the present case comes within the scope of the past case at all. That requires determining precisely what it was that the past court decided, what features of the situation before the past court were critical to its reasoning and decision, whether the present situation falls within the scope of the past case, appropriately characterized, and whether there are any distinct features of the present case that justify differential treatment despite its apparent similarity. Llewellyn thus distinguished between two uses of precedent.[18] The first, strict view, proceeds from the understanding that no court has the power to decide a matter not before it. Thus, all that a past case can truly be precedent for are propositions necessary to its decision. This enables a later court confronted with a past decision it does not favor to distinguish it away, to confine its holding to its facts. "It is the recognized, legitimate, honorable technique for whittling precedents away, for making the lawyer, in his argument, and the court, in its decision, free of them. It is a surgeon's knife."[19] It is also hard. "[T]here is difficulty in going underneath what is said, in making a keen reexamination of the case that stood before the court, in showing that the language used was quite beside the point, as the point is revealed under the lens of leisured microscopic refinement."[20] To those who lack the necessary insight or talent, it can seem like sophistry.

Courts and lawyers who find a past decision advantageous, by contrast, often resort to what Llewellyn called the loose view of precedent. This is not reliance on precedent strictly speaking – because the deciding court is not pushed in a direction it was disinclined to go – but precedent as a rhetorical device. Here the focus falls on what the past court said it was doing. Any proposition invoked may be leveraged as necessary to support reaching the desired conclusion in the present case. "In its extreme form this results in thinking and arguing exclusively from *language* that is found in past opinions, and in citing and working with that language wholly without reference to the facts of the case which called the language forth."[21] This, of course, is a more superficial, and therefore easier, style of reasoning.

For Llewellyn, the coexistence of these two contradictory approaches to the use of past decisions is a feature rather than a bug. The ability to minimize the influence of some past decisions while simultaneously expanding that of others allows the law to grow and adapt while still maintaining its connection to the past. And the differing skill levels required to implement the two processes in an effective manner – the fact that it is more difficult to minimize the effect of a past decision than to maximize it – provides a benefit as well. "The strict view—that view that cuts the past away—is hard to use. An ignorant, an unskillful judge will find it hard to use: the past will bind him. But the skilful judge—he whom we would make free—is thus made free. He has the knife in hand, and he can free himself."[22] Llewellyn's assessment depends on at least two critical assumptions. One is that it is the judges themselves who are working with the material of past decisions and who are constrained by their reasoning unless they can find a way to distinguish them. Another is that a judge

[18] Karl N. Llewellyn, *The Bramble Bush* (Dobbs Ferry, NY: Oceana Publications, Inc., 1960) 66–68.
[19] Llewellyn, 'Bramble Bush', 66–68.
[20] Id.
[21] Id.
[22] Id.

who possesses the intellectual skill necessary to make the required distinctions will draw upon that skill in the right situations and for the right reasons.

On the surface, little of the doctrinal terrain of stare decisis has shifted in any meaningful way. The justices on the Supreme Court have engaged in skirmishes over precisely how the various factors to be considered in determining whether to overrule a past decision are to be weighted and prioritized. The law reviews continue to include new academic work exploring the contours of precedent and offering formulas for how the doctrine ought to be employed. These debates may, to be sure, affect the atmosphere in which precedent is implemented. Some eras will tend, on the whole, to be more respectful of the work of past courts than others. Sometimes shifts in the distribution of judicial power, as when the perceived political valence of a supreme court's majority flips after a long period of control by the other side, will lead those newly in possession of power to rethink their perspective on stare decisis. On the ground, however, the fundamental components of the analysis remain the same, and the role of discretion remains substantial. Ebbs and flows in the various forces that channel and constrain that discretion, and shifts in the identity of who exercises that discretion and how, more than the formal doctrinal frameworks within which it is exercised, seem to be what drive changes in the extent to which precedent itself constrains.

JUDICIAL OPINIONS

For the most part, or so we tend to imagine, judicial decisions and judicial opinions travel together. Especially at the appellate level, we expect significant decisions to be accompanied by written justifications. But that has not always been the case, most obviously in preliterate societies. In medieval Iceland, for example, the content of the law itself was orally preserved through a lawspeaker who recited it each summer at an annual assembly known as the Althing.[23] The lawspeaker was assisted in this by a fifty-member law council and other procedures designed to ensure that knowledge of the law was widely held. Its annual recitation served not only to provide authority for the resolution of the various disputes brought to the gathering but also to allow the public to know what the law was. The process thus served the same basic legitimating functions that modern judicial opinions do.

Writing of course allows for the easy dissemination of information, and it is no surprise that every modern legal system relies on written records of both legal rules and the decisions to which they are applied.[24] The written word is fixed in a way that oral speech is not, thereby allowing for continuity of content and reducing the

[23] Judy Quinn, 'From Orality to Literacy in Medieval Iceland,' in Margaret Clunies Ross, ed., *Old Icelandic Literature and Society* (Cambridge: Cambridge University Press, 2000) 30.

[24] Jack Goody, *The Domestication of the Savage Mind* (Cambridge: Cambridge University Press, 1977) 11; Walter J. Ong, *Orality and Literacy: The Technologizing of the Word* (New York: Routledge, 1982) 33–34.

likelihood of transmission error as the text is distributed. Moreover, because a reader need not devote effort to storing content in memory, more cognitive resources are available for understanding and analysis. But it is not inevitable that a system would become as dominated by the written word to the extent and at the pace that it happened in the United States. That appears to have been a product of the comparatively great distances and sparse population characteristic of the country's development.[25] It simply wasn't feasible for lawyers to travel to be present to make arguments in court while also meeting their other obligations, and heavy reliance on writing was in that sense an accommodation to practicality rather than something regarded as a necessary ingredient of the judicial process.

What seems natural to us, then, was once an innovation. Even when written reports of decisions eventually emerged, they were not the direct product of judges. Judges instead announce their decisions and justifications orally at the conclusion of a case. A reporter present in the courtroom would, with what one imagines were varying degrees of fidelity and comprehensiveness, transcribe the judge's remarks and prepare them for circulation, only sometimes after arranging for review by the judge.[26] The movement toward judicially authored opinions was the product of a desire to provide a better foundation for the development of the common law and to encourage judges to be thorough and thoughtful in their work. The form of written opinions also varies. Early courts in the United States followed the English practice of seriatim opinions, meaning that each judge on a multi-member court would provide an explanation of their reasoning in a case. That practice ended with John Marshall's appointment as Chief Justice in 1801.[27] Marshall believed that the Supreme Court's stature would benefit from its speaking with a single voice, and the custom took hold.

But of course not all judicial decisions are justified in written opinions. Many decisions made by trial judges, with evidentiary rulings made on the fly at trial serving as an obvious example, are hardly justified at all, much less in writing. Indeed, for the most part, trial judges enjoy broad discretion over whether to write.[28] There are few firm requirements, and the norms are imprecise. Timing matters, as does the complexity of the case or the issue and the likelihood of appeal. A judge may want to defend a ruling against the prospect of reversal or highlight aspects of a novel situation for the appellate court. Discretion exists at the appellate level as well. As an extreme example, from 1989 to 1996, the US Court of Appeals for the

[25] Suzanne Ehrenberg, 'Embracing the Writing-Centered Legal Process,' (2004) 89 *Iowa Law Review* 4, 1159, 1171–78.

[26] John H. Langbein, Renee Lettow Lerner, and Bruce P. Smith, *History of the Common Law: The Development of Anglo-American Legal Institutions* (Boston: Aspen Publishing 2009) 822.

[27] Scott Douglas Gerber, 'Introduction: The Supreme Court before John Marshall,' in Scott Douglas Gerber, ed., *Seriatim: The Supreme Court before John Marshall* (New York: New York University Press, 1998) 1, 20.

[28] Chad M. Oldfather, 'Writing, Cognition, and the Nature of the Judicial Function,' (2008) 96 *Georgetown Law Journal* 1283, 1289.

Third Circuit disposed of approximately 60 percent of its caseload via one-sentence summary orders affirming the decision below.[29] While that was an aberration, all the federal courts of appeals have, to varying degrees, engaged in the practice. And while the Supreme Court writes opinions in all the cases it accepts, its decisions not to grant certiorari are rarely accompanied by a written statement, and the same holds for other work that forms part of its "shadow docket."[30] Actual practice reflects a rough cost–benefit analysis in which courts balance the time and effort required to generate an opinion against the benefits to the parties, the public, and the system of having a written statement of the rationale for the court's ruling.

A survey of the literature on the functions of judicial opinions reveals that they serve three primary functions in the contemporary American system.[31] One is to provide the parties to a dispute, and the public more generally, with an explanation of the court's reasoning. Judicial judgments, after all, are ultimately backed by the force of the court's reasoning; they must rely on the legislative and executive branches to provide the tools of enforcement. If a court's reasoning fails to persuade, then the parties and the public can respond. A legislature might change the law, adjust the courts' funding, or impose procedural requirements on the judiciary. Lawyers and academics can monitor the courts' decisions on a larger scale and provide qualitative critique of a specific line of decisions or, as we saw in Chapter 2, large-scale empirical assessments of decisions that reveal trends and tendencies that are less visible to those engaged in the day-to-day work of the courts.

A second function is to create precedent. In a system in which courts are presumed to be obligated to decide current (and future) cases consistently with past cases, it's critical for judges and lawyers to have easy access to a record of what courts in those past cases actually decided. That's true not only for purposes of resolving those cases that are currently before the courts but also to enable lawyers to counsel their clients in a way that best enables them to structure their affairs in a way that allows them to avoid running afoul of the law.

The third is to serve as a source of discipline for judges. The act of providing an explanation can dispel what psychologists call "the illusion of explanatory depth." People who think they have a firm grasp on a concept often find that an attempt to put their understanding into words reveals that they understood less than they thought.[32] And the effect goes beyond that. Writing, to a greater degree than speech,

[29] Mitu Gulati and C.M.A. McCauliff, 'On *Not* Making Law,' (1998) *Law and Contemporary Problems* 157, 162.

[30] Stephen Vladeck, *The Shadow Docket: How the Supreme Court Uses Stealth Rulings to Amass Power and Undermine the Republic* (New York: Hatchette, 2023).

[31] This discussion relies heavily on Chad M. Oldfather, 'Remedying Judicial Inactivism: Opinions as Informational Regulation,' (2006) 58 *Florida Law Review* 743, 788–93.

[32] David Dunning, 'The Trouble of Not Knowing What You Do Not Know,' in Nathan Ballantyne and David Dunning, eds., *Reason, Bias, and Inquiry: The Crossroads of Epistemology and Psychology* (Oxford: Oxford University Press, 2022) 208.

is a controlled process.[33] It allows for precision and revision and thereby facilitates the resolution of complicated problems. Done well, for anything more than the simplest tasks, writing involves more than simply exporting thought to the page. The sophisticated writer constantly checks their thoughts against the words they have written, ensuring not just that the written word accurately conveys the substance of the writer's thoughts but also that those words do so with appropriate precision and in the right register, understanding all the while that readers will have access only to the words on the page and not to any of the additional cues, such as gesture and intonation, available to a conversational partner. A writer may use a word, recognize that it will be unfamiliar to many readers, and in the process of attempting to provide clarity realize that they do not themselves have a firm grasp on its meaning. The process of writing thus both transforms and serves as a check on thought. The acts of organizing thought and then breaking it down on the page reveal gaps in reasoning and thus often lead to the refinement of rationale and occasionally, as revealed in the common expression that an approach "won't write," to more dramatic shifts in reasoning or conclusions.

The typical judicial opinion depicts the decision it justifies as the product of a purely deductive exercise. It will recite the facts, present the issue to be decided, survey the applicable legal authority, work through the application of that authority, and announce its conclusion. Judges often maintain that their opinions truly reflect how the process works, and that the reasons offered in their opinions are indeed the real reasons driving their decisions.[34] One imagines that is sometimes true. A judge faced with an issue from an unfamiliar area of law in a situation where the judge has no reason or inclination to favor a decision one way or the other might well engage in what feels like a paint-by-numbers exercise.

But things are often not so clear. The law is often incomplete or ambiguous. Judges bring their preferences, both conscious and unconscious, to each case. The cognitive apparatus that helps us navigate daily life can blind judges to the ways in which there is more to a situation than first meets the eye. Reaching even a tentative top-level decision about which party should prevail can be difficult. An attempt to provide an account of justifying reasons one way or the other can in such cases serve to test out initial inclinations. "Beyond that," as Judge Henry Friendly described the process, "all kinds of questions open up. After the result, is it a case in which we should say as little as possible? Is it a case in which we should try to elaborate the more important reasons? Let your mind roam, is it useful to say more than necessary because of the problems before the lower courts?"[35] The decision thus cleaves into

[33] For discussions of the transformative effects of writing, see Ronald T. Kellogg, *The Psychology of Writing* (Oxford: Oxford University Press, 1994); Carl Bereiter and Marlene Scardamalia, *The Psychology of Written Composition* (New York: Routledge, 1987).

[34] Ruggero J. Aldisert, *The Judicial Process* (St. Paul, MN: West Publishing Co., 2nd ed. 1996) 604.

[35] Howard J. Woodford, Jr., *Courts of Appeals in the Federal Judicial System* (Princeton: Princeton University Press, 1981) 130.

something with multiple dimensions. To the parties, it matters who wins. To future litigants and judges, it matters why.

There is thus a distinction between decision and justification that cuts across all three functions of opinions.[36] Analytically, if not always as a description of reality, the judge first reaches the decision. That might be a product of hunch or intuition, it might follow from a studied consideration of the applicable authorities, it might be a combination of both or something else entirely, such as ideology. Except insofar as the past internalization of professional norms and craft values serves as a source of discipline – and as we will explore in Chapter 6, it might be a valuable source of discipline indeed – the judge in deciding is unconstrained other than by the obligation to justify the decision in an opinion. Only once the judge has decided, whether firmly or with some degree of tentativeness, can the process of justification begin. The justification will ideally serve all three of opinions' functions. It will provide the parties and the public with an assurance that the judge's decision has an appropriate legal basis, and that the parties' arguments were at least accounted for even if they do not prevail. It will set forth the court's decision, and the grounds for that decision, in a way that future lawyers and judges can account for in advising clients and deciding cases, and it will do so by setting parameters that bind future courts. And in writing the justification in a way that is mindful of the needs to satisfy the expectation that the parties' arguments will be heard and accounted for and to fit this decision in among preceding decisions while also anticipating possible future cases, the judge will almost necessarily find that the process serves as a source of discipline.

Here, we must consider the question of judicial candor.[37] How forthcoming should a judge be about the true reasons for a decision? Full candor is both theoretically and practically impossible to attain. None of us has the level of self-knowledge necessary to provide a truly complete account of why we have done anything we've done, and even were such knowledge attainable, the effort required to reduce it to writing – assuming that would even be possible – would be far out of proportion to the benefits of doing so. And yet surely some substantial correspondence between the reasons that, from the judge's perspective, actually motivated the decision and those identified in the judge's justification seems desirable if not necessary. Imagine a judge whose process of deciding involved flipping a coin, choosing a winner based on which party's counsel the judge thought was better dressed at argument, or relying on some other improper factor such as race or ideology. That judge could often tell a facially plausible story about why the law led to the favored result. But it would

36 For discussions of the distinction, see Ruggero J. Aldisert, *Opinion Writing* (Durham, NC: Carolina Academic Press 1990) 31–34; Bruce Anderson, *"Discovery" in Legal Decision-Making* (New York: Springer, 1996); Martin P. Golding, *Legal Reasoning* (Peterborough, ON: Broadview Press, 1983); Richard A. Wasserstrom, *The Judicial Decision: Toward a Theory of Legal Justification* (Stanford: Stanford University Press, 1961).

37 For an overview, see Chad M. Oldfather, 'Defining Judicial Inactivism: Models of Adjudication and the Duty to Decide,' (2005) 94 *Georgetown Law Journal* 121, 155–60.

fail in its obligations to the parties and the public by not being a faithful account and would accordingly mislead future actors about what things to account for in structuring their affairs or making arguments to that judge or court. For the regime to work, it must not merely be the case that the judge can tell a story, but do so sincerely.[38] In other words, the judge must believe that the reasons the judge has offered are reasons that an appropriately situated member of the legal community would accept as legitimate reasons, even if the judge does not personally accept the reasons. Put differently, a judge might provide three distinct reasons in justifying a decision, but only find two of them convincing. Referring to the third is appropriate so long as the judge believes that a substantial portion of the legal community regards it as a legitimate step in a legal argument that would apply to this case.

However much we regard candor as a desirable feature of judicial opinions, one hardly needs to spend much time with them to recognize that most judicial opinions fall somewhere short of any ideal. Here, too, is a situation where modern research serves primarily to support and refine long-recognized insights. Llewellyn, as we saw at the outset of Chapter 3, invoked William James: "The completed decision wipes off memory's slate most of the process of its attainment." Professor Dan Simon recounted his awe and puzzlement as a first-year law student reading opinions that systematically marshaled law and logic to bring even the most difficult questions readily to heel. "Each opinion read like a tour de force, bursting with knowledge, skill and acumen .... Tough and bewildering cases were put to rest by means of singly correct legal answers, which were apparently embedded, almost unnoticeably, within the legal materials."[39] And yet these opinions were often followed by dissenting opinions, each just as confidently and compellingly marching through the applicable authorities on the way to reaching the opposite conclusion.

Simon and his co-author, Nicholas Scurich, contended that this phenomenon can be explained by the psychological processes a judge goes through in the process of deciding. A decision-maker, including a judge, initially faces a complex bundle of facts, concepts, and values, which must each be assessed and integrated into a coherent framework. Once that process begins, a series of feedback loops come into play. The evaluation of a single piece of evidence leads to adjustments in the overall framework. The study of a single past decision, for example, may lead the judge to rethink the nature of the underlying principles in the applicable body of law. That in turn affects not only how the judge will evaluate the next piece of information, whether it's another case or something else, but also potentially what other evidence the judge deems appropriate to consider at all. The perceived strength of the evidence on one side gradually grows, while the countervailing arguments and materials come to seem less and less compelling. The result is that the judge comes to regard the arguments on one side as convincing, perhaps overwhelmingly so, and

38 Micah Schwartzman, 'Judicial Sincerity,' (2008) 94 *Virginia Law Review* 987.

39 Dan Simon and Nicholas Scurich, 'Judicial Overstating,' (2013) 88 *Chicago-Kent Law Review* 411.

those on the other side as weak or misguided. What at first seemed like a difficult decision now strikes the judge as obvious.

For the most part, this takes place beyond conscious awareness. From the judge's subjective vantage point, the explanation for the clarity they have discovered must be the law itself. Simon and Scurich contend that while judges "perceive the law as constraining, objective, and certain," the reality is that "these properties are merely artifacts of the judges' cognitive processing. Coherence is not a property of the legal materials, but a feature imposed upon them."[40] Once the decision is reached and the judge has concluded that the answer is clear, it becomes natural to line up as many additional arguments as are available – in other words, to pad the opinion. None of this necessarily means decisions are wrong, by whatever metric that is to be assessed. But the result is opinions with the characteristics Simon recalls encountering as a first-year, and another drawback is that the incorporation of the post-hoc justifications makes it difficult for readers to discern which factors were the ones that truly made a difference for the judge.

Notably, all of the above assumes that judges write their own opinions, that they are the ones shaping the raw material out of which decisions are made. But that is rarely the case. In most chambers, it is law clerks, rather than judges, who write the first drafts of opinions.[41] Writing in 1960, before the clerks' role as initial authors had fully taken hold, Llewellyn praised the institution of the law clerk.[42] Among its primary virtues, in his estimation, is the mechanism it provides for judges to keep up with developments in academic legal work by putting them in close contact with a stream of new law school graduates who have been recently immersed in that work. And as a happy byproduct, at the completion of their terms, those clerks will enter practice secure in the knowledge that the appellate courts function well, having just witnessed their functioning themselves. Llewellyn believed their presence in the bar, both in their own right and as ambassadors spreading word of the legitimacy of the judicial process, would thereby help to solidify the courts' institutional standing.

But Llewellyn's optimistic perspective was not universally shared, even then. In 1957, William Rehnquist, then a young lawyer who had clerked for Justice Robert Jackson a few years prior, published an essay in which he expressed concern about the role of law clerks at the Supreme Court and the possibility that liberal clerks were manipulating conservative justices.[43] He disavowed "[t]he specter of the law clerk as a legal Rasputin, exerting an important influence on the cases actually decided by the Court." The justices have time to devote to the study of such cases, he averred,

40 Simon and Scurich, 'Judicial Overstating', 423.

41 The discussion of the role of law clerks in the following paragraphs draws heavily on Chad M. Oldfather and Todd C. Peppers, 'Judicial Assistants or Junior Judges: The Hiring, Utilization, and Influence of Law Clerks,' (2014) 98 *Marquette Law Review* 1.

42 Llewellyn, 'Common Law Tradition', 321–22.

43 William H. Rehnquist, 'Who Writes Decisions of the Supreme Court,' *US News and World Report*, December 13, 1957, at 74.

and in any case, it struck him as implausible that anyone with a resume sufficient to land them on the Supreme Court would be susceptible to being swayed by a clerk fresh out of law school. He was less sanguine about clerks' neutrality in the Court's processes of deciding which cases to take in the first place via the review of petitions for certiorari. Here, the justices lack the ability to give each case close attention and must therefore rely on memoranda prepared by their clerks. Rehnquist was careful not to claim that clerks were intentionally slanting their work in such a way as to improperly influence their justices. But he did contend that the potential for unconscious bias presented a true cause for concern, and because the group of clerks with whom he served leaned, in his estimation, far to the left of both the justices and the public in general, so, too, was the influence they exerted.

Rehnquist's piece generated a substantial number of responses. Professor Alexander Bickel accepted Rehnquist's claim that clerks could exercise influence but regarded that as a feature. In phrasing that echoed Llewellyn, Bickel characterized the law clerk as something that "is in its modest way one of the influences that keep judicial law rationally responsive to the needs of the day."[44] A former clerk to Justice Stanley Reed argued that clerks' work was limited to "the drudgery of judging—looking up citations, examining old cases for apt quotations, general research."[45] The impulses behind these efforts to minimize the significance of the clerks' role are understandable. Law clerks lack the knowledge and experience possessed by the judges they serve. And it's the judges, after all, who hold the appointment, and theirs is not a role in which the office alone confers authority in the sense that legislators hold authority. A legislator simply by virtue of having been elected to the position is empowered to cast votes for or against proposed legislation; there is no formal or informal requirement that a vote be accompanied by any sort of justification. Judges, by contrast, cannot generally exercise *ex cathedra* authority. Justification is a condition to the wielding of judicial power, and one might accordingly question the exercise of that power if the process of justification is delegated.

As it happened, Llewellyn's rosy depiction of the role of law clerks came at the outset of the massive increase in caseloads that led to the systemic triage discussed earlier. One component of the courts' adaptation was an increase in the amount of work delegated to law clerks. In 1968, Second Circuit Chief Judge Edward Lumbard wrote that his "court cannot adequately handle the prospective increase in its business for the next few years unless it is given sufficient supporting personnel" and that "additional law clerk help is imperative."[46] His essay acknowledged, though it did not highlight, that clerks drafted opinions, but assured readers that responsibility stayed with the judge, because clerks "know enough to be of great help, but

44 Alexander M. Bickel, 'The Court: An Indictment Analyzed,' *New York Times*, April 27, 1958, § 6.

45 William Rogers, 'Do Law Clerks Wield Power in Supreme Court Cases?,' *US News and World Report*, February 21, 1958, at 114, 116.

46 J. Edward Lumbard, 'Current Problems of the Federal Courts of Appeals,' (1968) 54 *Cornell Law Review* 29, 39.

not quite enough to do much judging."[47] The trend was not limited to the federal courts. State courts had also increasingly turned to law clerks, with the use of clerks almost always connected to a surge in caseload.[48] By 1973, there was a Law Clerk Institute (sponsored by the Appellate Judges Conference of the Division of Judicial Administration of the American Bar Association and held at the Louisiana State University Law School) devoted to preparing soon-to-be clerks for the role,[49] and in remarks related to the establishment of the Institute, Professor Paul Baier canvassed the available evidence relating to the duties of clerks in both federal and state courts. He noted that some judges remained whose opinions were entirely a product of their own hands, but his discussion more generally both recognizes and celebrates the fact that most clerks do a lot of writing, including opinion drafts, thereby leaving for the judge "the harder task of judging."[50] Even so, Baier acknowledged the tendency of the clerk to want to incorporate all their research into an opinion draft – which he called "Treatise-itis" – and he urged resistance.

By 1993, Kronman offered a pessimistic view of law clerks. In his estimation, the rise of the law clerk led to an increase in the aggregate number of opinions produced as well as a change in their style. Clerks tend to write longer opinions that, despite Baier's admonition, lean too heavily on footnoting and jargon. Beyond that, clerks lack experience and thus what Llewellyn described as "horse sense." Lacking developed professional judgment and discernment, they must rely on surrogates for it, resulting in an uncritical acceptance of and reliance on "the opinions of their seniors," as well as "on general rules and principles, which even a beginner with intelligence but no experience can comprehend."[51] The effect, Kronman argued, was subtle but devastating. Clerk-drafted opinions will be different, displaying less practical wisdom and more "youthful traits such as cleverness and dialectical agility."[52] And, he continued, as those opinions become the norm, the characteristics they exhibit will become the characteristics that are valued and emulated.

Clerks' incentives matter, too. A clerkship becomes a permanent part of a resume and often brings an associated brand. One is forever a Ginsburg clerk, a Scalia clerk, or a Posner clerk, and even those whose judge may not have a high national profile

47 Lumbard, 'Current Problems', 40.

48 Paul R. Baier, 'The Law Clerks: Profile of an Institution,' (1973) 26 *Vanderbilt Law Review* 1125, 1133–34.

49 Baier, 'Profile of an Institution', 1133–34.

50 Id., 1153.

51 Id., 349–50. Judge Richard Posner echoed this point over two decades later, invoking Aristotle in observing that although law clerks are often "smarter and harder working" than their judges, that does not mean they would make better judges because "the young, being analytically sharp but inexperienced, rely on analysis rather than experience to make judgments." Richard A. Posner, *Divergent Paths: The Academy and the Judiciary* (Cambridge: Harvard University Press, 2016) 226–27.

52 Anthony T. Kronman, *The Lost Lawyer: Failing Ideals of the Legal Profession* (Cambridge: Harvard University Press, 1993) 350.

will fit into one of the various boxes for those who clerked on the Ninth Circuit, the Southern District of New York, or the Supreme Court of Georgia. Some clerks will recognize this and regard their year or two with their judge as an opportunity to enhance that judge's standing.[53] In addition, the nature of the judge-clerk relationship is one that tends to create substantial and longstanding loyalty.[54] To a large degree, this is a natural product of the vast difference in knowledge and experience that will characterize the relationship. The recent graduate, no matter how talented they were as a law student, will not be able to see all that the experienced judge can see, whether in terms of what's really at stake in a case, what the broader implications of a decision are for related areas of law or for the law in operation in the world, or otherwise, and will accordingly come to regard the judge, as well as the more experienced lawyers with whom they work closely in their early years of practice, as an especially wise and knowledgeable person. All of this, plus more traditional personal and professional incentives to do a good job in the eyes of one's employer, creates a dynamic in which a clerk will be more inclined to seek out, credit, and incorporate into an opinion draft the arguments and authorities that support the judge's initial inclination than those that run contrary to it.[55]

Judges, then, end up as editors of drafts written by assistants who are often talented enough to craft a plausible justification for a wide range of results. While editing done well can perhaps entail the same depth of engagement as writing,[56] it does not do so as a matter of course.[57] It is not hard to imagine a judge faced with a crowded docket and a rhetorically well-crafted justification of the position they were already inclined to take undertaking a somewhat perfunctory review. The judge as editor can avoid engaging with the complications, qualifications, and competing considerations that a true effort to grapple with existing case law and the parties' characterizations of it might uncover. As Fiss suggested, a significant part of the process that has long worked to discipline judicial thought is absent, or at least not present to the same degree. This, in turn, creates more room for ideology or other nonlegal factors to influence decision-making.

A related development concerns the role of ideology in law clerk hiring. Among my cohort of law students in the early 1990s, it was understood that tailoring one's resume was appropriate for applications to some judges. Evidence developed since then supports the conclusion that many judges do indeed tend to favor clerks who share their ideological outlook.[58] Fifth Circuit Judge James Ho's stated refusal to

[53] Paul Horwitz, 'Clerking for Grown-Ups: A Tribute to Judge Ed Carnes,' (2018) 69 *Alabama Law Review* 663, 665.

[54] Horwitz, 'Tribute to Carnes'.

[55] Richard A. Posner, *How Judges Think* (Cambridge: Harvard University Press, 2008) 286.

[56] For a very skeptical take, see David McGowan, 'Judicial Writing and the Ethics of Judicial Office,' (2001) 14 *Georgetown Journal of Legal Ethics* 509.

[57] Oldfather, 'Writing, Cognition', 1344.

[58] Adam Bonica, Adam S. Chilton, Jacob Goldin, Kyle Rozema, and Maya Sen, 'The Political Ideologies of Law Clerks,' (2017) 19 *American Law and Economics Review* 96.

hire clerks from Yale Law School based on his perception that the school "actively practices" the cancellation of conservative views[59] lends further support to the idea that ideology plays an increasing role, as does the rise of the Heritage Foundation's Judicial Clerkship Training Academy, which focuses exclusively on conservative legal theory.[60]

Expectations may shape reality. A recent study by Judge Jeremy Fogel, Professor Mary Hoopes, and Justice Goodwin Liu[61] suggests that most judges do not emphasize ideology in selecting clerks, and that some have a preference against clerks with agendas. The authors noted, though, that their sample appeared not to include "the substantial number of judges who utilize the Federalist Society network in hiring clerks."[62] And many judges reported that aspiring clerks tend to self-select, such that it has become more difficult to assemble an ideologically diverse set of clerks even for those judges who want to. Fogel, Hoopes, and Liu observe that the phenomenon is compounded by hiring practices at the Supreme Court, where the justices tend to hire ideologically compatible clerks who have served under ideologically compatible circuit court judges.

ATMOSPHERIC CHANGES

None of the changes discussed so far in this chapter necessarily have a tangible effect in any given case. Instead, something like the distinction between climate and weather is at work. The existence of climate change is not inconsistent with the occurrence of good weather, sometimes during seasons when it is least expected. The shifts appear in averages and tendencies.

There are other atmospheric changes at work when it comes to judging. One has to do with developments that affect the nature of the system's most basic ingredient – the people who become judges. In contrast to civil law systems, in which the judicial role is a distinct career path with distinct training,[63] nearly all American judges come to the bench after a career as a lawyer in a practice that typically includes a substantial litigation component. They were advocates, mentally accustomed to advancing a cause. For today's judges, that experience came in a context that is quite distinct from their predecessors from a couple generations ago.

In part, this is a product in the nature of the practice of law. Not even a century ago, most lawyers in private practice were generalists or solo practitioners. Law firms were loose affiliations of individual practices rather than coordinated collections of

59 Debra Cassens Weiss, 'Why this conservative federal appeals judge will no longer hire clerks from Yale Law School,' *ABA Journal*, October 3, 2022.

60 See www.heritage.org/training#clerkship.

61 Jeremy D. Fogel, Mary S. Hoopes and Goodwin Liu, 'Law Clerk Selection and Diversity: Insights from Fifty Sitting Judges of the Federal Courts of Appeals,' (2023) 137 *Harvard Law Review* 588.

62 Fogel, Hoopes, and Liu, 'Law Clerk Selection', 617.

63 Paul M. Li, 'How Our Judicial Schools Compare to the Rest of the World,' (1995) 1 *Judges' Journal* 17.

specialists, and even the largest among them topped out at around a couple dozen lawyers.[64] Judges who came of professional age in the 1950s and 1960s were members of law firms that provided the full range of services to their clients, and as lawyers, they did not have narrow specialties but often served as both counselors and litigators. There was less emphasis on income and billable hours, and the nature of their relationships with clients was such that true counseling – in the sense of comparatively deep integration into a company's management including the ability to say "no" without fear that the client might seek a more accommodating lawyer elsewhere – was consistently possible. Lawyers in large law firms were often deeply involved in the profession, through bar associations and otherwise. As Chapter 6 will explore further, this entailed a fundamentally different orientation to the law and the profession, and in a way that undoubtedly affected the way such lawyers approached the judicial role.

Today's private practitioner is much more likely to be a specialist, and beyond a certain level of seniority is often likely to act as a manager of more junior lawyers rather than to be a lawyer in the full sense of those who practiced a century ago. Those lawyers were able to stay up-to-date on the output of the courts in their jurisdiction and could claim at least some general familiarity with the entire scope of law. Those lawyers likewise had a sense for the entirety of their clients' interests, because they tended to be involved across a wide swath of them. Their counterparts today are more likely to know only a piece, and to lack familiarity not only with the full nature of their clients' affairs but also with the broader legal framework within which those clients operate. Many of today's senior lawyers spend little time researching and writing about the law, those that do are often confined to a narrow slice of it, and no lawyer can claim broad knowledge of the law's many corners. As Kronman put it over three decades ago, today's lawyer, especially at large law firms, is more often a technocrat than a wise counselor.[65]

Economic pressures matter as well. Information about the earnings of one's peers and one's clients is readily available, and it fuels an emphasis on compensation. Because lawyers charge for their time, the only paths to greater compensation are higher rates and increases in the number of hours worked. The typical lawyer at a large firm becomes focused on meeting billable hour requirements and generating work to feed those requirements. Less time remains for service to the profession whether through the organized bar or otherwise. So, too, when it comes to time for reflection about the content of the law, the nature of the professional role, and the functioning of legal institutions or otherwise. Three decades ago, the practice of law still included built-in pauses. Overnight delivery, fax machines, and messenger services enabled the quick delivery of documents, but it was not yet instantaneous.

64 Lawrence M. Friedman, *American Law in the Twentieth Century* (New Haven: Yale University Press, 2004) 29–33.

65 Kronman, 'Lost Lawyer', 289.

A document that left the firm would likely not return with reactions from clients or opposing counsel until at least a day or two later. And it was generally understood that people became unreachable beyond a certain point in the day. The lawyer could take work home, but work would not be able to follow them there.

Large law firms make up only a portion of the profession, of course. The work of those engaged primarily in criminal practice, or as personal injury or in-house lawyers, may in many respects largely resemble that of their predecessors. But the elite segments of the profession undoubtedly affect its culture as a whole, and what those lawyers value, and what they don't, inevitably affects their peers. And it in turn affects the behavior of those lawyers who become judges. The judge who has been primarily a manager or an editor of work written by more junior lawyers will see nothing unusual in using law clerks in a similar manner. All of this, Kronman suggested, "entails a reduction in the demand that his or her own work makes on the judge's imaginative powers and the consequent enfeeblement of these powers themselves."[66]

These changes in the profession have occurred in the midst of larger social changes that also touch on aspects of the core of judging. In 1994, when the internet's use was still limited mostly to scientists, Sven Birkerts decried a decline in the depth of reading. In the then-long-past world where books were rare and other sources of distraction scarce, readers had little choice but to revisit works they had read before, to ponder the language and the structure, to extract depth, and, in a sense, to create it.[67] But the world in which he wrote offered comparatively limitless access to reading material, and this tempted, if it did not compel, the reader to skim across the surface, to proceed laterally rather than vertically. And this, he contended, produced a collective loss of depth, of "a sense of the deep and natural connectedness of things."[68] And with the loss of depth came a loss of wisdom, which, in Birkerts's view, is a product of vertical thought. "Wisdom has nothing to do with the gathering or organizing of facts .... Wisdom is a seeing *through* facts, a penetration to the underlying laws and patterns. It relates the immediate to something larger ...."[69]

The three decades since Birkerts wrote have of course featured an acceleration of the trends he decried. In 2008, Nicholas Carr published *Is Google Making Us Stupid* in The Atlantic, and a more developed version two years later in *The Shallows: What the Internet is Doing to Our Brains*. Carr, too, lamented the loss of depth facilitated by the slower pace of past worlds. In his view, the problem is not simply that the internet has increased the extent of information overload, but that its delivery mechanisms fundamentally change the way we approach and engage with

66 Id., 326.

67 Sven Birkerts, *The Gutenberg Elegies: The Fate of Reading in an Electronic Age* (New York: Farrar, Straus and Giroux, 1994) 72.

68 Birkerts, 'Gutenberg Elegies', 94.

69 Id., 175.

the world. "[W]hen we go online, we enter an environment that promotes cursory reading, hurried and distracted thinking, and superficial learning."[70] The effect is not temporary but instead leads to a reworking of our neural circuitry, and in such a way that diminishes our ability and taste for reflective, linear thought. "And, thanks once again to the plasticity of our neuronal pathways, the more we use the Web, the more we train our brains to be distracted—to process information very quickly and very efficiently but without sustained attention."[71]

The judicial process certainly includes features that, in their ideal form, provide protection against the superficial thinking our modern world engenders. But as we have seen, those protections have in important respects weakened. We might imagine that judges as a group would be more immune to these effects. And that may be so. But here, I'll offer an anecdote. I happened to be corresponding with Judge Richard Posner about another matter when Carr's article in *The Atlantic* came out. I brought it to Posner's attention, and among his remarks in response was to relay his sense that "the Web is having the same effect on my brain as the author of the article describes on his."[72] That someone with Posner's tremendous intellect felt affected suggests that the rest of us are not immune.

Any significant new technology – written language, the printing press, radio, television – will inevitably change habits of thought and patterns of social activity and will trigger some to conclude that this time the end is truly nigh. But there are always gains that come alongside whatever is lost, the world becomes accustomed to the change, and a new equilibrium takes hold. Those of us who lived in the pre-internet world can remember what it was like, and that we managed to function perfectly well. Yet when our phone is lost or disabled, we're left to wonder how we did it. Individually and collectively, we've lost the habits, skills, and social infrastructure that enabled us to coordinate our activities even without being in instantaneous contact.

So, too, with the workings of the law. The habits and skills have evolved. But much of the institutional and procedural architecture remains the same or, as explored earlier, has itself evolved in response to other pressures and developments, and in ways that might exacerbate the effects. Viewed from a distance, the mechanisms of adjudication seem to have remained constant, at least in broad form. But, as we have already seen, a closer look reveals a range of small changes that, taken together, have substantially altered the system. Consider, for example, the way legal research is conducted. At least superficially, the existing structures and practices of litigation continue to reflect an equilibrium reached in a world in which legal research could be conducted only through books. That

70 Nicholas Carr, *The Shallows: What the Internet is Doing to Our Brains* (New York: W.W. Norton and Company, 2010) 124.

71 Carr, 'The Shallows', 194.

72 Email from Judge Richard Posner to Chad Oldfather, June 18, 2008.

process entailed a certain sort of engagement with the material, and that type of engagement and the nature of the understanding it engendered formed part of the atmosphere in which equilibrium was reached. Computerization has altered the atmosphere, and a small-but-robust literature has attempted to tease out the nature of those differences.[73]

That automation would affect the judicial process was apparent as early as 1960, when one commentator, echoing the optimism behind predictions that television would serve primarily educational purposes, imagined that automation would free up judges to do more time thinking and less time researching.[74] The prognostication had taken on a different tone by the time Westlaw and Lexis had gained a firm foothold. Scholars writing at roughly the same time as Kronman and Birkerts foresaw significant intellectual shifts due to computerization's disruptive effect on the structuring of knowledge. Law's organization in the print world was dictated by the curricular divisions first imposed by Dean Christopher Columbus Langdell as refined by the conceptual structure by which the West Publishing Company organized decisions. Finding cases relevant to one's situation required that one first determine where in this framework to look, a process that would often begin with review of a treatise or other secondary source that provided a comprehensive overview of the pertinent area of law. From there, one would turn to the digests and search through a series of paragraph-long glimpses into the cases' treatment of what one hoped was the point at hand. The process was often tedious and time-consuming, and the crudeness of the conceptual scheme together with an apparent editorial preference for over- rather than underinclusiveness meant that too many of the digest entries seemed to point toward cursory restatements of a well-established point of law. But it also enabled sometimes-productive serendipity. All of this work involved text laid out on a page adjacent to other text. And as one scanned those pages, something else, whether in a digest or an opinion, might catch the eye and provide helpful insight or, perhaps, trigger a reconceptualization of the problem. The simple fact that the process took more time undoubtedly produced the same sorts of benefits that Birkerts lamented the passing of. More time enables more thought, both conscious and unconscious, and thus a deeper appreciation of an issue.[75]

73 The discussion here draws primarily on Barbara Bantliff, 'From Creativity to Computerese: Thinking Like a Lawyer in the Computer Age,' (1996) 88 *Law Library Journal* 338; F. Allan Hanson, 'From Key Numbers to Key Words: How Automation Has Transformed the Law,' (2002) 94 *Law Library Journal* 563; Casey R. Fronk, 'The Cost of Judicial Citation: Empirical Investigation of Citation Practices in the Federal Appellate Courts,' (2010) *University of Illinois Journal of Law, Technology, and Policy* 51; Aaron S. Kirschenfeld and Alexa Z. Chew, 'Citation Stickiness, Computer-Assisted Legal Research, and the Universe of Thinkable Thoughts,' (2022) 19 *Legal Communication and Rhetoric* 1.

74 Vincent P. Biunno, 'History of Electronic Methods for Legal Research,' (1960) 2 *Modern Uses of Logic in Law* 99, 102.

75 Nicholson Baker wrote a similarly spirited lament about the demise of library card catalogs. Nicholson Baker, Discards, *The New Yorker*, April 4, 1994, at 64.

Computer-assisted research enables a different sort of approach. It allows for searches that are fact- rather than concept-driven. A lawyer with a case involving an alleged breach of contract in connection with the delivery of groceries, construction materials, or software can begin the research process by looking for cases involving similar fact patterns and thus thinking about the case not as some generic type of contracts case but rather as a case about groceries, construction materials, or software. The process makes it faster and easier to find cases to support one's preferred position, and without having to spend time reflecting on legal principles or wading through a mass of cases with no apparent relevance to that position – thereby, of course, depriving the lawyer of what time for reflection might have provided, namely the understanding that some apparently unrelated case was relevant after all. It supports superficial analysis rather than consideration of the deeper structure of law and legal relationships and, in the words of a commentator writing in 2002, has led to "an emerging conception of the law as a collection of facts and doctrines that is organized loosely if at all."[76] In addition, it erodes the distinction between primary and secondary sources of authority and facilitates the use and reliance on sources from outside the narrow domain of law. The overall effect, many of these observers predicted, was a decline in the force of precedent and the rise of even more of the ideologically driven decision-making the Realists and the Crits had long contended lurked behind the law's façade. The larger effect would be to splinter our collective conceptions of what law is and how it works in favor of a more individualistic world in which new organizational patterns emerge to displace old ones.[77]

To a large degree, changes of the sort that early commentators predicted can be hard to assess. Operationalizing something like a worldview, or depth of thought, for purposes of empirical measurement seems considerably more difficult to do than for something like judicial ideology. Some of the changes resulting from a shift from print to electronic resources may be so diffuse or even imperceptible as to resist quantification or characterization. *That* things have changed seems clear. *How* they have changed is undoubtedly more elusive.

Efforts to measure the effect of the shift have produced mixed results. One approach has involved measuring citation patterns. Casey Fronk studied two sets of federal appellate opinions from 1957 to 2007, one of which was a sampling from across the federal judiciary and the other of which focused on two long-serving judges. The study yielded several interesting results. The average number of

[76] Hanson, 'Key Numbers to Key Words', 564.

[77] As F. Allan Hanson put it: "Paradoxically, although information accessed electronically may have enhanced meaning for individual users because it is tailored more specifically to their particular purposes, it is less meaningful as a basis for collective consciousness and professional specialization in social groups precisely because of its individualistic quality. Worldview is a social phenomenon … [and] a close relationship exists between worldviews and classification systems because people have a tendency to imagine that the world really is organized the way their socially established classifications say it is." Hanson, 'Key Numbers to Key Words', 599.

citations per opinion nearly doubled over the fifty-year period.[78] The use of string cites – reference to several cases to support a proposition – decreased over the period studied, with the sharpest break in the practice coinciding with the use of computer-assisted research on a large scale. Meanwhile, the depth with which opinions tended to discuss the cases they cited grew, and the overall length of opinions grew with it. In all, this seems consistent with the idea that the savings on time spent in research led to an increase in the time spent on justification.

More recently, Professors Aaron Kirschenfeld and Alexa Chew examined what they labeled as "citation stickiness" – the overlap among the cases cited by the parties and the court.[79] They examined a sample of cases from 1957, 1987, and 2017 and expected to find what earlier writers on the shift from print to computer predicted, namely a reduction in overlap that would reflect an atomization facilitated by electronic research tools. What they found instead was the opposite. Whether measured in terms of cases that were cited in both one party's brief and the opinion ("sticky" citations) or those cited in both parties' briefs and the opinion ("super sticky" citations), the amount of overlap increased over time. Rather than seeming to move away from the agreed-on premises thought to be a feature of Langdell's conceptual universe as refined by West Publishing, the cases in their sample appeared to move toward consensus.

Kirschenfeld and Chew suggest several possible explanations for what they observed. One is that as computer-aided research evolved, it came to measure the depth of treatment. Print digests and citation-based research tools for the most part did not distinguish among citations, such that a citation providing incidental support for a mundane proposition would appear the same as a decision that went into considerable depth in its analysis of that same case. The only way to find the latter cases was to wade through them all. The researcher using contemporary computerized research services, by contrast, finds the cases with the more in-depth treatment appearing at the top of the list. The search costs are accordingly lower, and the risks of missing a significant case are reduced. A second explanation is improved research and writing instruction in law school. What was once largely ad hoc is now professionalized, and the new lawyers and law clerks who do the bulk of the research and writing are well-trained in how to make the best use of the available resources. Together, these developments may simply have increased the likelihood that everyone will converge on the right, or at least the same, set of cases.

78 Fronk, 'Cost of Judicial Citation', 69–71. As Fronk notes, the increase is probably not entirely due to automation, and the trend toward increased citation started in the 1940s. Other likely contributing factors include the increased availability of precedent to cite as past decisions accumulated, and the increased resources, primarily in the form of law clerks and other court staff, available to judges to increase their productiveness.

79 Kirschenfeld and Chew, 'Citation Stickiness'. I undertook a project that used a text-similarity methodology to investigate the overlap among briefs and opinions, which appears as Chad M. Oldfather, Joseph P. Bockhorst, and Brian P. Dimmer, 'Triangulating Judicial Responsiveness: Automated Content Analysis, Judicial Opinions, and the Methodology of Legal Scholarship,' (2012) 64 *Florida Law Review* 1189.

A final potential explanation merits consideration. A friend recently lamented that the music service Spotify's algorithms provide him with "a blander version of myself."[80] So it may be with computer-assisted research. As Kirschenfeld and Chew put it, the algorithms "may have changed to push advocates and courts closer to one another."[81] Algorithms, no less than West Publishing's Key Number system (and perhaps more so), rely on categorizations.[82] Those categorizations both shape and are shaped by users. They are also invisible to users, and as artificial intelligence becomes more sophisticated are increasingly invisible to anyone.[83] Yet they provide the researcher with a set of cases that are, in effect, characterized as the most pertinent, the only ones that need to be considered. The opportunity for serendipitous discovery of other sources and lines of argument remains, because the lawyer must still read the opinions. But it is reduced. And discovering those lines of argument, which often rely on deeper, structural analogies rather than the more superficial factors likely to gain the attention of algorithms, takes the time, effort, and space for reflection that are at a premium for practicing lawyers in our digital world.

As I write, the profession stands on the cusp of another transition as lawyers, law schools, and courts begin to integrate into their practice increasingly sophisticated artificial intelligence drawing on large-language models. However AI develops, it is likely to make the analysis in this chapter seem quaint, and to increase the distance between the law as it was put in practice and how it will be. The nature of judges' relation to their work, and to the law more generally, will inevitably change further as well.

80 Text message from Andrew Kincaid to Shorewood Association of Darts (SAD), July 11, 2023 (screenshot on file with author).

81 Kirschenfeld and Chew, 'Citation Stickiness', 16.

82 For overviews of scholarly work relating to the social effects of algorithms, see David Garth Beer, 'The Social Power of Algorithms,' (2017) 20 *Information, Communication & Society* 1; Emanule Arielli, 'Taste and the Algorithm', *Studi di estetica*, anno XLVI (2018).

83 Frank Pasquale has addressed in a broader way the concerns that arise out of the opacity of the algorithms that pervade our lives. Frank Pasquale, *The Black Box Society: The Secret Algorithms That Control Money and Information* (Cambridge: Harvard University Press, 2015).

5

External Constraints on Judicial Behavior

Judicial independence, as we have seen, does not mean that courts are free to do as they please or to operate according only to the restrictions they set for themselves. They are instead subject to a range of forces and incentives produced largely by actors outside the courts. Any distinction between the discipline provided by forces that we might consider "internal" to the judiciary – such as those discussed in Chapter 4 – and those that are "external" will necessarily be somewhat artificial. Some of the procedural and institutional arrangements that work to constrain judicial power have both internal and external components. Even those that fall clearly on one side or the other do not work in isolation. The effectiveness and desirability of any given source of constraint will depend in part on the robustness of others.

An obvious source of external influence is the other branches of government. At the federal level, the Constitution speaks only of the Supreme Court and "such inferior Courts as the Congress may from time to time ordain and establish"[1] and even in the case of the Supreme Court it provides Congress with the power to make exceptions to the Court's appellate jurisdiction and to subject the Court's exercise of that jurisdiction to regulation. History is filled with threats by members of Congress unhappy with the federal courts' decision-making in certain types of cases to take away the courts' jurisdiction over those cases. To be sure, the judiciary has historically resisted legislative efforts to interfere directly in its core business, such as in *Plaut* v. *Spendthrift Farms, Inc.*,[2] in which the Supreme Court declared unconstitutional a statute that purported to revive cases the judiciary had already dismissed. But legislatures have plenty of tools at their disposal to respond to what they perceive as poor decision-making. They can amend statutes if they conclude that courts have misconstrued or misused them, and constitutions, too, can be changed. Courts can be expanded in response to rising caseloads, or not. Judicial salaries can be increased and courthouses modernized, or not. Term limits and other adjustments

[1] United States Constitution, Article III, § 1.

[2] 514 US 211 (1995).

to judges' terms of service can be imposed, at least at the state level. Impeachment remains rare in reality, but real as a threat.

The executive branch, too, can influence the courts. At the federal level, the most powerful tool is the ability to use the nomination power to determine who will staff the judiciary, and state executives often have the power to appoint judges even in systems where judges are ordinarily elected (such as to serve out the remainder of the term of a judge who has retired). The executive also has enforcement discretion. Courts lack the independent ability to enforce their orders and must rely on the executive branch to do so. If it is reluctant or unwilling, there is not much a court can do. The instruments are sometimes blunt, but they can still be effective.

These mechanisms have not themselves changed, but the atmosphere and norms in which they're wielded have shifted over time. In this deeply polarized era, in which, as we will see, judicial selection has become increasingly partisan, it is unsurprising to find courts increasingly perceived as partisan institutions, and in turn to see that the political branches react accordingly. These sorts of efforts, and their effects, tend to be targeted. The message is a version of "we don't like how you've handled this issue, and as a result we are going to make it more difficult for you to continue along that path, or at least to make your lives less pleasant."

There's much to be said about each of these.[3] The focus here will instead be on three phenomena with more general effects – judicial selection processes, standards of judicial ethics, and media coverage. As with the forces discussed in Chapter 4, each has changed in its nature and effectiveness (or in the nature of its effectiveness), and each, or so I will argue, in ways that largely undermine its effectiveness in providing the desired channeling effects.

JUDICIAL ETHICS

Both in a broad sense, and in terms of the more precise prescriptions embodied in the various codes of judicial conduct, ethical norms are an important part of the answer to questions concerning how we address the realities of legal and factual indeterminacy and more generally work to shape judicial behavior toward its more desirable manifestations. Because legal questions do not always have a single, clearly correct answer, it's difficult, at best, to assess the accuracy or quality of judicial decisions.

Part of what defined the decades-long run up to *Rucho*, for example, was disagreement among the justices not only about how to gauge when partisanship in gerrymandering has gone too far but also about whether it is possible for a court to do so at all. One might strongly believe there is a correct answer to that question, but its correctness in that sense will be a product of reasoning that proceeds from certain

[3] For one such discussion, see Richard A. Posner, *How Judges Think* (Cambridge: Harvard University Press, 2008) 125–57.

premises – about the proper way to interpret the Constitution, the role of the judiciary, and so on – that are themselves contested. Someone who accepts a different set of premises will just as strongly believe that another answer is the correct one. Once one abandons the notion of a timeless, universal, brooding omnipresence of law in favor of an understanding of law as a product of social and political priorities and needs, it becomes impossible to pin law, or at least important parts of it, down. Those priorities and needs shift over time and come into conflict with one another in varying ways, making it unsurprising that observers will often fail to agree on how to make the best sense of them, and their embodiment in imprecise legal rules, in the context of resolving any specific dispute. Even in cases where there is a clearly correct answer, it isn't always easy to confirm that that's the case. An opinion that depicts a clear set of facts that leads to the clear application of a clear legal rule might turn out on investigation to be misleading. The facts may not be so established as the opinion suggests, or the law might not be as settled.

We turn to proxies as a result. Some of these are the internal restraints discussed in Chapter 4. The adversarial process ensures that judges confront both sides of the arguments. The understanding that decisions must be justified, typically via a written opinion, ensures a connection to the governing standards. Neither device, even in its idealized form, provides full constraint. A judge who wants to cut corners will still be able to do so. But adherence to process provides some assurance that, on the whole, the system functions as we want it to. It sets the parameters for how the job should be done and decreases the likelihood of inadvertent failures. Ethical rules serve a similar function.

Here, a brief detour into the world of sports might be helpful.[4] Consider first sports such as baseball, football, and track and field. To be sure, officiating in those sports unavoidably involves, to varying degrees, elements of judgment. All, for example, call for penalties to be imposed on athletes who interfere with their competitors, with interference being very much a matter of context and degree requiring the exercise of judgment in its application. But the ultimate scoring determinations – whether the ball crossed the goal line or cleared the fence, who crossed the finish line first or jumped the farthest, and the like – are easily verified. No specialized knowledge is required to get a call right, and the primary advantage that officials enjoy over fans is that they are closer to the action. An official who gets such a call wrong can easily be identified, and one who gets calls consistently wrong will fail to advance through the ranks.

In those sports, there is less need to rely on proxies to provide assurance that the officials are approaching their job in the appropriate way, and consequently less

4 I develop the comparison at some length in two pieces: Chad M. Oldfather, 'Aesthetic Judging,' (2018) 52 *UC Davis Law Review* 981; Chad M. Oldfather, 'Aesthetic Judging and the Constitution (Or, Why Supreme Court Justices Are Less Like Umpires and More Like Figure-Skating Judges),' (2020) 72 *Florida Law Review* 391.

concern about things such as conflicts of interest. The fact that an official might have grown up as a fan of a specific team doesn't seem to matter. Other sports, with figure skating and gymnastics serving as the most prominent examples, have a component of aesthetic judgment at their core. Most fans watching those sports do not have the expertise necessary to score those events. In providing a score, the judge will be drawing on expertise and criteria that are, at best, only partially articulable. One can say with clarity to even the most casual fan what it takes to score a basket or a touchdown, and what the point value is for doing so. The same doesn't hold in aesthetic sports. Apart from egregious errors, there is no set of fixed and precise criteria by which to demonstrate that a judge's decision was wrong. As with law, there will be differing judgments that proceed at least in part from different premises concerning what ought to count as excellence in the sport. Some judges will belong to one school of thought (that, say, values athleticism), others to another (that places more emphasis on artistic expression), and both will fall within the acceptable range of professional judgment.

In such a context, there is more room for improper factors – favoritism, personal prejudice, bribery – to influence decisions, and there is no obvious way to determine that something is amiss. Unsurprisingly, those sports place considerably more emphasis on ensuring that officials comply with proxies. Their rules include restrictions on relationships that might create or appear to create conflicts of interest, requirements that judges not serve as judges over competitors with whom they have had prior relationships, and prohibitions on communication among judges during the course of a competition. All are designed to maintain the appearance of impartiality and sporting justice.

In the legal system, the trappings of the judicial role itself serve as a source of ethical constraint. Judges consistently report immediate changes in their day-to-day lives once they assume their role. Their peers no longer treat them as peers, and their name changes from whatever it had been to "Judge." Casual professional interaction is harder to come by. Once likely just a face in the crowd, the judge must be vigilant to the possibility that any misstep will be noticed and publicized.[5] The proceedings and architecture of the courtroom underscore this. All rise upon the entrance of the black-robed judge, often into a room designed to impress upon those who enter it the distinctive and significant nature of what takes place within.[6] The judge's day-to-day life is filled with reminders that they occupy a distinct role with distinct responsibilities.

At the same time, however, the opportunities for lapses increase. Judges exercise a great deal of power within an institutional framework that, because of the priority

5 For examples of candid accounts of the change in role, see James P. Gray, *Wearing the Robe: The Art and Responsibilities of Judging in Today's Courts* (Garden City, NY: Square One, 2009); Neal Dicker, 'Avoiding Judicial Arrogance: A Personal Essay,' (2005) 44 *Judges' Journal* 21.

6 Keith J. Bybee, 'Judging in Place: Architecture, Design, and the Operation of Courts,' (2012) 37 *Law and Social Inquiry* 1014.

it places on decisional independence, features few of the incentives and other accountability mechanisms that discipline most officeholders. There are no raises or bonuses for good performance, no bosses keeping a close eye on the clock, and only the more egregious forms of malfeasance get punished. At the trial court level, in particular, a judge has a considerable ability to wield authority over individuals, whether they are parties, lawyers, court staff, or others over whom a judge wishes to exercise control. There are many people who wish to curry favor with a judge, and very few who have the ability or the inclination to tell the judge "no." "Treat someone as omniscient long enough and he may come to believe it himself. People who think themselves omniscient become impatient, disdainful, and cantankerous."[7] They come, in other words, to suffer from "black robe disease."

In a broad sense, what we expect of judges has not changed and can be derived from both the standard model and Shapiro's triad. Professor Charles Geyh has identified a set of values that recur throughout history: honesty, impartiality, independence, competence, diligence, and temperamental suitability to the role.[8] At least when stated in such a broad way, these seem intuitively indisputable and in need of little elaboration. Of course, we want judges who possess those characteristics.

What do they mean? Honesty entails that judges not accept bribes or gifts or otherwise use the position for personal gain, and it also points in a more general way to a certain baseline of being aboveboard in one's approach to the job. Impartiality implies a receptiveness to reasoned argument and a lack of extralegal preference not just for individual parties but also for the various social, racial, and other groups of which they are a part. Independence, which we have of course already considered, entails judges who are institutionally insulated from pressures that might otherwise drive them to make decisions based on improper factors and psychologically inclined to use the resulting space to follow the law according to their best lights. The final three values fall within the more general expectation that a judge will be capable. The underlying idea is that a judge will bring appropriate skills, dedication, and thoughtfulness to the task. As with much of what we have seen already, the ultimate goals are instrumental. These are not obligations imposed on judges simply because they are goods in their own right. There's certainly a case to be made that all of them are, but just as the judicial power exists not for its own sake but to serve social functions, so, too, do the norms serve instrumental purposes that are subordinate to those same functions.

It comes as no surprise, then, that although the norms are of long standing, the understanding of those norms and the ways in which they have been implemented have varied over time. For a prominent example of a different ethical landscape, we need to look no further than perhaps the most bedrock case in all of United States

7 Carl T. Bogus, 'Culture of Quiesence,' (2004) 9 *Roger Williams Law Review* 351, 353.

8 Charles Gardner Geyh, *Courting Peril: The Political Transformation of the American Judiciary* (Oxford: Oxford University Press, 2016).

constitutional law: *Marbury* v. *Madison*.[9] The dispute in that case arose from the Secretary of State's failure during the waning moments of the Adams administration to complete the delivery of a commission for a position as justice of the peace. William Marbury, whose commission was at stake, sued the incoming Secretary of State, James Madison, in the Supreme Court. The Court's opinion was of course written by the new Chief Justice, John Marshall, who had for a time held that position together with the job he had just left – as Secretary of State. He was, in other words, intimately involved in the dispute over which he presided as Chief Justice. However much our norms may be in flux today, it continues to seem unthinkable that a modern justice would not recuse in such a situation.[10] But that was a different era, and a different world. Just as today's rural judges cannot help but preside over cases in which they have more than a passing familiarity with the parties and lawyers, so must the legal system of the time have necessarily tolerated a closer web of relationships.

The familiar modern, code-based apparatus of judicial ethics is a relatively recent innovation. The American Bar Association (ABA) first approved its Canons of Judicial Ethics in 1924, triggered by repercussions from the "Black Sox" scandal in Major League Baseball.[11] In the wake of the scandal, in which members of the Chicago White Sox were bribed to throw the 1919 World Series, the league named Judge Kenesaw Mountain Landis as its commissioner. Landis kept his federal judgeship, which led the House Judiciary Committee to conduct an inquiry into impeachment. Landis resigned his judgeship before the Committee completed its work, but the episode illustrated the limitations of impeachment as a mechanism for enforcing ethics requirements. The ABA in turn commenced the process that led to the Canons, which have evolved – with each step a reaction to some newly perceived problem, often triggered by the actions of the Supreme Court or an individual justice – from their initial hortatory character to their present form, which relies on "shall" rather than "should" as the key verb.

The ABA's Model Code of Judicial Conduct serves as the template for the codes adopted by states and is generally echoed by the Code of Conduct for United States Judges. It features four canons, each of which it makes more concrete via a set of rules, which are in turn accompanied by comments providing further elaboration on the rules. The Canons are as follows:[12]

> Canon 1: A judge shall uphold and promote the independence, integrity, and impartiality of the judiciary, and shall avoid impropriety and the appearance of impropriety.

[9] 5 US (1 Cranch) 137 (1803).

[10] For detailed discussion of the ethical dimension of *Marbury*, see James J. Sample, 'Supreme Court Recusal from *Marbury* to the Modern Day,' (2013) 26 *Georgetown Journal of Legal Ethics* 95, 105–08.

[11] Charles Gardner Geyh, 'The Architecture of Judicial Ethics,' (2021) 169 *University of Pennsylvania Law Review* 2351, 2360–61.

[12] American Bar Association, *Model Code of Judicial Conduct* (2020).

Canon 2: A judge shall perform the duties of judicial office impartially, competently, and diligently.

Canon 3: A judge shall conduct the judge's personal and extrajudicial activities to minimize the risk of conflict with the obligations of the judicial office.

Canon 4: A judge or candidate for judicial office shall not engage in political or campaign activity that is inconsistent with the independence, integrity, or impartiality of the judiciary.

The language of the canons is, understandably, capacious. As the standards are stated, it is difficult to disagree. To be opposed to independence, integrity, and impartiality, to competence and diligence, or to favor a permissive approach to conflicts of interest would be to be opposed to our system as a whole. Each is a core part of maintaining the integrity of the triadic structure; the absence of any, especially on a large scale, would further the impression that the judge or judges who fail to satisfy the requirements are not truly neutral.

The challenge comes as the task of definition moves closer to the retail level. What does it mean for a judge to be impartial, or for a judge to avoid impropriety and the appearance of impropriety? Take first impartiality, which a leading treatise describes as "the judicial capacity to decide cases with an open mind and without bias for or against those who appear before the judge."[13] Is it enough that judges do not have any predisposition toward any of the parties that appear before them? Does it mean that judges must take care to preserve a lack of predisposition – to maintain the triadic structure – until the conclusion of a case? Should we – can we – expect judges to avoid forming conclusions about legal questions until such time as they have a case that squarely presents them? What about a judge's methodological commitments? Must a judge who has concluded that originalism is the only proper approach to constitutional interpretation revisit that conclusion each time a constitutional question arises?

The Supreme Court took a cut at these questions in *Republican Party of Minnesota* v. *White*.[14] It struck down, on First Amendment grounds, a Minnesota rule prohibiting candidates for judicial office from announcing their "views on disputed legal or political issues." The Eighth Circuit had upheld the rule on the grounds that the state's interests in maintaining a judiciary that was and was perceived to be impartial were compelling enough to satisfy strict scrutiny. Justice Scalia's majority opinion leaned heavily on his efforts to define impartiality. The traditional use of the term, he noted, connotes a lack of bias or predisposition against any of the parties to a case. But that interest would not be furthered by a rule targeted at speech concerning issues in a general sense. To be opposed to crime is not to be categorically biased against criminal defendants or any given defendant. A second approach would

[13] Charles Gardner Geyh, James J. Alfini, and James J. Sample, *Judicial Conduct and Ethics*, (New York: LexisNexis, 6th ed., 2023) §1.02.

[14] 536 US 765 (2002).

define impartiality as involving a lack of preconceptions about specific legal views. Here the problem was not that the clause failed to further the interest, but that the interest was not a sufficiently compelling one. All judges come to the bench with some preconceptions about the law. It would be impossible for it to be otherwise, and it would be undesirable even if it were possible, because it would mean the prospective judge had given the law a disqualifyingly small amount of consideration. The Court lingered only briefly over a third candidate, which it characterized as "openmindedness," a willingness to consider opposing views and be open to persuasion. Such a thing might be desirable in the judiciary, Justice Scalia allowed, "but we need not pursue that inquiry, since we do not believe the Minnesota Supreme Court adopted the announce clause for that purpose."

Even so, the Court considered a related argument, which was that the prohibition on candidate announcement of views furthered openmindedness because a candidate who announced a position during a campaign would feel committed to that position. It's essentially the justification that Justice David Souter offered in his confirmation hearings for his refusal to engage with the validity of *Roe* v. *Wade*. For a judge to afford a litigant a fair hearing, Souter offered, "requires a willingness of the court not only to listen, but to genuinely examine the position which the court is inclined at that point to take."[15] Voicing an opinion to the Senate Judiciary Committee, he continued, would subvert that end. Everyone, he continued, has had the experience of changing their position on something after they thought they had made up their mind. And everyone knows that it is more difficult to do so once one has publicly committed to the position – especially, one imagines, when that commitment is "to the Senate of the United States and, for all practical purposes, to the American people." Souter, who was part of the three-justice joint opinion that, as we saw in the Introduction, was lauded for its wisdom by both Kronman and the *Dobbs* dissenters, may well not have known where he would come out on the question. Had he taken a position, he may well have felt bound to adhere to it.

Justice Scalia rejected that logic as applied to Minnesota's rule. Candidates for judicial office, he explained, will have publicly committed themselves to many legal and political positions before becoming candidates. To prohibit them from making such statements only from the moment they become candidates, then, would be "woefully underinclusive." A campaign promise, on the other hand, might be different, but that was covered by a different Minnesota rule. The line might be thin, but it was one that worked to Justice Scalia's benefit. In his own confirmation hearing, Senator Edward Kennedy asked, "Do you expect to overrule the *Roe* v. *Wade* Supreme Court decision if you are confirmed?" Then-Judge Scalia responded that he did not think it would be appropriate for him to answer that question. His reasoning:

15 United States Senate, Committee on the Judiciary, *Hearings on the Nomination of David H. Souter to be Associate Justice of the Supreme Court of the United States* (1990) 194.

> Let us assume that I have people arguing before me to do it or not to do it. I think it is quite a thing to be arguing to somebody who you know has made a representation in the course of his confirmation hearings, and that is, by way of condition to his being confirmed, that he will do this or do that. I would be in a very bad position to adjudicate the case without being accused of having a less than impartial view of the matter.

For a different angle on impartiality, consider again the proposed prohibition on federal judges joining the Federalist Society and the American Constitution Society. The proposal was grounded in Canon 4 of the Code of Conduct for United States Judges, which expressly allows judges to engage in a range of extrajudicial activities but carves out those "that detract from the dignity of the judge's office, interfere with the performance of the judge's official duties, reflect adversely on the judge's impartiality, lead to frequent disqualification" or run counter to a set of more specific criteria that follow. The argument against allowing membership is that, especially in our deeply polarized society, it signals affiliation with one of the sides in the various political battles of the day. There is no uniformity of belief in either organization's membership, to be sure, but there are broad families of belief and allegiance. The effect may not be as specific as placing a sign for a specific candidate in one's yard, but it is the equivalent of pledging one's general loyalty to Team Red or Team Blue. The concern is with the third type of impartiality, the one the *White* Court chose not to pursue: openmindedness. And the rule's requirement does not stop at impartiality itself. It's the perception of partiality that matters, regardless of how the organization or the judges themselves understand the nature and significance of their affiliation or activity.

Although the committee that initiated the matter backed down due to the strong reaction against it and the lack of consensus that reaction reflected, its members clearly remained convinced of the wisdom of their rule. The memorandum announcing the committee's withdrawal of its proposed Advisory Opinion noted the ever-changing landscape of polarization and admonished judges "to remain vigilant about problems associated with membership in organizations" and cautioned that "each individual judge should take care to make all membership decisions in a way that is consistent with the highest ideals of the profession as expressed in the Code of Conduct."

The "appearance of impropriety" standard likewise generates both constraint and disagreement. Proponents of the rule applaud its prophylactic effect.[16] A focus on appearance will undoubtedly be overinclusive and will lead to recusals in situations where the judge would be perfectly capable of acting in an appropriate manner. But doing so serves another interest, one at the core of the triad, which is that judges be understood by the public not to be acting improperly or operating from a position in which they will be tempted to do so. And in practice, it allows for the saving of face.

[16] For example, M. Margaret McKeown, 'Don't Shoot the Canons: Maintaining the Appearance of Impropriety Standard,' (2005) 7 *Journal of Appellate Practice and Procedure* 45.

A litigant seeking a judge's recusal need not contend that the judge has acted in an improper manner, or search for evidence supporting that claim. The argument instead can be about how things look rather than how they are: "I'm not saying you'd do such a thing, your honor, but surely you can appreciate how this might look from the perspective of a neutral observer."

But, others contend, the costs associated with an amorphous standard such as the "appearance of impropriety" are too high.[17] Vagueness invites speculation and overuse. Frivolous charges make it difficult to identify truly unethical behavior, and over time will devalue the charge. In cumulative effect, "the power to unfairly criticize a judge as violating the appearances of impropriety serves to bring the judiciary into disrepute."[18] The better approach, critics contend, is to define unethical behavior more precisely. And indeed, the trend, which Judge Richard Posner associated with "the decline of consensus in law and the concomitant growth in judicial discretion,"[19] has been toward tightening up the rules.

One more detour into sport. The author, Bruce Weber, a former umpire, argues that "a prime function of officials is to relieve players of the burden of honor."[20] Because officials are there to enforce the rules, players are free to get away with as much as they can. The player who didn't quite catch the ball need not feel obligated to correct an official who rules otherwise. Deception is central to sporting competition, Weber reasons, and competitors' interest in maximizing any deception that will help them win is a large part of the explanation for why we have umpires and referees in the first place.

When it comes to judges, relief from the burden of honor seems undesirable. Yet an emphasis on increasingly precise ethical codes seems likely to have just that result. The risk is that judges, and the public, will come to regard what is ethical as equivalent to what is permitted under the rules rather than regarding the rules as specific manifestations of more general aspirations. As Professor Geyh has put it, the risk of a code-driven approach is that it can encourage judges to view their ethical obligations "through the eyes of a Holmesian 'bad man,' set aspiration aside, and structure their behavior to comply with the minimum standards necessary to avoid discipline. Such a code thus invites a race to the bottom and effectively makes 'bad men' of all subject to its authority."[21]

Consider, for example, recent controversies surrounding conduct by justices on the Supreme Court.[22] Justices Alito and Thomas turn out to have taken lavish trips

17 Ronald D. Rotunda, 'Judicial Ethics, the Appearance of Impropriety, and the Proposed New ABA Judicial Code,' (2006) 34 *Hofstra Law Review* 1337.

18 Rotunda, 'Judicial Ethics', 1376.

19 Richard A. Posner, *The Problems of Jurisprudence* (Cambridge: Harvard University Press, 1990) 127–28.

20 Bruce Weber, 'A Boy Scout Pulls a Fast One,' *New York Times*, September 18, 2010.

21 Geyh, 'Architecture of Judicial Ethics', 2397.

22 For a general discussion, in the context of reporting on a hearing concerning the potential adoption of an ethics code for the Court, see Abbie VanSickle, 'Prominent Retired Judge Calls for Ethics Rules for Supreme Court Justices,' *New York Times*, May 2, 2023.

courtesy of beneficiaries who, at least in an indirect sense, have a considerable interest in the Court's output. Several of the justices have received lavish book deals, and Justice Sotomayor has used Court staff and resources to promote her book.[23] There are, undoubtedly, other examples involving other justices. Nearly all of it seems self-evidently to involve leveraging the office for personal gain and to demonstrate what can readily be described as bad form.

A common response from those defending the justices' behavior is that it did not violate any rules. The instinct, in other words, is that the formal rules governing the justices conduct, such as they are, are the only things that matter. That the justices might have a duty of honor and that it perhaps ought to have occurred to them to avoid engaging in much of the scrutinized conduct regardless of what the rules say, are not ideas that have received much express play in the discussion. The push has not been for the reinvigoration of norms that would keep the justices broadly away from such behavior, but instead for the imposition of a more comprehensive set of ethical rules.[24]

A related critique of an overemphasis on the rules of ethics is that the types of things they address are not always, or perhaps even often, the things that matter most in the day-to-day operation of the courts. Former Judge Alex Kozinski contended that most of the thrust of the Canons and the structure of the rules implementing them were misguided.[25] He could not imagine, he contended, that his ownership of stock in a company would affect his vote on a matter in which the company was a party. And yet he was required to file a financial disclosure every year. Most of the parts of the Canons that receive attention, he contended, are of this sort. Satisfying the appearance of impartiality is not necessary to keep judges from acting unethically, but it creates the implication that judges who satisfy the appearance standard are also indeed acting in an ethical manner.

But that, Kozinski asserted, is not so at all. The real issues, the temptations that judges confront daily, are elsewhere. He provided a host of examples. Rising caseloads mean that judges must make choices about how to allocate their time. The result is that "important" cases get the most judicial attention, while "routine" cases get the least. That makes sense in the abstract. Most cases are indeed easy, and their resolution adds nothing of significance to the law. The problem is that the cases do not reliably announce themselves as easy or difficult. Most of the time, the ones that seem easy actually are, and this creates a temptation to conclude that the easy-seeming ones always are. "But then, once in a while, it turns out that what looked like an easy case is actually quite difficult .... After more than two decades of judging I have found no way to separate the sheep from the goats, except by taking a

[23] Steve Eder, Abbie VanSickle, and Elizabeth A. Harris, 'How Supreme Court Justices Make Millions From Book Deals,' *New York Times*, July 27, 2023.

[24] Carl Hulse, 'Democrats to Press Supreme Court Ethics Rules Over G.O.P. Opposition,' *New York Times*, July 17, 2023.

[25] Alex Kozinski, 'The Real Issues of Judicial Ethics,' (2004) 32 *Hofstra Law Review* 1095.

close look." The choice of whether to make the effort is an ethical one, but it is not one that can be regulated by rule or monitored from any vantage point other than the judge's conscience. So, too, with questions about how much work to delegate to law clerks and court staff, how closely to review opinion drafts from clerks, what to do when a dispassionate application of the law leads to an obviously unjust result, whether there is ever an ethical obligation to dissent, how to account for the reputational consequences of a decision, and so on. In Kozinski's view, "Judicial ethics, where it counts, is hidden from view, and no rule can possibly ensure ethical judicial conduct. Ultimately, there is no choice but to trust the judges."

There is, as those who follow the federal judiciary will know, a very real sense in which Judge Kozinski disproved his own conclusions. Kozinski resigned his position in the wake of allegations that he sexually harassed several of his law clerks, engaged in untoward sexual behavior toward a wide range of other women, and was an abusive boss.[26] His initial reaction to the allegations was, as the editorial board of the *Los Angeles Times* put it, "dismissive."[27] In announcing his retirement after the number of women claiming to have been his targets accumulated, Kozinski did not acknowledge the wrongfulness of his behavior but rather claimed to have no intent to make his clerks uncomfortable and attributed the situation to his "broad sense of humor and a candid way of speaking" coupled with the fact that he "may not have been mindful enough of the special challenges and pressures that women face in the workplace."[28] The problem with trusting the judges, it seems, is that the judges who most need to internalize the ethical lessons embodied in things like the Canons often lack the self-awareness to realize that they fall into that category. No one is a villain in their own eyes, as the acting advice has it. And the bromide applies to judges, too.

In the wake of the allegations against Judge Kozinski and others, Chief Justice Roberts called for the establishment of a working group "to example the sufficiency of the safeguards currently in place within the Judiciary to protect all court employees from inappropriate conduct in the workplace."[29] The working group concluded that, despite the features of the federal judiciary that "are likely to lessen the risk of employee harassment," there are features of the judicial workplace that increase the risk of misconduct or work as obstacles to the reporting or proper addressing of misconduct when it occurs. One of these is the dramatic power disparities between judges, court staff, and law clerks who are typically at the beginning of their careers

[26] Matt Zapotosky, 'Prominent Appeals Court Judge Alex Kozinski accused of sexual misconduct,' *Washington Post*, December 8, 2017; Matt Zapotosky, 'Nine more women say judge subjected them to inappropriate behavior, including four who say he touched or kissed them,' *Washington Post*, December 15, 2017; Matt Zapotosky, 'Federal appeals judge announces immediate retirement amid probe of sexual misconduct allegations,' *Washington Post*, December 18, 2017.

[27] 'Editorial: Alex Kozinski's retirement doesn't end the discussion about sexual harassment in the judiciary,' *Los Angeles Times*, December 19, 2017.

[28] Editorial, 'Kozinski's retirement'.

[29] Report of the Federal Judiciary Workplace Conduct Working Group to the Judicial Conference of the United States, June 1, 2018.

and thus may regard the risks of reporting misconduct as too high. In addition, the emphasis on confidentiality throughout the judicial decision-making process may enhance the sense that everything that happens in the context of the judge-clerk relationship must remain secret. Judges, meanwhile, enjoy life tenure and the considerable prestige that comes with the role. The working group accordingly recommended, and the judicial conference approved, a set of amendments to the Code of Conduct for United States Judges that clarified that abusive and harassing conduct, discrimination, and retaliation all fall within the definition of misconduct, as does a failure to come forward with reliable information about likely misconduct.

JUDICIAL SELECTION

Judicial selection is a vast topic, and one that allows for only limited generalization. There is, of course, a basic distinction between selection mechanisms in the states and in the federal system. But that accounts for only so much difference. Surely the most salient form of selection is that for Article III federal judges, in which the President nominates and the Senate confirms, for a position that features life tenure. But not all federal officers who bear the title "judge" attain their position through that process. States, as we will see, utilize a wide variety of mechanisms, each of which operates in its own, unique way, whether as a product of formal structures or on-the-ground practices.

These differences matter, though not always in ways that are easy to identify. The nature of a selection system will, sometimes subtly, affect the identity and characteristics of those who become judges. Some methods might be more effective than others in making the position seem prestigious. Others will favor those who have been politically active, or involved in other ways, such as through bar associations. Still, others will reward those who are willing and able to devote a substantial amount of time to campaigning. Any significant difference will affect the mix of people who consider seeking a judicial position, who undertake the steps toward obtaining one, and who are successful in doing so. Those differences in turn will impact the way judges behave in the role.

First, the states. Generally speaking, dominant methods of judicial selection in the states have shifted over time. Appointment was the norm in the nation's early years, but a desire to enhance judicial independence vis-à-vis the other branches led to a shift to elections that began in the early decades of the nineteenth century, and a century after that, many states moved toward making those elections nonpartisan.[30] Today, states employ "a dizzying assortment of methods."[31] The majority – thirty-nine

[30] Jed Handelsman Shugerman, 'Economic Crisis and the Rise of Judicial Elections and Judicial Review,' (2010) 123 *Harvard Law Review* 1061.

[31] Brennan Center for Justice, *Judicial Selection: Significant Figures*, May 8, 2015 (updated April 14, 2023), [perma.cc/N7F8-P34V]. For a general overview of current selection practices and the history

states – use some form of election for at least some of their judges. Some of those elections are head-to-head partisan contests, some are at least formally nonpartisan, and others are retention elections in which the choice put to the voters is simply whether the judge (who first received the position via appointment) should continue in office for another term. In twenty-six states, the governor makes initial appointments, usually from a slate of candidates generated by some sort of nominating commission, and in two states, the legislature does. In total, sixteen states provide for some role for the legislature or another body other than the governor. In those states in which appointed judges do not have to stand for retention election, some may be reappointed at the end of the term, and in a few others, an appointed judge serves until a specified retirement age or has life tenure.[32]

The United States is one of only three countries to have judicial elections, and it does so on a much larger scale than the other two (Switzerland and Japan).[33] By one count, nearly 90 percent of all state judges must stand for some sort of election.[34] There are obvious objections to selecting judges in this way. One is that it raises a different set of concerns about judicial independence, in that elections simply replace loyalty to appointive officials with allegiance to donors and interest groups. Another is that judging involves the application of professional expertise, which by its very nature is beyond the ability of those who lack that expertise to assess. Voters will necessarily rely on proxies instead, and those proxies – things such as charisma or even past experience in another judicial role – will be imperfect indicators at best. This raises the concern that elections, whether partisan or nonpartisan, tend to discourage or perhaps even exclude from the pool of potential judges those without an inclination toward or a history of political involvement.[35] A segment of the bar will be disinclined to seek judicial office. This can have undesirable demographic effects and might also work against those whose intellectual orientation is, as Chapters 7 and 8 will explore, especially conducive to being a good judge.[36] Appointive processes raise similar concerns, with the added dimension of a fear that the political aspects do not disappear but instead take place out of public view.[37]

and patterns that produced them, on which much of the discussion in these paragraphs draws, see Herbert M. Kritzer, *Judicial Selection in the States: Politics and the Struggle for Reform* (Cambridge: Cambridge University Press, 2020) 12–30.

32 Charles Gardner Geyh, 'The Endless Judicial Selection Debate and Why It Matters for Judicial Independence,' (2008) 21 *Georgetown Journal of Legal Ethics* 1259, 1263.

33 Bert Brandenberg and Roy A. Schotland, 'Justice in Peril: The Endangered Balance Between Impartial Courts and Judicial Election Campaigns,' (2008) 21 *Georgetown Journal of Legal Ethics* 1229.

34 Matthew J. Streb, ed., 'The Study of Judicial Elections,' in *Running for Judge: The Rising Political, Financial, and Legal Stakes of Judicial Elections* (New York: New York University Press, 2007) 1, 7.

35 Robert J. Cottrol, 'Creative Uncertainty,' (2002) 81 *Texas Law Review* 627, 648–49.

36 Margaret S. Williams, 'In a Different Path: The Process of Becoming a Judge for Women and Men,' (2006) 90 *Judicature* 104, 113.

37 Judith L. Maute, 'Selecting Justice in State Courts: The Ballot Box or the Backroom,' (2000) 41 *South Texas Law Review* 1197.

The “Missouri Plan” has been the most popular effort to combat the effects of direct elections. Its core features include judges who are initially appointed to their positions, typically after having been screened by a nominating committee that forwards an approved set of candidates to the governor for final selection, and who then must stand for periodic retention elections in which the voters are simply asked whether the judge or justice should be retained in office. Traditionally, retention elections have been comparatively calm affairs, with judges raising little money and engaging in minimal advertising or other campaigning. But that changed in 2010 with the successful effort to oust justices on the Iowa Supreme Court who had held that the state’s constitution protects a right to same-sex marriage.[38] In the wake of that incident, conservative groups began to inject more money into retention elections, specifically in opposition to judges with what those groups perceived to be liberal voting records, and those races, too, have come to resemble more traditional political campaigns. More generally, the Missouri Plan has lost momentum as an alternative to head-to-head elections, due mostly to Republican opposition. Professor Herbert Kritzer posits that this switch in Republican preferences – Republicans used to be among the proponents of the Missouri Plan – is a product of two factors.[39] The first is a general sense that, because the plan’s appointment mechanisms privilege input from the legal profession, it tends to produce a bench that is more liberal than politicians or the public as a whole for the simple reason that the profession tends to be more liberal than either group. As Professor Brian Fitzpatrick put the point, “In short, I am skeptical that merit selection *removes* politics from judicial selection. Rather, merit selection may simply *move* the politics of judicial selection into closer alignment with the ideological preferences of the bar.”[40] The second is a narrower sense on the part of business interests that targeted advertising can be effective in getting the public to vote in ways that are consistent with their preferences.

Whatever the precise nature of the dynamic, there appears to be broad agreement on the proposition that different selection mechanisms will produce judiciaries that feature, in addition to whatever other differing characteristics they have, differing ideological mixes. Many commentators believe that these effects on the identity of those who are willing to seek judicial office have only intensified in the wake of *Republican Party of Minnesota* v. *White*, discussed earlier, and *Citizens United* v.

38 David Hughes, ‘New-Style Campaigns in State Supreme Court Retention Elections,’ (2019) 19 *State Politics & Policy Quarterly* 127.

39 Kritzer, ‘Judicial Selection in the States’, 358–64. Kritzer cites three primary sources in support of his claim that conservatives have come to favor head-to-head elections. The first is a Federalist Society white paper. Michael DeBow, Diane Brey, Erick Kaardal, John Soroko, and Frank Strickland, ‘The Case for Partisan Judicial Elections,’ (2002) 33 *University of Toledo Law Review* 393. The other two are works by Professors Brian Fiztpatrick and Stephen Ware. Brian T. Fitzpatrick, ‘The Politics of Merit Selection,’ (2009) 74 *Missouri Law Review* 675; Stephen J. Ware, ‘The Missouri Plan in National Perspective,’ (2009) 74 *Missouri Law Review* 758.

40 Fitzpatrick, ‘Politics of Merit Selection’, 676.

Federal Election Commission,[41] in which the Supreme Court held that limitations on independent political expenditures by corporations and labor unions violate the Constitution. Spending in state judicial races has increased, and much of that is driven by independent expenditures. As Debra Erenberg and Matt Berg put it, "The shift of campaign cash toward independent television advertisements is particularly troubling because these groups go to great lengths to conceal the sources of their funding and sponsor an alarming number of misleading attack ads that reduce public confidence in the courts."[42] Consider for example the independent expenditures that led to the Supreme Court's decision in *Caperton* v. *A.T. Massey Coal Co.*,[43] in which it held that outsized expenditures can require recusal when their source is involved in litigation that will come before the winner of a judicial election. The donor, Don Blankenship, was the president of a company that had won a substantial verdict against Massey Coal in a case pending before the West Virginia Supreme Court. Blankenship created a nonprofit organization to which he contributed over $3 million and which in turn spent it in support of a challenger who defeated the court's incumbent chief justice. The case was about a mining contract. The nonprofit's name was "And for the Sake of the Kids."

A final point worth noting in the context of state judicial selection is the disparity between what the public appears to want and what the system seems increasingly to deliver. Professor Kritzer, building on a small body of preceding research, conducted a survey designed to gauge the characteristics members of the public find most important in judges.[44] The results demonstrate a broad preference for the importance of professional over political characteristics. For state Supreme Court justices, over 80 percent of their respondents rated "deep legal knowledge," "expressed commitment to protecting legal rights," and "reputation for integrity/high ethical standards" as "essential" characteristics. Over 60 percent included "excelled in law school," "substantial experience practicing law in the courtroom," "reputation as a good listener," and "respected by leaders of the legal community." By contrast, not a single political characteristic broke 50 percent, and the only one that (just over) 40 percent deemed essential was "respected by elected political officials." Not quite a quarter placed "expressed willingness to be sensitive to community preferences"

41 558 US 310 (2010).

42 Debra Erenberg and Matt Berg, 'The Dark Knight Rises: The Growing Role of Independent Expenditures in Judicial Elections After *Citizens United*,' (2013) 49 *Willamette Law Review* 501, 503. For a specific discussion of the role of *White*, see Rachel Caufield, 'Judicial Elections: Today's Trends and Tomorrow's Forecast,' (2007) 46 *Judges' Journal* 6. The precise nature of the magnitude, nature, and effects of independent expenditures in judicial elections in the wake of *Citizens United* remains a complicated puzzle. See, for example, Brent D. Boyea, 'Citizens United and Independent Expenditures in State Supreme Court Elections,' (2020) 41 *Justice System Journal* 323; Nicholas LaRowe, 'Independent Spending in State Supreme Court Elections After *Citizens United*,' (2016) 100 *Judicature* 46.

43 556 US 868 (2009).

44 Kritzer, 'Judicial Selection in the States', 364–68.

and "strong support from the leaders of my preferred political party" among the essential characteristics. The distribution of results was different when the questions related to trial judges – with a greater desire for those judges to be aware of and sensitive to community preferences – but on the whole, professional characteristics continued to dominate the list of those regarded as essential. All of this is consistent with social scientific research indicating that the public overwhelmingly prefers the legal model of decision-making.[45] In short, judicial elections increasingly seem to deliver something other than what either the public or the profession find desirable.

In the federal system, Article III judges occupy the most prominent role, and it is their selection that people have in mind when invoking the federal model. Its basic components are the power to nominate, vested in the President, and the power to confirm, held by the Senate. In operation, however, the process is more complex. And as with state court mechanisms, the norms and practices have shifted over time. The process begins with the creation of a vacancy. Sometimes those occur by chance, as when a judge unexpectedly dies while in office. But often, they are a product of political factors. A sitting justice or judge may time their departure so as to allow a President from one party or the other to nominate their successor. Occasionally, vacancies arise through the creation of additional judgeships. Politics matters in that situation for the simple reason that Congress is unlikely to expand the judiciary except in situations where the President and both houses of Congress are held by the same party.

The particulars of getting a nomination depend on at least two factors. One is the level of the judiciary at which the vacancy exists. In the case of the Supreme Court, the process is driven almost entirely by the executive. With respect to the lower federal courts, however, things are different. District judges are inherently tied to states, and most circuit court judgeships are by custom associated with a specific state. As a result, the Senators from the applicable state typically play a significant role in determining who gets the nomination. The specific state involved is the second factor. For some states, the process is entirely informal, and having a connection to a Senator can be a significant factor. Others have a formalized application process, created by agreement of the state's senators, which typically involves a nominating commission that provides a list of candidates from which a selection is usually, but not always, made.

Significant vetting of potential appointees by the White House is the norm as well, with the intensity of scrutiny corresponding to an opening's level in the judicial hierarchy. This includes an FBI-conducted background check as well as

[45] See, for example, Tom R. Tyler and Gregory Mitchell, 'Legitimacy and the Empowerment of Discretionary Legal Authority: The United States Supreme Court and Abortion Rights,' (1994) 43 *Duke Law Journal* 703, 784 ("Willingness to empower the Court is related only to judgments about how the Court makes decisions, not to either agreement with its past decisions about abortion or general agreement with its decisions."), 788 (noting general approval of a court in which "the law, not personal values and opinions, should drive outcomes").

consultation with prominent political figures from the President's party within the state. In the case of Supreme Court vacancies, and increasingly for lower-court seats, considerable ideological screening takes place as well. This involves scrutiny of a potential nominee's writings as well as interviews and the completion of written surveys. On the whole, the process results in most federal judicial appointees having some history of political activity.

Once the President has selected a nominee, the focus shifts to the Senate. Its process starts in the Senate Judiciary Committee, which can itself derail a nomination simply by failing to act on it, as was the case with President Obama's nomination of Judge Merrick Garland to the Supreme Court. In the context of lower-court nominations, by longstanding tradition, the committee chair distributes "blue slips" to the Senators from the state to which a judgeship relates, and a Senator can thwart a nomination simply by declining to return the slip.[46] But that practice, which when honored can serve as a moderating force in situations where one or both of a state's senators are from a different party than the President and Senate majority, has eroded. In 2017, Senator Charles Grassley announced that he would not adhere to the blue-slip tradition in the case of circuit court nominees where he perceived the objections to be "political or ideological."[47] Although the blue slip process remains at least formally in place, its continued viability remains in question. When it holds hearings on lower-court nominations, which has traditionally been the case for the vast majority of nominees, they have tended to be relatively low-key affairs with few witnesses and little press coverage.

The final step is for the nomination to go before the full Senate. Until relatively recently – 2013 in the case of lower-court nominations, and 2017 in the case of the Supreme Court – the possibility of a filibuster meant that sixty votes were required to ensure confirmation, but following the Senate's exercise of the "nuclear option," in both cases, a simple majority vote suffices for confirmation. Before the elimination of the filibuster, a single senator could block a nomination simply by placing a "hold" on it, which in effect was a statement of intent to filibuster. Although holds have not been formally eliminated, their effectiveness has been considerably reduced.

The process has never been free of politics. Indeed, the Senate rejected John Rutledge, nominated to be Chief Justice by President Washington in 1795, largely if not entirely on political grounds.[48] An 1880 *New York Times* editorial strongly conveys a sense that this is unremarkable: "That the President, as a rule, should appoint to important Judicial positions those who are of his own political faith is but natural

[46] Carl Tobias, 'Senate Blue Slips and Regular Senate Order,' (2018) 37 *Yale Law and Policy Review Inter Alia* 1.

[47] Karoun Demirjian, 'Grassley schedules contentious judicial nominees for hearing,' *Washington Post*, November 16, 2017. Grassley claimed that adherence to the blue slip tradition had always been subject to exceptions.

[48] David A. Strauss and Cass R. Sunstein, 'The Senate, the Constitution, and the Confirmation Process,' (1992) 101 *Yale Law Journal* 1491, 1501.

and proper. Consciously or unconsciously, the most upright of judges, in construing the law, are sometimes influenced by their political convictions."[49] More than a half-century later, President Roosevelt's court-packing scheme resulted from political frustrations, and senators occasionally pushed back against his nominees when they felt they had not been given enough input in the selection process.[50] In that sense, politics has been ever-present.

Even so, Professor William Ross, writing in 2002 after having surveyed presidential elections dating back to 1860, concluded that "[j]udicial issues rarely have played a prominent role in presidential campaigns and elections."[51] The reasons for this include generalized public ignorance about government coupled with the relative subtlety of the issues that come before the courts, as well as the likelihood that a focus on judicial issues would likely reproduce the divide among the electorate that already exists over the candidates.

Still, most observers, including Ross, agree that partisan interests have come to exert a more pronounced influence on a more frequent basis.[52] Many observers point to President Reagan's failed nomination of Judge Robert Bork to the Supreme Court as the moment that sparked a trend toward greater politicization. Prior to the Reagan administration, Supreme Court nominations were generally not driven by ideology in some comprehensive sense. Attorney General Edwin Meese, in particular, was interested in the development of conservative ideas in addition to achieving more immediate political victories,[53] and he emphasized the importance of appointing judges who would facilitate the advance of conservative causes over the long term.[54] Bork was thoroughly screened with respect to his judicial philosophy prior to his appointment, and his confirmation hearings were likewise ideologically focused, with more than 400 interest groups weighing in.[55] Nearly everyone agrees that the process has become increasingly politicized since, with the only question being who is to blame. Conservatives blame liberals, liberals blame conservatives, and others blame both sides for succumbing to a general decline in civility.[56]

49 *New York Times*, February 2, 1880.

50 Lee Epstein and Jeffrey A. Segal, *Advice and Consent: The Politics of Judicial Appointments* (Oxford: Oxford University Press, 2005) 2–3.

51 William G. Ross, 'The Role of Judicial Issues in Presidential Campaigns,' (2002) 42 *Santa Clara Law Review* 391, 472–73.

52 William G. Ross, 'Participation by the Public in the Federal Judicial Selection Process,' (1990) 43 *Vanderbilt Law Review* 1.

53 Steven M. Teles, 'Transformative Bureaucracy: Reagan's Lawyers and the Dynamics of Political Investment,' (2009) 23 *Studies in American Political Development* 61, 66–69.

54 Neal Devins and Lawrence Baum, *The Company They Keep: How Partisan Divisions Came to the Supreme Court* (Oxford: Oxford University Press, 2019) 124.

55 John Anthony Maltese, 'Confirmation Gridlock: The Federal Judicial Appointments Process Under Bill Clinton and George W. Bush,' (2003) 5 *Journal of Appellate Practice and Procedure* 1, 8–9.

56 Benjamin Wittes, *Confirmation Wars: Preserving Independent Courts in Angry Times* (Washington, DC: Rowman & Littlefield Publishers, 2006) 10.

Still another group of commentators favors a structural explanation. For example, despite having concluded that judicial issues rarely played a role in presidential politics, Ross saw an increased likelihood that they would matter in the future. This was due in part to the larger range of divisive issues subject to judicial authority, which has resulted in more media attention to the judiciary than in the past.[57] And, he argued, voters can have more confidence that their vote will influence the judiciary due to the fact that increased vetting of candidates has made it considerably less likely "that judges will defy the expectations of the Presidents who appoint them." Judges appointed by Republican administrations will be faithfully conservative, and those appointed by Democrats will be faithfully liberal.

Ross's prediction was accurate, as most prominently exemplified by the approach of then-candidate Donald Trump, who pledged to nominate Supreme Court justices from a list generated by the conservative Federalist Society.[58] As Professors Lawrence Baum and Neal Devins point out, this move provided Republican voters with assurance that they could count on Trump's nominees being every bit as conservative as those that would come from those of his opponents, such as Ted Cruz, whose ideological consistency was more well-established. And it represented something of a natural culmination of a Republican focus on ideological purity in judicial appointments that began with Meese, whose early support for the Federalist Society helped enable it to develop the gatekeeping authority it wields today. (We will further consider the Federalist Society in Chapter 6.).

The result of all of this, in the words of Professor Keith Whittington, is that "[t]he politics of federal judicial appointments is as heated and as high-profile as it has ever been in American history."[59] Both parties have come to pay greater attention to judicial appointments, and over the past thirty years, the Senate has been unusually likely to obstruct circuit-court nominations. The Senate's norms have changed from confirming nominees via voice votes, last regularly practiced during the Reagan administration, to roll call votes that, depending on one's perspective, either require or allow Senators to go on record with their opposition to a nominee. Doing so becomes politically useful, which in turn creates the expectation that Senators will oppose nominations made by presidents from the other party.[60] Given

[57] See also Bradley W. Joondeph, 'Law, Politics, and the Appointments Process,' (2006) 46 *Santa Clara Law Review* 737.

[58] Lawrence Baum and Neal Devins, 'Federalist Court: How the Federalist Society Became the De Facto Selector of Republican Supreme Court Justices,' *Slate*, Jan 31, 2017, available at scholarship .law.wm.edu/cgi/viewcontent.cgi?article=1406&context=popular_media.

[59] Keith E. Whittington, 'Partisanship, Norms, and Federal Judicial Appointments,' (2018) 16 *Georgetown Journal of Law and Public Policy* 521–35.

[60] An examination of senators' behavior in asking questions during confirmation hearings provides an interesting window into how politics shapes the process.

> We find that senatorial power dynamics and constituent preferences influence senators' behavior during the hearings. Specifically, our results suggest that senators modify their level of engagement with the nominee as the government shifts from unified to divided. Nominees presented

this environment, combined with the lack of any ideological overlap between the two parties' senatorial delegations, Whittington characterizes it as almost inevitable that the Senate has done away with its custom of requiring sixty votes to confirm a nominee with any significant opposition, because otherwise few nominees would be confirmed at all. This works well enough in a world in which the President and the Senate majority are from the same party. It remains to be seen what will happen when they are not. Whittington's characterization of the situation is apt: "Both parties feel justified in doing whatever is necessary to advance their favored nominees and block their disfavored nominees, not only because they can point to a history of grievances in which the other side did the same but also because every nominee in an age of polarization seems like an extremist to the opposite party."[61]

All of this threatens the independence and integrity of the judiciary, and of the rule of law more generally. When the judiciary is viewed as another site for partisan battles, and when ideological purity becomes a necessary precondition to securing a nomination, the most likely nominees are not simply those with a history of political involvement, but those whose history places them toward the extreme ends.[62] It thus becomes not just the appointment process that is polarized, but the judiciary itself. Professors Adam Bonica and Maya Sen, following a study in which they applied political science measures of ideology to lower-court judges, offered this striking conclusion: "The lower courts have polarized alongside the Supreme Court, to the extent that federal district and circuit court judges are now nearly as polarized as the parties in Congress."[63]

These developments have consequences both inside and outside of the federal judiciary. An overtly partisan and contentious selection process conveys an understanding, if not an expectation, that judges' decisions will be consistent with the ideology of those who appointed them.[64] The sorts of commitments that Justices Souter

> during unified government experience a coronation. In-party senators (i.e., those in the nominating president's party) ask only enough questions to showcase the nominee's qualifications and reinforce the president's narrative that this nominee is the best nominee, while out-party senators engage in more intense conversations with the nominee as they seek to mitigate the damage causes by the inevitable successful confirmation. Under divided government, however, the out-party can threaten a nomination, and both parties consequently partake in more contentious hearings with significantly more exchanges. We also show that public opinion in a senator's state can temper this behavior; in-party senators from states that support the nominee draw less attention to themselves and engage with the nominee less frequently, regardless of the institutional setup.

Jessica A. Schoenherr, Elizabeth A. Lane and Miles T. Armaly, 'The Purpose of Senatorial Grandstanding During Supreme Court Confirmation Hearings,' (2020) 8 *Journal of Law and Courts* 333, 333–34.

61 Schoenherr, Lane, and Armaly, 'Senatorial Grandstanding', 533.

62 Adam Bonica and Maya Sen, 'Estimating Judicial Ideology,' (2021) 35 *Journal of Economic Perspectives* 97.

63 Bonica and Sen, 'Estimating Ideology', 110.

64 Vicki C. Jackson, 'Packages of Judicial Independence: The Selection and Tenure of Article III Judges,' (2007) 95 *Georgetown Law Journal* 965, 969–74.

and Scalia declined to make to the Senate Judiciary Committee are no longer the source of concern; they have been implicitly made at a much earlier stage. The judiciary is thus increasingly filled with "movement judges" whose conception of their role is far from that of the triadic neutral.[65]

An obvious consequence within the federal judiciary is the increased ability for parties bringing controversial claims to judge shop. Lawyers have of course long engaged in efforts to get a favorable forum, whether in terms of advantageous law or what they perceive to be hospitable judges and juries. But the practice seems to have reached a new level, with lawsuits challenging the Biden administration routinely filed in federal courts with no natural connection to the case but with a judge the plaintiffs regard as favorable. This led the Justice Department, in a motion for the transfer of some of those cases, to decry the "ongoing tactic of filing … lawsuits against the federal government in single-judge divisions or divisions where they are almost always guaranteed to procure a particular judicial officer undermines public confidence in the administration of justice …."[66] Outside the federal judiciary, one effect seems to have been to encourage state court judges – or at least those with aspirations to a federal appointment – to write "audition opinions" that mimic the combative style of some of the more high-profile federal judges and justices and more generally create an incentive for those judges to behave in ways that will appeal to an increasingly partisan federal-selection audience. And these judges, whether through their opinions or otherwise, necessarily serve as role models for the young lawyers entering the profession.

THE MEDIA

At its best, the media serves as an important check on the judiciary. In theory, news coverage functions as a conduit between the specialized world of the courts and a public that lacks an expert's sophistication but wishes to be informed about the workings of government. In an ideal world, the result would be the noiseless transmission of information to an electorate that would in turn exert pressure for appropriate change, whether through their elected representatives or, in states that have elected judiciaries, through the selection and retention of judges. We of course do not live in such a world and never have. Journalists often do not have the knowledge or resources necessary to accurately convey the workings of the legal system. Much of the public lacks a general desire to be informed. Even in an uncrowded market for attention, one imagines, the sensational enjoys an inherent advantage over the mundane. In a crowded market, the advantage is substantial.

65 Robert L. Tsai and Mary Ziegler, 'Abortion Politics and the Rise of Movement Jurists,' (2024) 57 *UC Davis Law Review* 2149.

66 Perry Stein, 'The Justice Department's fight against judge shopping in Texas,' *Washington Post*, March 19, 2023.

The Supreme Court has understandably drawn the bulk of the media's attention over time, and scholars have consistently found that portions of the Court's docket receive a disproportionate share of the coverage.[67] Cases in areas such as civil rights and the First Amendment receive more attention than, say, business cases, and observers have come to different conclusions about how comprehensive and accurate that coverage is. Writing in 2003, Professors Rorie Spill and Zoe Oxley found differences in the nature of the treatment provided by newspapers and television and posited that these differences might account for the differing levels of support for the Court manifested among members of the public. "The most attentive members of the public tend to receive their information from both newspapers and television; the less attentive are usually only exposed to the latter form."[68] Among other things, the latter audience does not reliably receive the cues that the Court provides about the nature of its work – such as that it is the law rather than the justices that drive the Court's decisions. This is because it is newspapers, to a much greater extent than television, that provide a greater depth of coverage of the sort more likely to discuss the Court's rationale for its decisions.

More recently, Professors Barry Sullivan and Cristina Tilley studied print media coverage of *Brown* v. *Board of Education*[69] and *Parents Involved in Community Schools* v. *Seattle School District No. 1*,[70] two cases relating to the use of race in public school assignments decided fifty years apart.[71] The difference was stark. The coverage of *Brown*, they found, "mainly discussed constitutional text, precedent, and statutes as the presumed drivers of judicial decision-making."[72] What's more, "the press gave little if any attention to the individual Justices' personal backgrounds or political orientations, and few third-party interest groups were asked to comment on the political implications of the case."[73] Coverage of *Parents Involved*, by contrast, "focused on the political leanings and backgrounds of the Justices as important drivers of the Court's decision."[74] Throughout the case, "third-party interest groups were quoted at length, explaining the case in political terms; the relevant legal texts received much less attention."[75] All of this provides cause for concern. A public that views the justices as engaged in what is ultimately another form of political struggle will lose faith in the Court as an institution. It also brings the risk of becoming

[67] Rorie L. Spill and Zoe M. Oxley, 'Philosopher Kings or Political Actors – How the Media Portray the Supreme Court,' (2003) 87 *Judicature* 22–29. Spill and Oxley provide a brief overview of the work that had been done by that date.

[68] Spill and Oxley, 'Philosopher Kings', 29.

[69] 347 US 483 (1954).

[70] 551 US 701 (2007).

[71] Barry Sullivan and Cristina Carmody Tilley, 'Supreme Court Journalism: From Law to Spectacle?,' (2020) 77 *Washington & Lee Law Review* 343.

[72] Sullivan and Tilley, 'Supreme Court Journalism', 350.

[73] Id., 350–51.

[74] Id.

[75] Id.

self-fulfilling – if that depiction of the judicial role gains general acceptance, then both the selectors and the selected become more likely to act in accordance with it rather than the role expectations described throughout this book.

The effects hold in roughly the same way when the media covers courts beyond the Supreme Court. Professor Jennifer Robbenolt and Christina Studebaker reviewed research examining the media's coverage of civil litigation generally and concluded that it presents a "systematically distorted picture of civil litigation."[76] The cases that receive the most attention tend to be outliers, and the coverage as a whole focuses on an unrepresentative sample of the larger work of the civil justice system. The world it depicts is one with more trials, more verdicts in favor of plaintiffs, and higher damage awards than is true in reality. This distortion in turn affects the decision-making of actors inside and outside the system, at least potentially including judges.

Of course, much of the past work considering the relationship between the media and the operation of the courts took place in a different world. The "Greenhouse effect" discussed in Chapter 3 was the product of an establishment media characterized by a generally uniform worldview. The landscape has fundamentally transformed over the past several decades due to changes in technology, journalism practices, and media business models. Beginning in the 1980s, cable television greatly expanded options for news, while legal and regulatory changes enabled increased consolidation of media ownership into large conglomerates. The introduction of the internet and social media in the early 2000s further revolutionized how news and information are produced and consumed. These shifts have resulted in a twenty-four-hour, fast-paced news cycle focused on breaking events, scandals, and infotainment. To attract viewers and generate profits, cable news channels such as Fox News and MSNBC rely on partisan, opinion-based coverage that pushes ideological narratives. Journalists often do not have the knowledge or resources necessary to accurately convey the workings of the legal system, and now more than ever face incentives to focus on the sensational over the mundane. Much of the public lacks a general desire to be informed but remains happy to learn about aberrational or high-profile matters that take place or end up in the court system. The Greenhouse effect no longer creates pressure toward changing the judicial climate in general but instead operates at the level of the microclimates of fragmented political and judicial audiences – again as more fully discussed in Chapter 3.

As noted at the outset, the sources of constraint explored in this chapter are not the whole picture. The external forces shaping judicial behavior include not only the tools wielded by the executive and legislative branches, as discussed at the beginning of this chapter, but also – especially in the case of the Supreme Court – the

76 Jennifer K. Robbenold and Christina A. Studebaker, 'News Media Reporting on Civil Litigation and Its Influence on Civil Justice Decision Making,' (2003) 27 *Law and Human Behavior* 1, 5–27.

possibility that the public or political branches will choose to ignore or resist the courts. There are recent innovations as well. For example, many states have implemented judicial performance evaluation (JPE) programs to serve the dual purposes of quality control and professional development.[77] JPE programs are typically run by independent commissions composed of attorneys, judges, and lay citizens, and they involve periodic evaluations of judges seeking retention or reappointment. The commissions typically collect information through surveys of lawyers, jurors, court staff, litigants, and others who interact with judges. They also analyze case management data, interview the judges, observe them in court, and review their written decisions. All of this is compiled into a report that is provided to the judge in a manner intended to serve as constructive feedback, and is often made publicly available to enhance public trust through transparency and to allow voters to inform themselves. The intentions are inarguably good, but questions remain, including about whether the results of JPE surveys and assessments reflect ideological and other biases as much as performance. As with the other forces impacting courts, the effects are varied and imprecise.

77 See, for example, David C. Brody, 'Use of Judicial Performance Evaluation to Enhance Judicial Accountability, Judicial Independence, and Public Trust,' (2008) 86 *Denver University Law Review* 115.

6

The Importance (and Erosion) of Norms

Article II, Section 1, Clause 5 of the United States Constitution limits eligibility to be President to those who are "a natural born Citizen." There is little evidence concerning precisely what the drafters meant by the phrase, and it thus presents at least two interpretive questions, one easy and one not. "Natural child birth," as the phrase is used today, connotes a delivery without painkillers or other medical assistance. Despite that apparent linguistic fit, and despite the lack of conclusive evidence of what the framers had in mind, the question this presents is not hard to answer. Having been born by Caesarian section, say, has no logical bearing on whether someone should be eligible to be President. We know this not because the words themselves tell us, but because we have a firm sense of what sort of document the Constitution is and what it is designed to do. The more difficult questions occur with respect to situations like those of presidential aspirants John McCain, born in the Panama Canal Zone to parents who were US citizens, and Ted Cruz, born in Canada with one parent who was an American citizen and one who was not. It's only in those latter cases that more characteristic interpretation must take place. This is because we understand something about the nation's circumstances when the Constitution was drafted, which included concerns about foreign influence that no longer hold in the same way.

Consider two other examples. Article II, Section 2, Clause 2 of the US Constitution provides that the President "shall nominate, and by and with the Advice and Consent of the Senate, shall appoint Ambassadors, other public Ministers and Consuls, Judges of the supreme Court, and all other Officers of the United States." Neither the clause nor anything else in the document sets a timeline or even a rough timing requirement that applies to the Senate's action on nominations. In similar fashion, Article VII, Section 1 of the Wisconsin Constitution places the power of impeachment in the state assembly and the power to try impeachments in the state's senate. It further provides that "No judicial officer shall exercise his office, after he shall have been impeached, until his acquittal." Here, too, the document sets no express requirements as to timing.

These provisions undoubtedly, and appropriately, vest discretion in the respective senates on the question of when to act. But in application, they also raise questions as to whether there are limits on that discretion. When President Obama nominated Merrick Garland to fill the seat on the Supreme Court created by Justice Antonin Scalia's death, the Republican-controlled Senate chose not to act on the nomination for 293 days, claiming that the vacancy occurred too close to a presidential election. The incident raised questions about just how far the tactic could be pushed. What if, in a situation where the President and the Senate majority were from different parties, the Senate refused to consider any nominee regardless of its timing? Or consider the situation that some anticipated might happen in Wisconsin. During her 2024 campaign, state Supreme Court justice Janet Protasiewicz stated her view that the state's extremely gerrymandered election maps were "rigged." Meanwhile, the Democratic Party was one of the major spenders on her behalf in the election. When cases challenging the state's maps were filed shortly after she was sworn in, members of the Republican-controlled legislature began talking of impeaching her if she did not recuse herself from the case. The Wisconsin Constitution's allocation of impeachment power is parallel to that in the federal Constitution – the state assembly has the power to impeach, and the state senate is responsible for the trial of all impeachments. But neither document speaks to timing. This, in turn, led to speculation that the Senate might simply choose not to act on the impeachment. Because the state constitution prohibits judicial officers from acting while an impeachment is pending, this would have created an evenly divided court and left the Democratic governor unable to appoint a replacement.

The point of these examples is this: in law, there are sometimes interpretations that are linguistically possible but are simply understood to be out-of-bounds. And there are sometimes interpretations that are linguistically possible but of contingent validity, and limitations that are present only between the lines. Arguments about when confirmation hearings or impeachment trials should take place, or whether they must happen at all, often involve little invocation of traditional legal authority and instead consist of references to established practices and an implied obligation of good faith. Those arguments proceed from a host of understandings about, in these examples, matters such as the purpose and nature of written constitutions, the appropriate division of authority among the various actors in the system, and so on. Those understandings will shift, as will the willingness of the ultimate decision-maker to recognize and prioritize the arguments the competing sides offer.

In Professor Frederick Schauer's phrasing, "the recognition and non-recognition of law and legal sources is better understood as a *practice* in the Wittgensteinian sense: a practice in which lawyers, judges, commentators, and other legal actors gradually and in diffuse fashion determine what will count as a legitimate source – and thus what will count as law."[1] Schauer's immediate topic was the then-raging debate over the appropriateness of citation to foreign authorities in the US Supreme Court, and his point was that comparatively trivial disputes over what is and is not

[1] Frederick Schauer, 'Authority and Authorities,' (2008) 94 *Virginia Law Review* 1931, 1957.

considered proper to cite to a court are reflective of and connected to deeper questions about what law is. The shift from formalism and its brooding omnipresence to a world in which we are all realists, regardless of whether it was a change in kind or instead a change in emphasis, and regardless of whether the Realists are understood to have been making primarily a descriptive claim about how law actually works rather than a prescriptive claim about how it should work, likewise represents a shift in the nature of law. If, descriptively, we collectively come to understand that law involves something beyond mechanistic reasoning deploying a timeless set of principles, then, also descriptively, judges will be more receptive to, say, arguments rooted in social science, and lawyers will be more inclined to make them. A feedback loop can emerge, and the answer to the question "what is law?" will over time come to include a greater portion of authorities that prior generations would have regarded as invalid. In the context of questions concerning the timing of confirmation hearings and impeachment trials, the answers seem to include norms about acting in good faith and with due promptness, though increasing resort to hardball tactics suggests that such norms are shifting or eroding.

There is an important flipside to this. If changes in norms can produce changes in law, then the stability of norms can likewise produce stability in law. Norms, in other words, serve as an important source of constraint. The idea – variously referred to via terms like habits of mind, sensibilities, norms, customs, techniques, craft values, dispositions, or conventions – has consistently appeared in the writings of both judges and theorists. One of the central lessons of Justice Benjamin Cardozo's The Nature of the Judicial Process is "that the whole subject matter of jurisprudence is more plastic, more malleable, the moulds less definitively cast, the bounds of right and wrong less preordained and constant, than most of us ... have been accustomed to believe."[2] He notes that in his early years on the bench, he was "much troubled in spirit ... to find how trackless was the ocean on which I had embarked."[3] But, he concludes, while judges can never fully escape the pull of individual preference or prejudice, they are disciplined by training and temperament. The net effect of these will vary from one judge to the next. The system as a whole benefits from the balancing out of the "eccentricities" of individual judges, reaching an equilibrium "which has a constancy and uniformity and average value greater than its component elements."[4]

This is the "dark matter" of law I referred to in the Introduction. What counts as law will be influenced by, and to a considerable degree will include, often unspoken understandings about the ways and aims of the legal system. The notion that thought can include and be disciplined by the intangible and inarticulable has been recognized by a variety of thinkers from both within and outside the law. Four

[2] Benjamin N. Cardozo, *The Nature of the Judicial Process* (New Haven: Yale University Press, 1921) 161.

[3] Cardozo, 'Judicial Process', 29.

[4] Id., 177–78.

decades after Cardozo, Professor Karl Llewellyn, one of the major figures in the Legal Realist movement, wrote to address what he perceived to be the legal profession's crisis of confidence in the appellate courts.[5] Experienced lawyers bemoaned the death of stare decisis. "[G]enerations of law students assume, two thirds of them, as of course and despite all your effort, that *if* the outcome of an appeal is not foredoomed in logic it *therefore* is the product of an uncontrolled will which is as good as wayward ...."[6] He focused on the performance of appellate courts across the run of cases, and from that perspective, he contended, the processes and institutions and habits of the American judicial system provide real constraints. He identified fourteen features of the system that contribute to that restraint. Many, such as written opinions, the adversarial process, and the collective nature of appellate decision-making, were of the sort discussed in the Chapters 4 and 5. But roughly half involve the acceptance of and reliance on conventions, the understood ways of doing things that are themselves a source of regularity. They include the following:

- The fact that judges have training and experience as lawyers. That training and experience will not have been uniform in its particulars, but it will have conditioned them to view the world in a distinct way, to think like lawyers, and to approach problems in the ways that lawyers do.
- The existence of a set of accepted techniques for going about the task of extracting meaning and guidance from legal doctrine and materials, and the understanding that certain techniques are unacceptable.
- A shared sense that the entire enterprise of adjudication is meant to bring about results that are, in some fundamental sense, just.
- The fact that judges are known to lawyers, who can learn the judges' ways of looking at and thinking about legal questions, and who can thereby discern patterns beyond those that would be evident merely from reading opinions, and to adjust their arguments and advise their clients accordingly.
- That there are in most eras predominant ways of thinking and otherwise going about the business of law that both lawyers and judges will tend to have internalized and comply with.
- The nature of the judicial office is understood to entail certain sorts of responsibility and selflessness, and these attitudes are reinforced by things such as the wearing of robes and the architecture of courthouses and courtrooms.

Llewellyn recognized that none of these factors hold in any absolute sense in all cases, and that to the extent they set forth ideals, they are ideals that the system routinely falls short of reaching. And yet, he maintained, they collectively work to provide consistency and predictability. They provide no guarantees when it comes to the resolution of any individual case. But they nonetheless foster regularity in the aggregate.

5 Karl N. Llewellyn, *The Common Law Tradition: Deciding Appeals* (Boston: Little, Brown, 1960).
6 Llewellyn, 'Common Law Tradition', 4.

At the heart of Llewellyn's less tangible sources of discipline is the notion that he referred to as "situation sense," the cumulative result of the intellectual conditioning that results from training and experience as a lawyer, the "ways and attitudes which are much more and better felt and done than they are said."[7] The judge enjoys freedom in decision-making, to be sure, but it is constrained freedom. The number of available paths through the legal material is not infinite.

> For while it is possible to build a number of divergent logical ladders up out of the same cases and down again to the same dispute, *there are not so many that can be built defensibly*. And of these few there are some, or there is one, toward which the prior cases pretty definitely press. Already you see the walls closing in around the judge. Finally, when all is done, he does remain free to choose—in a sense. But not free in another—for he is a judge. As a human being, his "attitude"—the resultant of his life—conditions him. As a judge—and a potent factor in his attitude—his conscience conditions him. It is his job to decide which ladder leads to the just conclusion, or to the wise conclusion—when he sees two clear possibilities.[8]

Situation sense is the product of a process that can be almost imperceptible. It involves "the heaping up of concrete instances"[9] that is necessary to give shape and meaning to general propositions. Concepts such as "reasonableness" or "due process," which to a newcomer might be clear as abstractions but not in their application, take on a richer meaning as one moves through a career. The lawyer sees that a certain type of notice is adequate in some situations and inadequate in others, and over time becomes able to anticipate with considerable accuracy which will be which. The sense results as well from the judge's status as an inhabitant of a culture in general and a professional subculture more specifically. "The constraints and the socialization resulting from his membership in society and from his legal training guarantee the continuity of decisions, the continuity of legal norms, and the predictability of the 'freest' decision making."[10] The point is sociological. Again, these forces provide no strong guarantees in the context of any given individual case. The regularity they generate is more visible from a distance than up close.[11]

As Professor Paul Gewirtz has explained, in Llewellyn's view, it's this, rather than legal rules, that provides the regularity in law.[12] The judge's situation sense will have been formed and shaped by the study and implementation of rules, but it's that sense and its interaction with the facts of a case that produce the result. And it's that sense that allows the experienced lawyer to effectively analyze a new case – whether

[7] Id., 214.

[8] Karl N. Llewellyn, *The Bramble Bush* (Dobbs Ferry, NY: Oceana Publications, Inc., 1960) 73.

[9] Llewellyn, 'Bramble Bush', 12.

[10] Llewellyn, 'Common Law Tradition', 78.

[11] "[W]hat looks to the sociologist like constraint can look to the lawyer like completely free discretion. The sociologist sees the forest, the lawyer sees the trees." Llewellyn, 'Common Law Tradition', 11.

[12] Paul Gewirtz, 'Introduction,' in Karl N. Llewellyn, ed., *The Case Law System in America* (Chicago: University of Chicago Press, 1989) xviii–xxii.

new in the sense that it truly hasn't arisen before or simply in the sense that the lawyer lacks an intimate familiarity with the applicable legal framework – and do so in a way that will be consistent with most other experienced lawyers in terms of its identification of the appropriate questions if not always of the correct answers to those questions. "The sort of legal certainty that does exist is to be found in the predictable reaction of a trained lawyer, or of a judge with a certain degree of life experience, to what the ultimate *disposition* of a fact situation should be."[13] Rules do little work at all. "In other words, the legal rules do not lay down any *limits within* which a judge moves. Rather, they set down *guidelines from* which a judge proceeds toward a decision."[14] They are evidence of the content of the internalized norms and practices, and by convention, any new decision may depart only so far from them. As I have developed more fully elsewhere,[15] the process is deeply akin to making aesthetic judgments in that the way to determine whether an assessment is correct is to compare it to those made by acknowledged experts in the field. Outsiders could offer superficially plausible accounts of reasonableness, due process, or the provisions applicable to the examples that opened this chapter. But, because they would lack professional conditioning, they would be less likely to hit the mark, and there would be greater variability in their analyses.

Decades after Llewellyn, Professor Stanley Fish, a literary theorist, applied the notion of a "community of interpretation" to law.[16] For Fish, the primary constraints on judges come from their being socialized members of a profession, members of an interpretive community who, because of their training and practice, have internalized ways of reading, understanding, and applying legal texts that shape their behavior. Effectively implementing rules requires an appreciation for context and how one works with that set of rules. Fish illustrates the idea by reference to basketball. He posits a situation in which a basketball coach had taught someone to dribble and shoot the ball but with no reference to actually playing the game. That player will have pertinent skills but not be able to use them to full effect. If the coach tells the player to take good shots and elaborates on what a good shot is, it is likely that whatever the coach says will be too general – what counts as a good shot as time is running out will be different from what counts in the middle of the game, will depend on whether another player is in position to take an even better shot, and so on. The concept of a "good shot" is inherently contextual. Eventually, the player, after a heaping up of concrete instances, will internalize a sense of the game, and will be able to confront even novel situations in an appropriate way. Part of Fish's

[13] Karl N. Llewellyn, Paul Gewirtz, and Michael Ansaldi, 'The Case Law System in America,' (1988) 88 *Columbia Law Review* 989, 1011.

[14] Llewellyn, Gewirtz, and Ansaldi, 'Case Law System', 1011.

[15] Chad M. Oldfather, 'Aesthetic Judging,' (2018) 52 *UC Davis Law Review* 981; Chad M. Oldfather, 'Aesthetic Judging and the Constitution (Or, Why Supreme Court Justices Are Less Like Umpires and More Like Figure-Skating Judges),' (2020) 72 *Florida Law Review* 391.

[16] Stanley Fish, '*Fish* v. *Fiss*', (1984) 36 *Stanford Law Review* 1325.

goal is to make a point we have already encountered: rules can never be detailed enough to cover all the possible situations that could arise under them. Another point is that they don't need to be, so long as they exist against a backdrop of shared norms. Someone fully situated in the field will understand what the rule is designed to accomplish, what its limitations are, how it interacts with other rules, and so on. It is understanding how to play basketball, or how to do law, that serves as the ultimate source of constraint by making some options appear sensible and others not. "The person who looks about and sees, without reflection, a field already organized by problems, impending decisions, possible courses of action, goals, consequences, desiderata, etc. is not free to choose or originate his own meanings, because a set of meanings has, in a sense, already chosen him and is working itself out in the actions of perception, interpretation, judgment, etc. he is even now performing."[17] Thus, "to be a judge … is not to be able to consult the rules (or, alternatively, to disregard them) but to have become an extension of the 'know-how' that gives the rules (if there happen to be any) the meanings they will immediately and obviously have."[18]

Fish's analysis works best in the case of expert lawyers or judges acting within the domain of their expertise. As we will see in Chapter 7, that is a substantial qualification. For such a person, the act of guiding a client, or of deciding a case, may indeed be as Judge Posner has described: "Most judges evaluate cases in a holistic, intuitive manner, reaching a tentative conclusion that they then subject to technical legal analysis."[19] But this, surely, is a matter of degree. The expert in an area, the judge who has internalized all the law in an area, or who has mastered the complexities of some statutory or regulatory scheme, can undoubtedly reach the correct result on intuitive grounds, with resort to the underlying materials necessary only as a check to ensure that the judge hasn't inadvertently overlooked something. The judge with experience as a lawyer but not enough to have an expert's command of a subject area will likewise have intuitions, but they will be more in the nature of probabilities than certainties. "This is how I think the analysis will go, these are what I expect to find the critical questions to be, and so on." It's akin to the sentiment expressed by Justice Oliver Wendell Holmes, Jr.: "I have long said there is no such thing as a hard case. I am frightened weekly but always when you walk up to the lion and lay hold the hide comes off and the same old donkey of a question of law is underneath."[20] The underlying principles and the analytical moves involved in "thinking like a lawyer" are consistent enough across subfields to enable a reasonable degree of accuracy. Consultation of the legal standards is necessary not simply as a check

[17] Fish, '*Fish* v. *Fiss*', 1325, 1333.

[18] Id., 1334.

[19] Richard A. Posner, *Divergent Paths: The Academy and the Judiciary* (Cambridge: Harvard University Press, 2016) 1–2.

[20] Oliver Wendell Holmes, Jr., and Frederick Pollock, *Holmes-Pollack Letters: The Correspondence of Mr. Justice Holmes and Sir Frederick Pollock* (Cambridge: Harvard University Press, 2nd ed., 1961) 1874–1932.

but because there is a nontrivial chance those initial intuitions might have been wrong. And sometimes the lawyer or judge will confront something completely new, a recent, significant decision from a higher court, a new statute or set of regulations, or just a wholly unfamiliar area of law. In that case, the ensuing guidance or decision-making can often be regarded as entirely the product of the rule. It will be a formalistic necessity, because the lawyer or judge will lack the ability to draw on anything other than the semantic content of the rules to guide their action.

Another way to explain this dynamic is by reference to what philosopher Michael Polanyi referred to as "tacit knowledge."[21] Polanyi's key phrase – "We know more than we can tell" – captures the idea that only some portion of what we know can be captured in verbal formulations, that "strictly speaking nothing that we know can be said precisely."[22] Gaining complete knowledge of a topic thus requires more than simply learning rules or maxims, it requires repeated exposure to examples, ideally under the guidance of one who possesses the sought-after knowledge. "By watching the master and emulating his efforts in the presence of his example, the apprentice unconsciously picks up the rules of the art, including those which are not explicitly known to the master himself."[23] The judge and the lawyer will not always be able to explain the source or nature of their intuitive judgments and may point to rules and maxims as if they are doing all the work. But they will be mistaken. They will, of necessity, be drawing on knowledge that is ineffable, but no less real because of it.

A final way to think about all of this is as involving pattern recognition. As one develops knowledge and expertise in an area, one begins to notice and assign significance to recurring patterns within a domain. As a result, one can, in effect, intuitively reason that "when this type of situation presents itself, it signifies X, which means the appropriate response is Y." A considerable amount of research done on chess players, for example, reveals that much of what separates players of various levels is their ability to recognize and act on patterns in the arrangement of pieces on the board.[24] Skilled athletes likewise recognize that commonly recurring situations – a certain set of movements by the opposing team, a ball or puck that bounces in a specific manner, the combination of a teammate moving in one direction and an opponent in another – are best met with certain responses. The reaction will not always be accurate or successful – the opponent may have intentionally created the illusion of a familiar pattern or may have a superior counterresponse or simply have superior skills. But the relative expert will be able to intuitively grasp what is happening at a deeper level than the relative novice, who, at best, will have

[21] Michael Polanyi, *The Tacit Dimension* (Chicago: University of Chicago Press, 1966) 4.

[22] Michael Polanyi, *Personal Knowledge: Towards a Post-Critical Philosophy* (Chicago: University of Chicago Press, 1958) 87–88.

[23] Polanyi, 'Personal Knowledge', 53.

[24] For example, Merim Bilalić, Robert Langner, Michael Erb, and Wolfgang Grodd, 'Mechanisms and Neural Basis of Object and Pattern Recognition: A Study with Chess Experts,' (2010), 139(4) *Journal of Experimental Psychology: General* 728.

to consciously process the inputs the expert simply sees. The game "slows down," as the familiar phrase has it.

This, too, works as a description of how legal expertise develops. To the beginning law student, everything is new. There is a new vocabulary to learn, stylized forms of writing to become accustomed to, and only some long-held habits of thought are regarded as appropriate. Things feel unfamiliar and unwieldy, much like when one first takes up a musical instrument or a new sport. But it becomes easier to read opinions and to separate what matters from what does not. A sense of the deeper structure of law starts to emerge, of the full menu of considerations that go into the formulation of legal doctrines. The new law graduate enters practice with a modest grasp of how to put that knowledge to work in the context of what is likely a specialized practice area. Most cases, or deals, or applications, or whatever the right unit of engagement might be, will be novel, and the new lawyer will need guidance. Over time, the situations and questions start to repeat, the moves and countermoves become familiar, and a feel develops for what matters, how it might matter, and what the best course of action for the client is. The lawyer can start to take on more complicated work and more responsibility. In larger law firms, it may take as long as a decade for a lawyer to demonstrate mastery of the full range of skills, only some of which are purely legal in nature, necessary to be named a partner in the firm. Even then, the learning curve will have flattened, but it will not have disappeared.

One might, or might not, find this account intuitively persuasive. A question remains: does this knowledge, whatever one labels it, provide constraint? A promising illustration comes by way of a study conducted by Professor Dan Kahan and several colleagues.[25] The study involved having subjects – a group that included an 800-person representative sample of the general US population, 253 judges, 225 lawyers, and 250 law students – analyze legal situations designed to trigger political bias. The pool of subjects, both generally and when viewed at the group level, reflected social divides over contested policy issues such as those relating to climate change and marijuana legalization. Each of the situations involved a statute with language ambiguous enough to create uncertainty as to whether it applied, and each statute appeared in the context of cases where the facts were identical except for the identity of the party to whom it potentially applied. Those identities were designed to trigger motivated reasoning. Subjects' political tendencies were expected to lead them to be highly sympathetic to one side or the other and thus to create a temptation to allow those tendencies to drive their analyses of the legal questions.

One statute provided for civil penalties to be imposed for "littering, disposing, or depositing any form of garbage, refuse, junk, or other debris" in a national wildlife preserve. Subjects were provided a scenario set in the desert along the border

[25] Dan M. Kahan, David Hoffman, Danieli Evans, Neal Devins, Eugene Lucci, and Katherine Cheng, '"Ideology" or "Situation Sense"? An Experimental Investigation of Motivated Reasoning and Professional Judgment,' (2016) 164 *University of Pennsylvania Law Review* 349.

between the United States and Mexico, and in which the defendants admitted leaving plastic water containers that they intended would be used and refilled. The subjects were to assume the role of a judge ruling on a motion to dismiss, and the question put to them required determining whether the defendants' conduct fit within the scope of the statute. For half of the subjects, the defendants were described as having left the water containers for the use of people illegally entering the United States. For the other half, the defendants were portrayed as workers constructing a border fence who had left the containers for themselves.

A second statute criminalized knowing violations of a prohibition on the disclosure by a government official of "confidential investigatory information relating to an identifiable private citizen." The defendant in the scenario was a police officer who admitted to passing along what he knew was "confidential investigatory information," but who also claimed that in doing so he did not know he was violating the law. Legally, his lack of knowledge, if accepted, would matter if the requirement of a knowing violation was interpreted as requiring that he knew not merely that the information was confidential and that the person he disclosed it to was not a government official, but also that there was a law against such disclosure. The subjects were instructed to imagine themselves as appellate court judges reviewing a trial judge's decision not to instruct the jury that the defendant's ignorance of the law prohibiting disclosure was a defense. In this situation, half the subjects were told the disclosure was made to a family planning center that provides information about birth control and abortion, and that it concerned the possible infiltration of the center by an anti-abortion activist. The other half were told that the disclosure was to a family planning center that provides information about alternatives to abortion, and that it concerned possible infiltration by a pro-choice activist.

Given the design of the problem, the researchers' expectation was that members of the public would offer "rulings" that correlated with their political views – that, roughly stated,[26] liberal subjects would be much more likely to find that the statutes did not apply in the case of defendants assisting immigrants and the abortion-service provider and did apply to those assisting construction workers building a border wall and the pro-life family planning group, and that the "rulings" from conservative subjects would reflect the opposite tendencies. The results were largely as expected. The subjects who were members of the general public were almost evenly split on the abortion problem and the "construction worker" version of the water can problem and divided 65–35 in the "immigrant aid" version of the problem, with the majority concluding that there was a violation. Individual subjects' responses were correlated with their worldviews more generally.

The results were very different among the subjects who were judges and lawyers, nearly 80 percent of whom agreed that the police officer in both of the disclosure

[26] The subjects were not categorized in quite so reductionist a form as simply "liberal" or "conservative," but rather in terms of a more refined measure of "cultural worldviews."

scenarios had violated the law, and majorities of whom concluded that neither of the water can situations involved violations of the statute. The pattern of their results suggested a near-complete immunity to the "identity protective cognition" that appeared to drive the reasoning of the members of the general public. Law students' results fell in between the two groups and continued to exhibit the apparent influence of worldview.

Kahan and his colleagues found in these results a hopeful confirmation of the idea that the internalization of professional norms can fuel a form of judgment that overrides motivated reasoning. Judges and lawyers converged in their answers to questions that divided the general public, while law students, whose professional judgment is unsurprisingly immature, showed signs of an emerging immunity to ideological influence. "Legal training and experience … endows judges with a specialized form of cognitive perception—what Karl Llewellyn called 'situation sense'—that reliably focuses their attention on the features of a case pertinent to its valid resolution."[27] It does so "notwithstanding the tug of influences that might systematically focus the attention of the public on facts that are irrelevant—and indeed inimical—to impartial legal decisionmaking."[28] It supports the intuition, held by Cardozo, Llewellyn, Fish, and others, that the internalization of professional norms and conventions can serve as a powerful disciplinary force, that whether one regards legal reasoning as a distinct form of thinking or simply a stylized form of reasoning, it involves habits of mind that impose constraint.

For all this to work, of course, there must be a stable base of norms and conventions to draw on. There must be broad acceptance of interpretive conventions and other ways of "doing law," and further acceptance of the idea that the application of law will often lead decision-makers to resolve disputes in a manner contrary to their first-order preferences. My side, whether I conceive of it in ideological terms or otherwise, will frequently lose. If such acceptance exists, then constitutional questions concerning things like eligibility for office, the timing of confirmation proceedings and impeachment trials, and so on can be resolved by resorting to shared senses of what the documents are intended to achieve and how the offices and institutions created in the document are to operate and interact. Shared understandings enable lawmakers and lawyers drafting agreements to fall back on concepts like reasonableness having some assurance that they can foresee how those terms will be implemented. Kahan's study provides reason to believe that a base exists, and that it is solid enough to constrain decision-making even in ideologically charged situations.

But ours is a highly polarized world, and one in which members of the different ideological camps increasingly self-segregate.[29] The like-minded tend to live

[27] Kahan, Hoffman, Evans, Devins, Lucci, and Cheng, 'Ideology or Situation Sense', 382.
[28] Id.
[29] Gregory J. Martin and Steven W. Webster, 'Does Residential Sorting Explain Geographic Polarization?,' (2020) 8 *Political Science Research and Methods* 215.

and socialize among themselves. Each side consumes its own media and thus there are often starkly divergent views on what the facts of a situation are as well as what their significance is. Partisans take their cues on what to believe from those whose views they trust, and often those views seem to have been formed based on little more than an understanding that they should vehemently oppose whatever the other side supports. The legal profession is not immune. Recall the proposal, discussed in Chapter 4, to prohibit federal judges from being members of the Federalist Society or American Constitution Society (ACS). The proposal arose out of the sense that membership in one of the two groups is akin to signaling one's commitment to a side.

There is something to this. The Federalist Society began in the 1980s, founded by law students at Yale and the University of Chicago who, in the words of Professor John McGinnis, were "startled and depressed" over "the absence of debate about the fundamental issues of law" due to the fact that "the faculty and student body at their law schools and at elite schools across the nation were so uniformly liberal," which created an environment "shrouded in a pall of orthodoxy."[30] Whether something is "a pall of orthodoxy" or an established, desirable norm is, of course, in the eye of the beholder. Those who created the Federalist Society were, as we will see, very interested in changing the norms of the profession, and very successful in doing so.

To appreciate this, consider things from the perspective of a new law student. Even for those with past exposure to the legal system, the start of law school is likely to be overwhelming, with its new language and ways of thinking and the unwritten rules of a professional culture that, no matter how close they might have approached it via past experiences, they have only ever observed. And of course, many of these students will have had no relevant experience at all. Most of them will be young, and with much to learn more generally. There will be a great many things they do not know.

But one thing many of them will have is political opinions, and a political orientation. Not all of them, but a substantial number, will identify as conservative or liberal. They will know what they prefer in terms of policy, at least in some areas. They will have chosen a side, found their people, and drawn conclusions about which media sources they trust and which they regard as biased or otherwise untrustworthy. (Of course, it isn't just new law students who find themselves in such a position. Most of us have fully worked out understandings of a handful of issues at best. We likewise rely on proxies to a considerable degree in figuring out what specific beliefs to hold.) They will have a point of view.

What they will not know is whether or how these opinions cash out in terms of doing law. And they will lack the knowledge to decide in a sophisticated way for themselves. They will, after all, spend the entirety of their first year working to learn the building block concepts of law. As the first year of law school has traditionally been constructed,

30 John O. McGinnis, 'An Opinionated History of the Federalist Society,' (2009) 7 *Georgetown Journal of Law and Public Policy* 403.

it works to break down faith in big ideas. In its purest form, it works as captured by Professor Kingsfield's explanation of the Socratic method to his students in *The Paper Chase*: "At times you may feel that you have found the correct answer. I assure you that this is a total delusion on your part. You'll never find the correct, absolute, and final answer."[31] The level of knowledge appropriate to independently drawing confident conclusions about large-scale substantive and methodological questions is years, and more likely decades, away. Yet, at the same time, Kronman posits, newcomers will "tend to place greater confidence than more-experienced lawyers do in the power of abstract ideas to provide needed guidance amid the complexities of political and legal life."[32] Someone who can confidently and with apparent credibility offer the answers the new law student seeks will be very appealing.

And so the young law student will do the rational thing under the circumstances and turn again to proxies. As with any type of difficult social question, they will tend to look to those who they regard as sharing their values.[33] Especially in a world as polarized as ours, politically or socially inclined law students will seek out not merely like-minded peers but also the like-minded who are farther along in their professional journey: second- and third-year students, faculty, and members of the bar. Because law school faculties and student bodies tend on the whole to be liberal,[34] liberal law students are able to select from a range of student organizations and may even feel comfortable simply relying on the dominant opinion within their law school community. Conservative students, by contrast, typically have one significant option: The Federalist Society.

The organization is insistent about certain aspects of its existence: one is that it is a debating society. As Professor Amanda Hollis-Brusky has put it, "Animated by the belief that ideas *can* and *do* have consequences, the Federalist Society's focus has been on training and shaping its members through intellectual engagement, networking conservative and libertarian legal elites, and facilitating opportunities for members to put their shared legal principles into practice as 'citizen-lawyers.'"[35] The Society is also officially nonpartisan, but that is not to say it endorses no views. Its credo holds "that the state exists to preserve freedom, that the separation of governmental powers is central to our Constitution, and that it is emphatically the province and duty of the judiciary to say what the law is, not what it should be."

[31] Twentieth Century-Fox Film Corp. *The Paper Chase*. New York, N.Y.: CBS/Fox Video, 1973.

[32] Anthony T. Kronman, *The Lost Lawyer: Failing Ideals of the Legal Profession* (Cambridge: Harvard University Press, 1993) 158.

[33] Donald Braman and Dan M. Kahan, 'Cultural Cognition and Public Policy,' (2006) 24 *Yale Law and Policy Review* 149.

[34] One study, using political donations as a proxy, found that only 15 percent of law professors, as contrasted with 35 percent of members of the bar, are conservative. Adam Bonica, Adam Chilton, Kyle Rozema and Maya Sen, 'The Legal Academy's Ideological Uniformity,' (2018) 47 *Journal of Legal Studies* 1.

[35] Amanda Hollis-Brusky, *Ideas with Consequences: The Federalist Society and the Conservative Counterrevolution* (Oxford: Oxford University Press, 2015) 3.

As an organization, it doesn't officially take positions on issues. It wasn't, for example, formally the society that provided a list of potential Supreme Court nominees to candidate Trump – despite Trump's own claim as a candidate that his administration would feature judges "all picked by the Federalist Society."[36] It was instead Leonard Leo, an individual who just happened to be the Society's executive director. However one comes out on the effectiveness of the organization's efforts to avoid partisanship, it has long been the debate, and the specific structure of the debate, that is the key thing.

> The Society's emphasis on debate, rather than just sponsoring conservative speakers, was evident from the beginning. The original 'how to' document makes the motivation clear: 'You are more likely to convince people of your viewpoint if they feel the other side has been given a fair hearing.' As [Society co-founder Professor Steven] Calabresi recalls, 'If you just bring a famous conservative and the audience hears that but thinks, "Well, sounds good to me, but I think one of my professors probably could have critiqued it and then I would have understood where they were wrong." By having the professor there on stage with them they get to see it and evaluate the idea.'[37]

The focus on debate, Professor Steven Teles concludes, has been critical to the organization's success. It allows the Society to nurture "a reputation for intellectual seriousness and distance from short-term partisan politics" and thereby makes it "more effective in serving the political goals of its allies than a more directly partisan organization ever could have been."[38] In discussing the value of debate within the Society, McGinniss distinguishes between ideologically external and internal critiques of ideas. The former are useful primarily in spurring conservatives to develop "better rhetoric" for their ideas. But the latter "are likely to be taken sympathetically and really change steps in arguments on the ground."[39] Those exchanges likewise help facilitate the accommodation of both libertarian and traditional conservative perspectives within the movement, which is necessary to maintain the sometimes uneasy coalition between them.

There's more to it. Society members "are regularly reminded by their leaders to be cordial and well-mannered with their ideological opponents," an approach driven in part "by the assumption that ideology has a personal component, that people initially attracted to or repelled by the character of an ideological movement's representatives rather than their ideas."[40] The debates usually take place before an audience predisposed to accept the conservative position. In that context, and by design, an

36 Iain Milhiser, 'What Trump has done to the courts, explained,' *Vox*, September 29, 2020.

37 Steven M. Teles, *The Rise of the Conservative Legal Movement: The Battle for Control of the Law* (Princeton: Princeton University Press, 2008) 144.

38 Teles, 'Rise of the Conservative Movement', 163.

39 McGinniss, 'Opinionated History', 406.

40 Teles, 'Rise of the Conservative Movement', 164.

individual audience member will feel less compelled to evaluate the ideas for themselves because they will get the benefit of the group working together to convince its members of the flaws in the opposing position. The effect is an inoculation of sorts. The group exposes itself to contrary ideas in a controlled setting, hears a response from a likeminded person, arms itself with counterarguments, and concludes that it need not trouble itself with revisiting the merits of the position going forward. Professors Donald Braman and Dan Kahan contend that these types of mechanisms involve "a set of in-group/out-group dynamics" that can exacerbate polarization. A belief that initially holds only a slight majority within the group may nevertheless come to dominate. In Professor Cass Sunstein's phrasing, "group polarization means that members of a deliberating group predictably move toward a more extreme point in the direction indicated by the members' predeliberation tendencies."[41]

There is no doubt that, however carefully the Federalist Society avoids engaging in lobbying or taking official positions on contested issues,[42] the organization has and very effectively advances goals that are broadly ideological in nature. In McGinnis's words, the Society "serves as an encompassing interest for generating conservative and libertarian ideas and sustaining networks of conservatives and libertarians" and is "the most powerful political cultural force for conservative ideas about law that … the United States has ever known."[43] Professor Evan Mandery characterized the Society as "one of the most influential legal organizations in American history, with intellectual reach and political clout that no other legal group can match."[44]

This is because the Society's influence is hardly limited to bringing young conservative lawyers into the fold. It maintains lawyers chapters that provide opportunities for camaraderie, networking, and reinforcement of the ideas first encountered in law school. All of this is intended to bear fruit in terms of policy as those lawyers move through their careers and, in some cases, into roles in government. As already noted, the Federalist Society has come to play a key role in Republican appointments to the federal judiciary. In the words of member Michael Greve, "the Federalist Society

41 Cass R. Sunstein, 'Deliberative Trouble? Why Groups Go to Extremes,' (2000) 110 *Yale Law Journal* 71.

42 This is a stance quite intentionally adopted by the organization, and it is the centerpiece of responses to charges that the Society is ideological in nature. As McGinnis put it, "The refusal to take political positions has had the advantage of repelling the now constant attacks made on the Society as its members become more numerous and its ideas have gained influence …. But by remaining a debating Society at its core, the Society is able to deflect much of the incoming political flak." McGinnis, 'Opinionated History', 410. For an example of that approach, consider this from an address by Senator Ted Cruz: "By the way, the left doesn't understand this gathering. The left thinks this is a partisan gathering. There is ideological diversity in The Federalist Society. You've got conservatives, you've got libertarians. You've got a lot of libertarians. You've got paleocons, which I've never been able to figure out what they believe, but the name invokes dinosaurs so it's kinda cool." Ted Cruz, 'Second Annual Gregory S. Coleman Memorial Lecture,' (2020) 24 *Texas Review of Law and Policy* 283, 285–86.

43 McGinniss, 'Opinionated History', 410, 411.

44 Evan Mandery, 'Why There's No Liberal Federalist Society,' *Politico*, January 23, 2019, available at www.politico.com/magazine/story/2019/01/23/why-theres-no-liberal-federalist-society-224033/.

has a de facto monopoly on the credentialing of rising stars … on the left there are a million ways of getting credentialed; on the political right there's only one way in these legal circles."[45] This, too, was an explicit goal. Though the Society's primary tangible output is debate and discussion, and important and intended byproduct is people. As Professor Steven Calabresi, one of the Society's co-founders, put it: "There was a real desire to train a generation of people—a farm team—who might go on later on in future Republican administrations to have an impact and to hold more important positions."[46] Among the goals, as he put it on a different occasion, was to "create a network of alumni who will have been shaped in a particular way."[47] The underlying intuition was that having the right people reduced the need to monitor their performance in whatever role they were placed in. Committed conservatives could be counted on to act in conservative ways. And an express goal during the development of the movement was to highlight the incentives for becoming a committed conservative, to show young lawyers "that if they were loyal to certain fundamental principles, that they would get ahead because they would be recognized as effective and loyal servants of Reagan."[48]

The nomination of David Souter[49] to the Supreme Court cemented the Society's role as the centerpiece of the conservative legal movement. Souter was a relative unknown whose route to the Court was a product of having impressed two people from his small state of New Hampshire who happened to hold influential positions at the right moment – John Sununu as Chief of Staff under President George H. W. Bush and Senator Warren Rudman. Souter was undoubtedly conservative under many definitions of the word, but, as it turned out, not the one that mattered most to the movement. He was, together with Justices Anthony Kennedy and Sandra Day O'Connor, an author of the unusual joint opinion in *Planned Parenthood* v. *Casey*[50] that upheld the constitutional right to obtain an abortion, and by the end of his time on the Court, he was typically regarded as a member of its liberal wing. His appointment, as characterized by Professors Devins and Baum, demonstrates that even in 1990, "the number of well-credentialed conservatives was comparably thin and the conservative legal movement was not sufficiently entrenched to demand that Republican appointees come from the pool of vetted conservatives."[51] Within a short time, "No More Souters" became a mantra within the movement.

45 Hollis-Brusky, 'Ideas with Consequences', 152.
46 Steven M. Teles, 'Transformative Bureaucracy: Reagan's Lawyers and the Dynamics of Political Investment,' (2009) 23 *Studies in American Political Development* 61, 73.
47 Hollis-Brusky, 'Ideas with Consequences', 10.
48 Id., 74 (quoting Kenneth Cribb, assistant to White House Chief of Staff Edwin Meese).
49 Chad M. Oldfather, 'The Inconspicuous DHS: The Supreme Court, Celebrity Culture, and Justice David H. Souter,' (2020) 90 *Mississippi Law Journal* 183.
50 505 US 833 (1992).
51 Devins and Baum, 'The Company They Keep', 126.

By 2005, in contrast, the conservative bench was deep and the movement influential. Thus, when President George W. Bush nominated Harriet Miers for the opening on the Supreme Court created by Justice O'Connor's resignation, the movement was able to thwart it. Miers had a longstanding personal relationship with Bush and was his personal lawyer at the White House. Her practice background, however, had not involved constitutional law. This, McGinnis relates, "was seen as an insult to the many qualified nominees … who had seriously grappled with the hard issues of constitutional law" and who could be counted on to contribute to the appropriate development of constitutional law.[52] Those nominees "had been largely nurtured by the Federalist Society."[53] Miers, by contrast, was not even a member of the Society, having once illustrated the point that she avoided membership in "politically charged" organizations by saying, "For example, I wouldn't belong to the Federalist Society any more than – I just feel like it's better to not be involved in organizations that seem to color your view one way or the other for people who are examining you."[54] After she withdrew, Bush nominated then-Judge Samuel Alito, a member of the Society. The headline of the *New York Times* article discussing the nomination read: "In Alito, G.O.P. Reaps Harvest Planted in '82."[55] That was the year Alito joined the Reagan administration as a young lawyer, and it was also the year the Federalist Society held its first meeting. The article quoted lawyers involved in the Society's founding who were gleeful over the organization's having become more successful than they ever could have imagined. Professor Douglas Kmiec, referring both to Alito and the successful nomination of Chief Justice John Roberts, characterized it as "a graduation. These individuals have been in study and preparation for these roles all their professional lives."[56]

Devins and Baum argue that the development of a distinct elite network of conservative lawyers has changed the nature of judging once those lawyers reach the bench. They are, for one thing, more thoroughly conservative than past Republican appointees. A prospective judge's record of involvement in the Society provides evidence that they have been intellectually nurtured in the preferred way and have a durable set of beliefs. It also allows access to trusted voices able to vouch for their reliability and appropriateness more generally. (One imagines there are many members of the Society who have no realistic prospect of gaining any of its plum networking advantages. The fact that the Society is open to the expression and debating of all views does not mean that all views will be received in the same way. A given individual may not espouse the right subset of views within the Society's big tent, may lack the appropriate personality, or may have demonstrated themselves to be

52 McGinnis, 'Opinionated History', 411.

53 Id.

54 Al Kamen, 'Miers's Long-Ago Federalist Slap Still Stings,' *Washington Post*, October 21, 2005.

55 David D. Kirkpatrick, 'In Alito, G.O.P. Reaps Harvest Planted in '82,' *New York Times*, January 30, 2006.

56 Kirkpatrick, 'Harvest'.

otherwise unreliable or temperamentally unfit according to whatever standards are then held by those with gatekeeping authority.).

Once a judge has reached the bench, the Society provides continued incentives for them to maintain their conservative approach. It is, by design, an alternative judicial audience, a community within which conservative judges and justices can receive accolades, deliver speeches to receptive audiences, and mingle with the very set of people with whom they were socialized into the profession and who were key to their obtaining their position. They will, naturally, continue to seek the regard of those people. In Calabresi's view, referring to the Federalist-associated justices, "I think it absolutely keeps them in check. When one tries to think about what kinds of checks exist on officials as powerful as Supreme Court Justices I think the check of criticism by law schools, journalists, and conservative think tanks like the Federalist Society, criticism from those quarters is something that they notice."[57]

At the same time – and here we return to the importance of norms as a constraint on judicial behavior – the continued involvement of judges and justices in the Society facilitates the shifting of the legal Overton window,[58] the range of ideas and arguments that are plausible at any given time.[59] As Teles puts it, the Society's "activities facilitate the orderly development of conservative legal ideas and their injection into the legal mainstream, reducing the stigma associated with those ideas in institutions that produce and transmit professional distinction."[60] Because what counts as a good legal argument is contingent on an array of factors that are in a constant state of flux, a well-timed effort coupled with a receptive audience can lead to an argument once regarded, in Professor Jack Balkin's phrasing, as "off the wall" becoming not merely plausible but successful.[61] An example was the Affordable Care Act's individual mandate. The fact that most legal academics reflexively rejected the idea that the mandate was beyond the reach of Congress's power under the Commerce Clause is often offered as evidence of a lack of ideological diversity in the academy.[62] Yet, as Balkin has pointed out, the concept of the mandate was developed by conservatives as a free-market alternative to the more sweeping alternative floated during the Clinton administration.[63] Those conservatives, too, presumably

57 Hollis-Brusky, 'Ideas with Consequences', 21.
58 Joseph Lehman, *The Overton Window*, www.mackinac.org/OvertonWindow.
59 Cruz, 'Memorial Lecture', 287.
60 Teles, 'Rise of the Conservative Movement', 136.
61 "[T]he conventions that determine what makes an argument about the Constitution good or bad, what legal claims are plausible, and which are 'off the wall,' change over time in response to changing political, social, and historical conditions." Jack M. Balkin, 'Constitutional Hardball and Constitutional Crises,' (2008) 26 *QLR* 579, 579.
62 David A. Hyman, 'Why Did Law Professors Misunderestimate the Lawsuits Against PPACA?,' (2014) *University of Illinois Law Review* 805, 807–08. Hyman offers the explanation that this was due to "motivated reasoning in an echo chamber."
63 Jack M. Balkin, 'From Off the Wall to On the Wall: How the Mandate Challenge Went Mainstream,' *The Atlantic*, June 4, 2012.

once regarded a mandate as within the scope of Congress's power. Thus, when it was passed, "the idea that the Act's mandate to purchase health insurance might be unconstitutional was, in the view of most legal professionals and academics, simply crazy." But when such an argument finds support from the right sort of group, or prominent members of a group such as the Federalist Society, the likelihood of its acceptance increases. A judge or justice adopting a position can feel considerably more comfortable doing so when they can draw upon logic developed by respected members of their community and celebrated by that community. Professor Amanda Hollis-Brusky regards the scope of the Society's interest as even broader, saying that it "is helping to change constitutional culture outside the legal profession."[64]

None of this is to suggest that susceptibility to group dynamics and the development of an immunity to ideas that are ideologically incompatible with one's own are limited to conservative students and lawyers. Intellectual blinders are a pervasive feature of our society, and the world of legal education is no exception. As noted earlier, one of the primary motivations for the founding of the Federalist Society was the undoubtedly correct sense that law schools and the legal profession more generally had a predominantly liberal orientation.[65] (That has not always been the case. The bar as a whole served as a conservative force until the 1960s, at which point lawyers began to move to the left, with the trend manifesting itself especially in its more elite quarters.[66]) The liberalism of the legal profession persists.[67] Although there certainly is a conservative presence in legal academia, perhaps due in part to the efforts of the Federalist Society, law professors as a group are overwhelmingly liberal.[68]

Holding the dominant position within the profession has undoubtedly facilitated success. Justice Scalia's vitriolic dissent in *Lawrence* v. *Texas*, in which the Court held that the Due Process Clause protects a right to engage in consensual sodomy, inartfully made the point by characterizing the result as "the product of a Court, which is the product of a law-profession culture, that has largely signed on to the so-called homosexual agenda ...."[69] As the line of cases, including Lawrence, leading up to the Court's recognition of a right to same-sex marriage demonstrate, the same mechanisms for shifting the Overton window exist as much on the left as on the

64 Hollis-Brusky, 'Ideas with Consequences,' 159.

65 John McGinnis recounts what can be described as a feeling of profound alienation from the faculty and students at Harvard Law School, with his first attendance at a Federalist Society event being a life-changing event. McGinnis, 'Opinionated History'.

66 Christina Pazzanese, 'Gauging the Bias of Lawyers,' *The Harvard Gazette*, August 10, 2017 (interview with Professor Maya Sen).

67 Adam Bonica, Adam S. Chilton and Maya Sen, 'The Political Ideologies of American Lawyers,' (2016) 8 *Journal of Legal Analysis* 277.

68 James C. Phillips, 'Why Are There So Few Conservatives and Libertarians in Legal Academia? An Empirical Exploration of Three Hypotheses,' (2016) 39 *Harvard Journal of Law and Public Policy* 153, 206. Phillips concludes that "conservative and libertarian law professors are less common, more qualified, and more productive and influential."

69 539 US 558, 602 (2003) (Scalia, J., dissenting).

right. The result in *Lawrence* might not have been unthinkable when Scalia joined the Court – *Bowers* v. *Hardwick*[70] was a 5–4 decision, after all – but the notion that the Constitution protects a right to same-sex marriage, as a practical matter, was.

Yet in the years following *Bowers*, the currents of opinion shifted and some of that shift was driven by the academy. Whatever the nature and fate of most legal scholarship, some of it traces out reasoning that alters the course of a field, occasionally through some sort of dramatic, paradigm-shifting insight, but more often through a process of gradual accretion. Just as in the familiar phrase in the world of evidence law that "a brick is not a wall" – meaning that a single piece of evidence need not establish anything conclusively to be relevant, simply that it has some tendency to contribute to the making of an overall case – a single law review article or book is unlikely to shift the path of the law. But an accumulation of law review articles accepting the same premises and making related arguments, joined by shifting public opinion and a few courts willing to follow the suggested reasoning to the recommended conclusion, can constitute a movement.[71]

Even so, the sense, among liberals at least, is that they have no force that is the equivalent of the Federalist Society, no "answer to what has long been an asymmetrical fight in the legal world."[72] There is a nominal candidate. The ACS was founded in 2001 as a response to the Federalist Society, and in general, its operations look the same. It has student chapters at law schools and lawyer chapters at the city or state level. It does not, however, generally follow the model of having a speaker present an opposing perspective. And it does not have an effective monopoly as the organizational home for liberal law students because there are other student groups that serve more narrow interests. Nor has it succeeded in creating a network that liberal students and lawyers feel they must participate in if they seek to advance their careers in politically inflected ways. As Mandery put it, "The federal

70 478 US 186 (1986), in which the Court had rejected the claim that the Constitution includes a right to sodomy.

71 The point is analogous to one made by Professor Robert Ray, who was also a member of the grossly underappreciated band, The Vulgar Boatmen. In response to a question about lyrical differences in popular music in the 1960s and 1980s, Ray offered this: "My sense is that all cultural forms which circulate in a society – not a poem that you have written and put in your closet and no one sees – but all cultural forms which circulate and get reproduced, have some influence. That's an easy statement. The hard thing is to measure exactly what influence, and how quickly, how soon .... My Argument has always been that the way rock works, both in terms of its emotional effectiveness but also in terms of its politics, is at the level of sound. No matter how powerful you think 'Ohio' is, in terms of politics 'Tutti Frutti' is more politically profound. The problem is, for politicians, or for musicians who have political intent, or want to seem significant, the change effected by sound seems too subtle, too hard to measure, too slow. But it's profound. Coleridge once said that the way poetry, or art, can influence people is like the sap going through a leaf, and I think that's the way it works, like ink in a blotter, until It's gradually diffused into a whole culture's way of thinking about itself and the world." Ross Taylor, *Poet/Musician/Songwriter: Robert Ray of The Vulgar Boatmen*, Washington Review, July 1990, available at poetryandfictionandrockandroll.wordpress.com/2013/10/25/interview-from-the-washington-review-july-1990/ (permalink: https://perma.cc/N877-87AY).

72 Mandery, 'No Liberal Federalist Society'.

and state judiciaries are filled with Federalist judges, but there are no 'ACS' judges to be found on the Supreme Court or the federal benches. It's just not a thing."[73] In part because conservatives remain a minority within the profession, their network is more intimate, and the feedback loops among the academy, the profession, and the judiciary are tighter. Liberals have more options, which makes both the feedback loops and the mechanisms for monitoring and sanctioning more diffuse.

This manifests itself in the groups' messaging as well. The Federalist Society describes its main purpose as being "to sponsor fair, serious, and open debate about the need to enhance individual freedom and the role of courts in saying what the law is rather than what they wish it to be." Among other things, this entails an understanding of the judicial role that involves the application of aspirationally precise methodologies – textualism for statutes and originalism for the Constitution. If one is going to insist on a conception of the judicial role restricted to "saying what the law is," then one will naturally be drawn to methodologies that lend themselves to being portrayed as leading to identifiably correct answers. The ACS, by contrast, exists "to support and advocate for laws and legal systems that strengthen our democratic legitimacy, uphold the rule of law, and redress the founding failures of our Constitution and enduring inequities in our laws in pursuit of realized equality." Its vision for the judiciary includes interpretation of "the US Constitution through the backdrop of history and through the lens of lived experience." The aims are laudable. But the recipe lacks the crisp prescriptive bite of the Federalist Society's vision and does not confront the suggestion that it imagines judges making the law what they wish it to be.

Comparatively ineffective though it may be, it does not seem wrong to suggest that the existence of the ACS facilitates polarization. Just as the liberal speaker at a Federalist Society event often functions as a mechanism for solidifying the conservative viewpoint, the existence of the ACS helps cement the idea that there is a "we" and a "they," and that "we" believe there is an appropriate way to do law while "they" have fallen prey to motivated reasoning and the other pathologies that can lead thought astray. The differences between these two approaches are most evident in the context of high-profile, public law issues – the Second Amendment, election law, congressional power, and the like. But the starkness and intractability of the differences on those issues fuel a perception of a more comprehensive divide. "We" are principled, "they" are result-oriented. Our approach is consistent with the longstanding norms of legal practice, theirs is illegitimate. And so on. Groups go to extremes. Polarization begets polarization. The dark matter fractures.

Changes within both the academy and the profession have served, if not to catalyze, then at least to enable these developments. In the academy, the trend has been toward greater identification with the university. In earlier eras, by contrast, law professors identified strongly with the profession, and much of their scholarly output

[73] Id.

was doctrinal work designed to be of immediate usefulness to the bench and bar. By the early 1990s, however, things had changed. In 1992, Judge Harry Edwards, who had previously been on the faculty at the University of Michigan's law school, published an attention-grabbing[74] article entitled *The Growing Disjunction Between Legal Education and the Legal Profession.*[75] Law schools, he contended, "have abandoned their proper place, by emphasizing abstract theory at the expense of practical scholarship and pedagogy."[76] He did not disclaim theory entirely. Indeed, Edwards suggests that theory – used to inform critique or generate proposals for reform – is a necessary ingredient of good doctrinal work. His target instead were those within the academy who appeared to scorn doctrine altogether and law schools in which law professors increasingly "disdain law teaching as an endeavor in pursuit of *professional* education."[77] Among the negative consequences Edwards identified was that new lawyers come to "lack the basic doctrinal skills," such that they will "not understand how to practice as a *professional.*"[78] At elite schools in particular, faculty regularly "ignore or disparage legal doctrine, on the assumption that bar review courses will prepare students to pass the bar and that students will then learn whatever they need to know from their employers."[79]

Kronman, writing during the same period, offered a similar assessment and traced the intellectual currents involved all the way back to Dean Christopher Columbus Langdell's effort to treat the common law as a body of material that reflects an underlying set of rules.[80] The effort to treat law as if it were reducible to rules, Kronman contended, entails the rejection of a core aspect of the common lawyer's worldview. "The common lawyer instinctively mistrusts abstract speculation. He believes that general principles have a role to play in the law but doubts that most serious disputes can be decided by reference to them alone. In addition, he insists, hard cases require the exercise of practical wisdom: a subtle and discriminating sense of how the (often conflicting) generalities of legal doctrine should be applied in concrete disputes."[81] Modern legal education and scholarship, Kronman contended, tends to emphasize abstraction: "It is more concerned with concepts than with cases. It can be expressed in propositional form and taught by means that produce intellectual competence but no change of temperament or character, in contrast to the virtue of practical wisdom, whose acquisition implied a change of exactly this sort."[82]

74 Edwards discussed the reaction in a follow up essay. Harry T. Edwards, 'The Growing Disjunction Between Legal Education and the Legal Profession: A Postscript,' (1993) 91 *Michigan Law Review* 2191.

75 Harry T. Edwards, 'The Growing Disjunction Between Legal Education and the Legal Profession,' (1992) 91 *Michigan Law Review* 34.

76 Edwards, 'Growing Disjunction', 34.

77 Id., 34.

78 Id., 38.

79 Id., 39.

80 Kronman, 'Lost Lawyer', 167.

81 Id., 20–21.

82 Id., 21.

Judge Posner, having himself played a major role in the transformation of the legal academy, offered a similar assessment. Law faculties when he first encountered them in the 1960s were oriented toward the profession. Professors aspired to be first-rate lawyers and understood their primary responsibility to be turning their students into good, and possibly great, lawyers. This happened through "instructing them by precept but also by example, by being a role model; and the role was that of a practicing lawyer."[83] Accomplishing this required more than passing along abstraction and critique. It involved imparting knowhow – concepts, rhetorical devices, a talent for the creative reading of authorities, and "a subtle sense ('judgment') of just how far one can go in stretching the limits of established legal doctrines."[84] Professors who do not view themselves in this way, whose primary orientation is toward the academy more generally, will be less inclined, and often less able, to pass along such knowledge.

Of course, it does not necessarily follow that lawyers will fail to develop the necessary skills. There are still plenty of good and great lawyers in the profession, and they seemingly remain available to impart the relevant knowledge. But here, too, things have shifted. Changes in the practice of law, especially in the large-firm context, have contributed to the deterioration of old norms. Part of that is a product of an increasing emphasis on profitability. Edwards observed that "[w]hile the schools are moving toward pure theory, the firms are moving toward pure commerce …."[85] The practice, as he diagnosed it, had become increasingly materialistic, with firms in turn placing less emphasis on *pro bono* practice and the development of ethical lawyers. For the firms, Edwards contended, the changes in legal education are fortuitous, "because the unformed novices can be shaped to the employers' needs. New associates will 'learn' to misconstrue cases and statutes, to write obfuscatory briefs, to overpaper a case, and this 'education' will be all the smoother if they studied only pure theory in law school."[86]

Kronman similarly emphasized changes in the nature of the skills that lawyers are called upon to deploy. The increasingly specialized and atomized nature of practice means that fewer lawyers, especially in large firms, act as counselors in a robust sense of the term. They are called upon instead to address discrete types of situations – a client faces a specific problem, a transaction involves the acquisition of a certain sort of asset, and so on. The focus is narrow, the knowledge technocratic. The development of practical wisdom requires experience drawing upon the capacity for exercising it, and the opportunities for gaining that experience have decreased alongside the scope of lawyers' expertise. And the trends have continued. As Professor Margaret Raymond noted twenty years after Kronman wrote, "the

83 Richard A. Posner, 'In Memoriam: Bernard D. Meltzer (1914–2007),' (2007) 74 *University of Chicago Law Review* 435.
84 Posner, 'Meltzer', 437.
85 Edwards, 'Growing Disjunction', 34.
86 Id., 39.

practice, the opportunities it presents, and the constraints it imposes have changed in many of the ways Dean Kronman described with a haste that makes his observations of the early '90s seem both prescient and understated."[87]

Of course, large firms are not the only context in which the practice of law takes place. In-house lawyers, for example, are often called upon to answer a broad range of questions and to do so in a manner that takes full account of their clients' short- and long-term interests. The role very much entails acting as a counselor. Lawyers whose clients are small businesses and individuals must guide them through unfamiliar transactions and procedures in a manner that, ideally, involves the use of wisdom. Still, large law firms play a large role in setting the tone for the profession, both by providing initial professional homes for those who go on to fill other roles and by setting a baseline understanding of what the practice at its highest levels looks like.

And there's another sense in which the shift in the nature of large-firm practice matters. To the extent that new law professors have experience in practice, it tends to be at large firms, and then only for a couple of years. Beyond that, the conventional wisdom holds that time in practice becomes a liability for the aspiring academic – the concern is that a candidate who has been in practice for a longer period is simply looking for a lifestyle change, or discovered they weren't going to make partner, or is too far removed from the academic setting to be able to formulate and approach research questions in an appropriate manner. Whatever the reasoning, the result, given the changes in the nature of practice, is that most new professors will have had little experience acting as lawyers in any robust sense of the term and little opportunity to witness, much less engage in, the application of practical wisdom. They will have less experience with the collision between abstraction and practicality and less appreciation for the pressures that the simple need to get things done places on the desire to do so in an intellectually pure or elegant way.

In all, and to at least as great an extent now as was the case when Edwards and Kronman wrote, new law professors tend to come to the academy as academics rather than as lawyers. Most will have a pedigree that is, to a meaningful degree, elite.[88] Many will hold a Ph.D. in another discipline,[89] and many will have spent time as a fellow or visiting assistant professor in a program designed to socialize them to the academy. Few will enter directly from practice, and, as I have already suggested, few will have more than a token amount of experience in practice, typically in the sort of

87 Margaret Raymond, 'Lost and Found: The Lost Lawyer Twenty Years Later,' (2014) *Journal of the Professional Lawyer* 109, 111.

88 Milan Markovic, 'The Law Professor Pipeline,' (2020) 92 *Temple Law Review* 813; Eric J. Segall and Adam Feldman, 'The Elite Teaching the Elite: Who Gets Hired by the Top Law Schools,' (2018) 68 *Journal of Legal Education* 614.

89 In the period from 2011 through 2015, one-fifth of all entry-level hires at American law schools held a Ph.D. in addition to a JD. Lynn M. LoPucki, 'Dawn of the Discipline-Based Law Faculty,' (2016) 65 *Journal of Legal Education* 506. For a study of hiring at more highly ranked schools, see Justin McCrary, Joy Milligan and James Phillips, 'The Ph.D Rises in American Law Schools, 1960–2011: What Does It Mean for Legal Education?,' (2016) 65 *Journal of Legal Education* 543.

associate role in a large law firm where the day-to-day tasks are far removed from the exercise of judgment that is at the heart of what a fully formed lawyer brings to the role. Those professors, consistent with Kronman's assessment, are more likely to be drawn to abstraction and to admire certain traits in judges, such as the development and implementation of abstract theories. They will model that admiration for their students, some of whom will become judges.

All of this together forms a complex system. Changes in education facilitate changes in practice, and changes in practice alter the perspectives of those who become faculty and provide education. Because lawyers, and for the most part only lawyers, become judges, who in turn issue the opinions that form much of the raw material of legal education, these feedback loops extend into the judiciary. Consider, for example, Professor Anthony D'Amato's contention that Realism "was a disastrous setback for American law," and that its influence on the law school curriculum generated a self-fulfilling prophecy: it teaches the future judges, from the earliest moments of their professional socialization, that doctrine is manipulable, that "once he becomes a judge, he will not have to pay much attention to what the lawyers say about the law (any more than he did in the classroom). For the 'law' will be whatever he proclaims it to be."[90] Posner offered a slightly different version of the point. Realist professors, by explaining decisions as having been driven by considerations not mentioned in judicial opinions, leave students with the impression "that what is difficult and important and professional in law is not deriving decisions from a realistic appraisal of the situation …; it is making the decision seem the unalloyed product of formalist analysis."[91]

In a similar vein, Professor Scott Altman argued "that law becomes more or less constraining depending on individual judges' beliefs about law, judges' role conceptions, and expectations about law held by observers in various positions of power."[92] Altman argued, in effect, that it is beneficial for judges to believe themselves to be more constrained by law than they actually are, because judges who believe they are so constrained will, to a much greater extent, act as if they are constrained. Judges who are fully aware of the extent to which judicial decisions are the product of other factors – and who are consequently aware of the extent to which judicial decisions can be the products of something other than legal standards – would be more inclined to see the process "as a tactical game, the point of which is to pursue [their] own goals, whether or not [they believe] that the rule can be most reasonably understood that way."[93] The suggestion is not that judges who believe law constrains them more than it does will not reach decisions that are (at least in part) products of

90 Anthony D'Amato, 'A New (and Better) Interpretation of Holmes's Prediction Theory of Law,' Northwestern Public Law Research Paper No. 08-28 (2008), available at papers.ssrn.com/sol3/papers.cfm?abstract_id=1255522.

91 Posner, 'Divergent Paths', 302.

92 Scott Altman, 'Beyond Candor,' (1990) 89 *Michigan Law Review* 296, 303–04.

93 Altman, 'Beyond Candor', 310.

nonlegal factors, but that they will be unwilling to do so consciously and thus will be less inclined to do so overall.

Legal education, the practice of law, and judging are, of course, not things that take place in a vacuum. They are instead set within, and thus influenced by, larger social forces. All the actors in the legal system are members of their society and are not immune to the currents that run through it. What's more, the broader public is one of the audiences for judicial decisions, and at least occasionally a decision will attract its attention. A large body of literature explores the connection between public opinion and the Supreme Court's decision-making[94] and, as we have already seen, elected judges are influenced by the perceived electoral consequences of their decisions. In an age of social media and round-the-clock news, the ensuing reaction – or the anticipation of a reaction – can, one imagines, shape judicial behavior more quickly and effectively.[95]

My focus here will be on larger and slow-moving trends. In this regard, too, there have been significant shifts with implications for law and the judicial role. I do not claim here to present a comprehensive account of these developments. Nor do I mean to make any strong claims about causation. Law is a complex system embedded within a larger complex system, with causal relationships that are difficult to disentangle. The claim instead is simply that the developments thus far outlined in this chapter – polarization within society and the profession, coupled with changes in society and the profession, and the fracturing of shared norms – collectively provide a rich environment for the flourishing of certain types of legal argument, including those such as textualism and originalism discussed in Chapter 7.

Several recent commentators have identified and decried social trends that parallel the law's turn away from practical wisdom. Professor Tom Nichols decries what he calls "the death of expertise."[96] His targets include generalized ignorance, anti-intellectualism, and resistance to the idea that some may possess insights inaccessible to most. "Never have so many people had so much access to so much knowledge and yet have been so resistant to learning anything."[97] The problem, in part, is that there is too much information for any one person to process. Thinking one's way through an issue is difficult, and the ready availability of simplistic information that confirms our preexisting beliefs makes it seem unnecessary. "People do not do 'research' so much as they 'search for pretty pages online to provide

94 For an example including an overview of past work, see Christopher J. Casillas, Peter K. Enns and Patrick C. Wohlfarth, 'How Public Opinion Constrains the U.S. Supreme Court,' (2011) 55 *American Journal of Political Science* 74.

95 Maxine Goodman, 'Shame, Angry Judges, and the Social Media Effect,' (2014) 63 *Catholic University Law Review* 589.

96 Tom Nichols, *The Death of Expertise: The Campaign Against Established Knowledge and Why It Matters* (Oxford: Oxford University Press, 2017).

97 Nichols, 'Death of Expertise', 2.

answers they like with the least amount of effort and in the shortest time.'"[98] If there are "experts" who hold a contrary position, they must be biased or have some sort of agenda as agents of an undefined "they" who want you to believe something. This presents a problem for expertise rooted in professional judgment, tacit knowledge, or "situation sense." To the skeptical ear, a decision that relies on, or even acknowledges, intangible knowledge amounts to a "just trust us" assurance that reads more as a cover for partisan or other illicit motivations than as a depiction of a legitimate process.

At the same time as it has grown distrustful of this form of expertise, ours has become a society subject to what Professor Jerry Muller calls "the tyranny of metrics."[99] The logic proceeds from the same sources. "[J]udgment is understood as personal, subjective, and self-interested. Metrics, by contrast, are supposed to provide information that is hard and objective."[100] They replace individualized judgment with numbers generated via standardized methods, they enable transparency in their application, and they in turn provide an objective basis for meting out rewards and punishments.[101] The resulting assessments are ubiquitous: testing in education, moneyball in sports, Six Sigma in business, research into judicial behavior, and so on.

There can be no doubt that the systematic collection and evaluation of data provides valuable insights by revealing patterns and inefficiencies that are, so to speak, invisible to the naked eye. Businesses use data to analyze consumer behavior patterns, tailor marketing strategies, and optimize their operations. Governments can enhance public services by, for example, identifying areas with specific needs, such as through the deployment of resources based on crime patterns. The increasingly sophisticated use of data analytics enables sports teams to gain advantages over their competitors by adjusting in-game strategies (going for it more often on fourth down in football, lifting starting pitchers after facing the opponent's lineup twice in baseball, and the like) as well as by changing their approach to constructing a team (such as baseball teams placing more value on players who draw a lot of walks). Few areas of life remain untransformed.

Yet data analysis, like any measure, can mislead. We manage what we measure, as the saying has it,[102] "[b]ut what can be measured is not always what is worth measuring: what gets measured may have no relationship to what we really want to know."[103] Or it may have a misleading relationship with what we really want to know. And too often, we attend to the numbers without adequate reflection on the extent to which they tell us something meaningful.

98 Nichols, 'Death of Expertise', 111.
99 Jerry Z. Muller, *The Tyranny of Metrics* (Princeton: Princeton University Press, 2018).
100 Muller, 'Tyranny of Metrics', 6.
101 Id., 18.
102 Louis Lowenstein, 'Financial Transparency and Corporate Governance: You Manage What You Measure,' (1996) 96 *Columbia Law Review* 1335, 1342.
103 Muller, 'Tyranny of Metrics', 3.

Consider, in that regard, the infamous *U.S. News* rankings of law schools. Few people regard the rankings as anything but deeply flawed.[104] They're based on a formula that shifts, occasionally dramatically, from one year to the next, and that bears a questionable connection to what really matters in distinguishing one school from another. Because the differences between the schools in the middle of the distribution are slight compared to those at either end – as is routinely the case with statistically normal distributions of data – small changes can result in large rankings swings despite no discernible changes in the actual educational experience. And yet, as if they cannot help themselves, people rely on these rankings. Prospective law students do it, candidates for faculty positions do it, and established faculty members do it in the context of making decisions about where to place their scholarship and in assessing the value of others' work. All should, though no doubt to varying degrees, know better. Because they do not, law schools have strong incentives to operate in ways that play to the rankings, such as by emphasizing applicants' test scores and grade point averages over other indicators of suitability for and success in the profession.

These trends may be manifestations of something deeper still. One such account comes from Iain McGilchrist, who draws on a broad array of disciplines to outline a social shift, focusing – in part literally and in part metaphorically – on the differences between the way the human brain's two hemispheres encounter and make sense of the world and the way in which our society has come to value one form over the other.[105] Both hemispheres contribute to nearly the entire array of our cognitive functions, but they nonetheless have distinct roles. The right hemisphere deals with new information. It "sees the whole, before whatever it is gets broken up into parts in our attempt to 'know' it. Its holistic processing of visual form is not based on summation of parts."[106] Its context-sensitive approach fosters creativity, insight, and intuitive problem-solving. It is the source of empathy. The left hemisphere, by contrast, deals in decontextualized analysis of the parts extracted from the whole. It is better at reasoning that is explicit, linear, and sequential. Its responsibilities include analytical thinking, language processing, and a reductionist approach to the world. It "tends toward a slavish following of the internal logic of the situation, even if this is in contravention of everything experience tells us."[107] Roughly speaking, the differences McGilchrist identifies track those between System 1 and System 2 processing discussed in Chapter 3, as well as other models developed in cognitive psychology.[108]

[104] Jeffrey Evans Stake, 'The Interplay Between Law School Rankings, Reputations, and Resource Allocation: Ways Rankings Mislead,' (2006) 81 *Indiana Law Journal* 229.

[105] Iain McGilchrist, *The Master and His Emissary: The Divided Brain and the Making of the Western World* (New Haven: Yale University Press, 2019); Iain McGilchrist, *The Matter with Things: Our Brains, Our Delusions, and the Unmaking of the World* (London: Perspectiva Press, 2021).

[106] McGilchrist, 'Master and Emissary', 46–47.

[107] Id., 50.

[108] "In short, the assumption is widely shared in cognitive psychology that human minds use two modes of cognition (which are traditionally referred to as *head* and *heart* in spiritual literature): one more intuitive/holistic/relational/unconscious/better attuned to the body and senses, the other

A key part of McGilchrist's argument is "that the hemispheric differences are not just a curiosity, a bunch of neuropsychological facts, but actually represent two individually coherent, but incompatible, aspects of the world."[109] He illustrates the point by drawing on the German language's distinction between two types of knowledge. *Kennen* is knowledge that arises out of encounters, as with a person.

> It's the way we naturally approach knowledge of a *living being*; it's to do with *individuals*, and permits a sense of *uniqueness*; it's "mine," *personal*, not something I can just hand on to someone else unchanged; and it is not *fixed* or *certain*. It's not easily captured in *words*; the *whole* is not captured by trying to list the *parts* ("quick-tempered," "lively," etc.); it has at least something to do with the *embodied* person (the photograph); it resists *general* terms; it has to be *experienced*; and the knowledge depends on *between-ness* (an encounter). These are all, in fact, aspects of the world "according to" the right hemisphere.[110]

No collection of adjectives can fully capture the unique essence of another person, and one person's knowledge of Jane Smith will not be the same as another's, nor can the bulk of that knowledge be readily conveyed via language. *Wissen*, by contrast, is knowledge assembled from readily observable and categorizable facts. "Its virtue is certainty—it's fixed. It doesn't change from person to person or from moment to moment. Context is therefore irrelevant. But it doesn't give a good idea of the whole, just of a partial reconstruction of aspects of the whole."[111] It can be packaged and transmitted with relative ease.

Both types of knowledge are valuable. But, McGilchrist contends, Western society has come to overrely on left-hemispheric knowledge and to discount and devalue that generated by the right. The trends he associated with the dominance of left-hemispheric thinking include a reductionism that "sees everything as made up from fundamental building blocks, the nature of which is assumed to be obvious, or at least knowable in principle in isolation from whatever they go to make up."[112] Holistic thinking and the notion of experience-based craft knowledge are nearly invisible to this way of thinking. Were the left hemisphere's domination to become complete, this conception of expertise would be displaced in favor of theoretically derived "expert" knowledge, judgment would give way to algorithm, nonexplicit meaning would become incomprehensible, "and perhaps the very concept of reasonableness might become unintelligible."[113]

This is a brief summary of a sprawling and subtle set of arguments, but it recalls Kronman's laments over the legal profession's move away from practical wisdom.

more abstract/rational/conscious/linguistic/detached." Marius Dorobantu, 'The Master's Theory of Everything: A Review of Iain McGilchrist's *The Matter with Things: Our Brains, Our Delusions, and the Unmaking of the World*,' (2023) 2 *Reviews in Science, Religion, and Theology* 6.

109 McGilchrist, 'Master and Emissary', 94.

110 Id., 95.

111 Id., 95.

112 Id., 424.

113 Id., 432.

Kronman's lawyer-statesman consistently draws on what McGilchrist would categorize as right-hemispheric cognition. The practically wise lawyer's thinking entails not just raw analytical intelligence but traits such as sobriety, fair-mindedness, and incorruptibility that work to direct the exercise of that intelligence.[114] It recognizes that not all situations have answers that can be reached via calculation. Goals may be incommensurable, and there will often be no agreed-upon standard by which to assess which should be prioritized. The practically wise person possesses "a willingness to entertain the views of others, to make the positive effort that is required to see their values in the best possible light."[115] Or, as McGilchrist might put it, to draw upon *kennen* as well as *Wissen*.

McGilchrist contends that it is a mistake to regard these two forms of knowledge as properly confined to their primary spheres. In particular, the application of *kennen* to more than just living beings, which he believes was once more common, can serve as the source of important insights beyond those that come from the amassing and tabulation of facts. He offers up philosophical paradoxes as examples of the way in which left-brained reasoning can lead us astray. Consider, for example, the Sorites paradox, which I first discussed in the Introduction. The paradox is frequently illustrated by the example of the relationship between a single grain of sand and a heap of sand. Not only is a single grain not a heap, but it also seems inconceivable that any single grain could be sufficient to transform something that is not a heap of sand into something that is, leading logically to the conclusion that no accumulation of grains of sand could ever become a heap. The implication is that it is impossible to determine whether there is a heap. This, as McGilchrist sees things, is a product of Wissen, or left-brained reasoning: "It tries to relate two *things*: a grain of sand and a heap, as though their relationship were transparent. It also presupposes that there must either be a heap or not be a heap at any time ...."[116] But the better approach is the right brain's, which appreciates that "it is a matter of a shift in context, and the coming into being of a *Gestalt*, an entity which has imprecisely defined bounds, and is recognized whole ...."[117] *Wissen's* mistake is to demand precision from decontextualized consideration of grains and heaps, rather than to appreciate that "the heap comes into being gradually, and is a process, an evolving, changing 'thing'" that cannot be decomposed into "a never-ending series of static moments."[118]

As discussed in the Introduction, the Supreme Court's analysis in *Rucho* v. *Common Cause* exemplifies this sort of thinking.[119] Some partisanship in

[114] Kronman, 'Lost Lawyer', 43.

[115] Id., 94.

[116] McGilchrist, 'Master and Emissary', 138–39.

[117] Id., 139.

[118] Id.

[119] For a more developed analysis of partisan gerrymandering as an instance of the Sorites paradox, see Kevin Morris, 'Partisan Gerrymander after *Rucho*: The Proof is in the Procedure,' (2022) 105 *Marquette Law Review* 787, 806–09.

gerrymandering is acceptable; it's permissible to place multiple grains of sand together. The problem, then, is to determine how much is too much; when do the grains become a heap? Because it's impossible to say, independent of context and in a way that all observers would accept as correct, that a specific grain of sand, or a specific additional increment of partisanship, was the one responsible for the transformation, it must therefore be impossible to distinguish "heap" from "not a heap." This, of course, is fallacious. Ten grains of sand is not a heap; ten billion is. That there will be hard cases does not mean there will be no easy cases.

This potential to be misled inheres in all efforts to focus only on that which can be explicitly stated. Such a focus necessarily involves abstracting away from the unique features of a situation to place them into categories and turning "this situation" into "this *type* of situation." Often, especially in law, that is appropriate, and indeed, the creation and application of general rules are central to the endeavor. But usually is not the same as always, and sometimes to force a situation into a preexisting category, to reduce it to a collection of labels, is to overlook its essence. The approach "isolates the object of attention from its context—not just its surroundings, but the depth in which it lives. It opacifies it .... The price is that this sheering away of the context produces something lifeless and mechanical."[120] "Reductionism is an inescapable consequence of a purely left-hemisphere vision of the world, since the left hemisphere sees everything as made up from fundamental building blocks, the nature of which is assumed to be obvious, or at least knowable in principle in isolation from whatever it is they go to make up."[121]

To a considerable degree, of course, left-hemispheric thinking inheres in law. The functioning of legal materials depends on reductionism and decontextualization. "It depends" may be a classic lawyerly answer, but the nature of law is to identify certain features of recurring situations as significant. Doing so provides consistency in application and allows people to structure their affairs in reliance on the ability to focus on those features. At the same time, of course, discretion and situation-sensitivity are also pervasive, with the concept of "reasonableness" being perhaps their most frequent vehicle. To whatever degree law has historically given primacy to *Wissen*, it has also incorporated *kennen*.

Perhaps the most pervasive example of the intellectual developments Kronman and McGilchrist identify has been the rise and broad influence of what Professor Elizabeth Berman calls "the economic style of reasoning"[122] – "a loose approach to policy problems that is grounded in the academic discipline of economics, but has traveled well beyond it. It is often perceived as politically neutral, but it nevertheless contains values of its own—values like choice, competition, and especially, efficiency."[123]

[120] McGilchrist, 'Master and Emissary', 181.

[121] Id., 424.

[122] Elizabeth Popp Berman, *Thinking Like an Economist: How Efficiency Replaced Equality in U.S. Public Policy* (Princeton: Princeton University Press, 2022)

[123] Berman, 'Thinking Like an Economist', 3–4.

This approach has come to dominate policy discourse, and in doing so, it has displaced consideration of less-quantifiable social goods. It emphasizes efficiency, competition, and choice and regards its techniques as both comprehensive and precise. Values rooted in claims of rights, or suggestions that limitations on corporate power are appropriate, have little place in the analysis. The problem of incommensurability goes away because incommensurable values are dismissed. "Arguments based on claims about absolute rights which implied that cost should not be considered, lost legitimacy. So did positions that center the impact of policy on community, or democracy, rather than cost-effectiveness. So did positions that valued equality or stability more highly than efficiency. Instead, policies that made sense in economic terms came to be seen as the only alternative."[124]

Economics-driven arguments have certainly influenced the law. As Professor Lawrence Friedman puts it, the law and economics movement "has achieved an almost astonishing success in the academy .... [I]t had a real impact on scholarship, on the curriculum, and on attitudes toward law."[125] And here, too, it traveled under the banner of being value neutral.[126] One simply asks whether a policy is efficient or otherwise sensible in an economic sense. But for some, including Kronman, this represented another aspect of the shift away from the profession's time-honored approach, as embodied in the lawyer-statesman ideal. "For in deep and essential ways the discipline of economics is hostile to this ideal. It is incapable of acknowledging the phenomenon of moral incommensurability. It equates judgment with calculation. And it has no room for the notions of character and prudence that lie at the ideal's heart."[127]

To summarize: law is a craft, and its practice – including adjudication – involves drawing on shared norms, the application of inarticulable knowhow, and the invocation of "ways and attitudes which are much more and better felt and done than they are said."[128] All of this depends on a widely shared conception of the endeavor, of what the law is designed to accomplish and how it functions. That shared conception is imperiled. Polarization in society and the profession is both a symptom and a

[124] Id., 222. Binyamin Applebaum is direct in his critique: "But the market revolution went too far. In the United States and in other developed nations, it has come at the expense of economic equality, of the health of liberal democracy, and of future generations. Economists instructed policy makers to focus on maximizing growth without regard to the distribution of the gains – to focus on the size of the pie rather than the size of the pieces." Binyamin Appelbaum, *The Economists' Hour: False Prophets, Free Markets, and the Fracture of Society* (New York: Little, Brown and Company, 2019) 6–7.

[125] Lawrence M. Friedman, *American Law in the Twentieth Century* (New Haven: Yale University Press, 2004) 495. For a comprehensive survey of the influence of economic thinking, see Ash, Elliott, Daniel L. Chen, and Suresh Naidu, 'Ideas have consequences: The impact of law and economics on American justice,' No. w29788. National Bureau of Economic Research, 2022.

[126] Friedman, 'American Law', 496.

[127] Kronman, 'Lost Lawyer', 167.

[128] Llewellyn, 'Common Law Tradition', 214.

cause. So, too, are changes in society and the profession that lead to a devaluation of expertise and craft knowledge in favor of the tangible, articulable, and quantifiable.

Though I largely share the perspective of those who find these developments lamentable, they are to a considerable degree natural and appropriate reactions to the developments covered in earlier portions of this book. Reliance on the inarticulable leaves space for the operation of noncraft values such as ideology and prejudice, and the system's internal and external checks have weakened. A correction is in order, and the very developments considered in this chapter created an environment ripe for that correction to take the form of the determinate-seeming methodologies explored in Chapter 7.

7

Specialization and Methodology as Partial Solutions

Thus far, I have attempted to demonstrate that the mechanisms the legal system has traditionally relied on to channel judicial behavior have weakened. For a variety of reasons, today's judges are less directly engaged with the work of deciding cases than their predecessors. Judicial selection increasingly emphasizes ideology. The norms that have traditionally served to provide a baseline of cohesion have frayed as our society and the profession have become increasingly polarized. All of this increased the space available for improper factors – however one conceives of them – to influence judicial decision-making. At the same time, our culture more generally has come to be suspicious of the intangible and unquantifiable. Expertise that is not backed by empirical evidence or that cannot otherwise be captured via or reduced to a formula, in the eyes of many, is no expertise at all.

This chapter explores two additional mechanisms for shaping judicial behavior. Neither is new. Both have received increased emphasis in recent decades. The first is increased reliance on specialized courts. The second is a move toward increasingly muscular methodologies for the interpretation of statutes and the Constitution. Like the other mechanisms we have examined, both stand in implicit recognition of judges' susceptibility to human psychological frailty. And both, I will suggest, are at least consistent with, if not products of, the shifts in intellectual context explored in Chapter 6. The erosion of shared professional norms has left the legal community divided over the appropriate ends of government and less able to simply assume that judges are operating from a broad base of shared premises, and polarization within society more generally has reinforced this dynamic. Specialization addresses this by shrinking the scope of the necessary consensus. At the same time, the intellectual currents that facilitated the rise of economics-driven analytical methods and the discounting of less-tangible forms of judgment have enhanced the appeal of approaches that lend themselves to depiction as decisional algorithms. In other words, the logic of textualism and originalism can be concisely explained in a way that appeals to our collective taste for the quantifiable. This, in effect, enhances their marketability while papering over the considerable nuance involved in their application, the lack of agreement as to what actually implementing these methods entails, and the fact that both ultimately rely on the exercise of judgment.

THE CASSANDRA QUANDARY

One last bit of stage-setting remains before turning to these mechanisms. As touched on in Chapter 6, the world of contemporary American legal practice is a world of specialization. One is not merely a lawyer; some adjective inevitably precedes the title. One is a tax lawyer, a criminal defense lawyer, an estate-planning lawyer, a patent lawyer, and so on. And while some lawyers tend to take on work that ranges over a wide array of domains, such as commercial litigators or solo practitioners, they are almost certain to refer away work that calls for specialized knowledge that is unfamiliar to them. Any mildly sophisticated client would understand that they should have different lawyers do the work of obtaining a patent for their invention, setting up the company that will commercialize it, paying taxes on the proceeds, litigating disputes over its use, addressing claims by employees who allege unfair treatment, drafting a will and otherwise planning for the disposition of their estate, and so on. It is not that any one of those lawyers is incapable of the other tasks, at least in theory, but rather that there is a considerably greater chance that a specialist will do a better job and do it more efficiently.

And yet, most judges are generalists. A given judge might preside over cases involving any of these matters. Judges, and especially generalist judges, thus fill a role that by its very nature makes them what Professor Nathan Ballantyne calls "epistemic trespassers" – "thinkers who have competence or expertise to make good judgments in one field, but move to another field where they lack competence—and pass judgment nonetheless."[1] Generalist judges must decide cases in subfields where they lack the specialist's familiarity. All judges at least occasionally confront cases arising out of unfamiliar situations. The judge whose career was as a prosecutor will have had little exposure to complex corporate and commercial arrangements. A middle-aged (or older) judge's understanding of technology may not have kept pace with change. A judge whose life experience has not included exposure to the subculture out of which a dispute arose may misdiagnose the significance of the parties' interactions. In any of these situations, and more, a judge might bring their own, erroneous assumptions about people's meanings and motivations to their understanding of the situation or might otherwise fail to appreciate that the ground rules are different. Beyond that lies the possibility that the judge will unwittingly make errors of law. They may mistake a superficial understanding for a deep one – they will, say, not appreciate that the semantic content of some legal standard serves as a shorthand reference for a nuanced and complex body of law rather than as a hard-edged, inflexible rule.

[1] Nathan Ballantyne, *Knowing Our Limits* (Oxford: Oxford University Press, 2019) 195.

All of this brings to mind a quote most associated with former Secretary of Defense Donald Rumsfeld: "As we know, there are known knowns; there are things we know we know. We also know there are known unknowns; that is to say we know there are some things we do not know. But there are also unknown unknowns—the ones we don't know we don't know." Regardless of whether Rumsfeld's comment made sense in context,[2] it's taken on a life as a shorthand for an aspect of epistemological reality with intellectual roots extending back at least as far as Confucius.[3] Exercising good judgment requires metacognition. We must be attentive to our thinking, to the things we know and the things we don't know, and we must also be mindful of the possibility that there are aspects of our own ignorance that are invisible to us. It is this latter task that can be the most difficult.

As Professor David Dunning puts it, "knowing what one doesn't know, having a reasonable understanding of the shape and scope of one's ignorance, makes knowing a hard task."[4] In this regard, consider the Dunning–Kruger effect, a phenomenon that has caught the public's attention over the past decade or so – or at least the attention of a certain self-satisfied segment of the public. As it's popularly understood, the effect "is a type of cognitive bias in which people believe they are smarter and more capable than they are. Essentially, low-ability people do not possess the skills needed to recognize their own incompetence."[5] Invoking the Dunning–Kruger effect, in this sense, is a comparatively sophisticated way of calling someone stupid: this person is so dull as to be unable to comprehend the extent of their own ignorance. And indeed, the phenomenon so conceived is easy enough to recognize: the know-it-all uncle at a family gathering; the countless denizens of social media and website comment sections whose eagerness to offer simple solutions to complex problems reveals their inability or unwillingness to reckon with nuance and contingency, anyone who completely, but confidently, misdiagnoses what just went wrong.

But the effect is actually broader. In Ballantyne's phrasing, "People who lack first-order knowledge often lack second-order knowledge about their lack of knowledge."[6] As Dunning himself explains, "The claim is that people with poor expertise lack what they need to be able to recognize their shortcomings. It is not that they fail to recognize their deficits; instead, they are simply not in a position to recognize those

[2] David A. Graham, 'Rumsfeld's Knowns and Unknowns: The Intellectual History of a Quip,' *The Atlantic*, March 27, 2014, available at www.theatlantic.com/politics/archive/2014/03/rumsfelds-knowns-and-unknowns-the-intellectual-history-of-a-quip/359719/.

[3] David Dunning, 'The Trouble of Not Knowing What You Do Not Know,' in Nathan Ballantyne and David Dunning, eds., *Reason, Bias, and Inquiry: The Crossroads of Epistemology and Psychology* (Oxford: Oxford University Press, 2022) 205.

[4] Dunning, 'The Trouble of Not Knowing', 206.

[5] Kendra Cherry, 'What Is the Dunning-Kruger Effect? A cognitive bias that causes an overestimation of capability,' Verywellmind.com, November 8, 2022, available at www.verywellmind.com/an-overview-of-the-dunning-kruger-effect-4160740.

[6] Ballantyne, 'Knowing Our Limits', 216.

deficits and should not be expected to do so."[7] Properly understood, then, the effect isn't limited to the intellectually challenged. To be sure, it is most evident among relative neophytes to a discipline. "A little knowledge is a dangerous thing," as the saying has it, and indeed, those who have learned something about a topic often imagine themselves as being much closer to knowing everything about that topic than they are, and as a result, they tend to exhibit considerable overconfidence in their judgments. But it does not stop there. Anyone who steps outside the bounds of their own expertise and into another is susceptible. The opinion columnist. The person successful in business who imagines themselves to be highly capable in some general sense and therefore also suited to success in government, or as a teacher or pundit. The academic who leverages success in a narrow discipline into status as a public intellectual. Perhaps even the law professor with an undergraduate degree in psychology who is writing this book. Indeed, the risks may be even greater for those who have developed legitimate expertise of some sort. Success in one domain may make them more confident of their overall intellectual abilities and therefore less cautious about stepping into domains where they lack appropriate knowledge.

To put the point in a different way, expertise is not some general status that one attains, nor is it the product of broad underlying talent.[8] As Ballantyne observes, "Expertise is a status of thinkers and it is relative to a field at a particular time."[9] It is, as often phrased, "domain-specific."[10] What's more, "[t]here is little transfer from high-level proficiency in one domain to proficiency in other domains—even when the domains seem, intuitively, very similar."[11]

Most discussions of judicial expertise treat the concept as if its nature is self-evident. But on reflection, the notion is slippery, and it can be conceived of in a variety of manners. It might be tied largely to subject matter in ways that reflect divisions in practice. Judges, same as lawyers, could be regarded as having expertise in tax law, corporate law, criminal law, or what have you. This, to draw on a distinction raised in Chapter 6, consists to a greater degree of "expert knowledge" than expertise or practical wisdom. The judge knows more but does not necessarily know

7 Dunning, 'The Trouble of Not Knowing', 209.

8 Precisely what it means for someone to be an expert is a matter of some disagreement. Expertise can be described in relative terms – I'm an expert on the community where I live relative to someone who just arrived, but not to someone my age or older who has lived here their entire life – or in qualitative terms – as in the case of someone who has the ability to think differently about a problem. To the extent that it is a relative phenomenon, its benefits are largely those of efficiency. If experts are qualitatively different from nonexperts, by contrast, their judgments and decisions should be better. I have considered these matters in greater depth in Chad M. Oldfather, 'Judging, Expertise, and the Rule of Law,' (2012) 89 *Washington University Law Review* 847.

9 Ballantyne, 'Knowing Our Limits', 199.

10 Paul J. Feltovich, Michael J. Prietula and K. Anders Ericsson, 'Studies of Expertise from Psychological Perspectives,' in K. Anders Ericsson, Neil Charness, Paul J. Feltovich and Robert R. Hoffman, eds., *The Cambridge Handbook of Expertise and Expert Performance* (Cambridge: Cambridge University Press, 2006) 41, 47.

11 Feltovich, Prietula and Ericsson, 'Studies of Expertise', 47.

differently. Or it might be transsubstantive. For example, some have contended that judges develop a general expertise in decision-making. Judge Posner "unreservedly" accepted the idea "that our judges are specialized—to judging," which at the appellate level "comes from long practice in evaluating arguments of counsel, decisions of trial judges, and trial records …."[12] Judge Henry Friendly suggested that "[t]he process is more important than the subject matter; and the judge can lay claim to being a specialist in that."[13] Or it might involve a developed capacity for deploying practical wisdom and the ability to mediate conflicts among incommensurable values in the context of, and in recognition of, the unique features of a situation.

It is also difficult to determine who counts as an expert given the lack of objective grounds on which to do so. Measures such as reversal and citation rates are helpful, but they are to a degree products of context. Judges who are frequently reversed or frequently cited in one era will not be in another. In a fractured profession, what some consider expertise, others might regard as a product of ideological bias. Any judgment of expertise will necessarily be a matter of professional consensus. And however defined and assessed, any judge's expertise will have limits. It is inevitable that they will routinely be drawn beyond it, or into areas where some additional type of expertise would be beneficial or necessary, whether because a case involves an unfamiliar area of law or because the facts that gave rise to a case arose in an unfamiliar setting. Judges inattentive to their limits – those who fail to heed the possibility of unknown unknowns – are likely to miss the fact that they have outrun the boundaries of their expertise and ought to proceed with caution.

Definition might be tricky, but there are at least two implications of Dunning and Ballantyne's work pertinent to the judicial role. One is that a failure to recognize one's own ignorance makes one less likely to seek additional knowledge or the expertise of others when it is appropriate to do so. The effect compounds itself. Those who are least aware of the nature and extent of their own ignorance are also the least likely to seek assistance. And when they do, they are less likely to know who to ask or rely on, due to what Dunning and his colleagues have called "the Cassandra Quandary." As Dunning puts it, "Flawed expertise not only prevents people from seeing their own ignorance; it also prevents them from recognizing superior competence in others."[14] For example, mediocre chess players will often misjudge moves made by superior players and thus underestimate the superior players' level of talent, because they lack the ability to see and account for all the features of the game situation that are accessible to the expert. Highly skilled players, by contrast, have no difficulty assessing the talent level of inferior players.

[12] Richard A. Posner, *The Federal Courts: Challenge and Reform* (Cambridge: Harvard University Press, 1996), 248–49.

[13] Henry J. Friendly, 'Reactions of a Lawyer – Newly Become Judge,' (1961) 71 *Yale Law Journal* 218, 222.

[14] Dunning, 'The Trouble of Not Knowing', 219.

People thus tend to have "lopsided accuracy" – they are better at evaluating the competence of those who are less skilled than they are at evaluating the more skilled. "It takes one to know one" is usually pitched as an insult, but there's another dimension to it. Those who lack expertise often cannot see the complexity and nuance that the expert relies on in making judgments, and consequently, the nonexpert cannot make sense of the expert's decisions. As Ballantyne describes it, people "rely on their own knowledge in order to evaluate the knowledge of other people. They tend to treat any deviation or departure from their own thinking as evidence of other people's incompetence."[15] Not only does "game recognize game," it seems, but also to a degree *only* game can recognize game. An additional danger, then, is this: not only might a judge fall prey to the Dunning–Kruger effect and thus not realize their comparative lack of insight, but also they may at the same time be unable to recognize when some other person, be they a fellow judge, a lawyer, an expert witness, or whoever, possesses a deeper level of understanding.

The implications for judges extend beyond the resolution of individual cases. We might imagine, for example, that it is good for judges from time to time to reexamine and, to some greater or lesser degree, update their jurisprudential commitments. Yet there are obvious disincentives for doing so. Each of us brings finite time and finite abilities to a world with practically infinite information. We must accordingly engage in a form of blind triage, seeking to gain the knowledge that will be most beneficial while being unable to know until we have gained it just how useful it will be. Judges face the conundrum no less than others. Imagine, for example, a judge who has espoused a certain theory of interpretation since law school. It will be easier for that judge to avoid extended consideration of alternative perspectives, even if decades of experience might allow for a deeper appreciation of the matter than when the then-student first encountered and rejected them. Motivated cognition will make that avoidance seem justified. That the judge would be a better judge with the additional knowledge seems hard to dispute. Even one who rejected alternative perspectives would be a more sophisticated thinker. Sincere engagement with such perspectives will tend to soften the edges of substantive or methodological commitments, and perhaps occasionally may even lead to a more significant change in view. But the judge will not know the value of what they do not know. And they will understand that their time is limited, and their priors can easily lead them to think that making the investment is not worth the time.

It bears emphasizing that, as with the psychological phenomena discussed earlier, these are tendencies, and not all judges will manifest them to the same extent or in the same ways. The features of procedural and institutional design that mitigate those phenomena will help mitigate them as well. Yet, as Cardozo pointed out, any of us can see the world only through our own eyes, which makes it easy to misapprehend how it looks through others' eyes. As I have suggested elsewhere, even a judge

[15] Ballantyne, 'Knowing Our Limits', 235.

with as substantial an intellect as Posner was seemingly susceptible, in his case by failing to appreciate the extent to which others were not on his intellectual level.[16]

SPECIALIZED COURTS

One response to the challenges posed by an increasingly specialized world is the development of specialized courts.[17] Thus, to name a few, we have tax courts, bankruptcy courts, family courts, and the Federal Circuit. Posner suggested the trend toward specialization would continue, if for no other reason than because it would be the only way to respond to increasing caseloads.[18] The appeal is easy to appreciate. If part of the problem is that judges must too often step outside their expertise, then the solution is to create a system that tethers judges more closely to that expertise. Judges who are experts in, or at least deeply familiar with, a specific subject matter will be able to more efficiently process cases and, because they will do less epistemic trespassing, reach decisions that are in general better than those that would be reached by generalists.[19] In doing so, they will create a better law. Because specialized judges will be more familiar with and attentive to both the law, its structure, and its underlying logic, their decisions will reflect and develop a body of law that is more uniform and predictable.[20] Properly deployed specialization can thus help mitigate the effects of some of the phenomena discussed in this book. Judges who possess expert-level knowledge will perhaps not be as affected by having less direct engagement with opinion writing. Fewer issues will be new to them; most will be easier to place within a familiar legal framework.

But there are costs to specialization. A specialized court risks becoming insular, especially if a specialized bar develops along with it. Judges and lawyers within such a closed system will be "less inclined to question shared premises, more likely to develop an internal and potentially impenetrable language, and otherwise generally disposed to facilitate the evolution of their institution in such a way as to move it away from the mainstream."[21] They will have less exposure to trends and developments in other areas of the law and will accordingly have fewer raw materials from which to draw analogies. At the same time, there will be boundary problems related to the definition of the court's jurisdiction, which will lead not only to administrative difficulties – does every case with a tax issue end up in tax court, or just some of

16 Chad M. Oldfather, 'Limitations (A Response to Judge Posner),' (2013) 51 *Duquesne Law Review* 67.

17 Chad M. Oldfather, 'Judging, Expertise, and the Rule of Law,' (2012) 89 *Washington University Law Review* 847.

18 Richard A. Posner, 'The Role of the Judge in the Twenty-First Century,' (2006) 86 *Boston University Law Review* 1049, 1050.

19 Edward K. Cheng, 'The Myth of the Generalist Judge,' (2008) 61 *Stanford Law Review* 519, 524.

20 Ellen R. Jordan, 'Specialized Courts: A Choice?,' (1981) 76 *Northwestern University Law Review* 745, 748–50.

21 Oldfather, 'Judging, Expertise', 858.

them? – but can also lead to the development of parallel, and inconsistent, bodies of law if the boundaries are set up in such a way as to allow some issues to come before both specialized and generalist courts.

All of this assumes that there is such a thing as expertise (or tacit knowledge) in law, or at least that expertise is attainable in all areas of law. But that, too, can be questioned. In areas such as constitutional law, there are fewer shared premises and a greater range of incommensurable aims. What one camp perceives as expertise might thus be regarded as simple ideological preference by another.[22] Expertise, if it exists, may entail something like the lawyer-statesman's capacity for charting a course through the waters of incommensurability, and the increase in polarization since Kronman wrote makes restoration of that ideal an even less likely prospect than he envisioned. In areas where premises are contested, the consequence of a specialized judiciary may not be uniformity and predictability but rather a body of authority that experiences wide swings as competing camps move in and out of control.

Increased specialization may be inevitable. It seems likely to realize its promise of allowing the judicial system to handle an increasing volume of cases, and to do so in a manner that, in most contexts, increases the consistency and accuracy of results. But there will be accompanying costs. Implicit in the rule of law ideal is a notion of law as a common language, something that, in theory, if not in practice, is accessible to all. A generalist judiciary fosters that ideal of necessity. Specialized advocates must, in effect, translate from the dialects of their specialties, and generalist courts will generate decisions in the common tongue. Specialized courts, no longer tethered to the common language and the common concepts, will be free to drift. The result, if there is no mechanism in place to stop it, will be that there are bodies of law instead of a body of law. My goal here, of course, is not to provide a comprehensive treatment of specialization. It can solve some problems – narrowing the scope of a court's domain increases the probable scope of shared premises while decreasing the likelihood of epistemic trespassing. But it is no panacea. It cannot make decision-making algorithmic, and it cannot eliminate the need for judgment.

THE TURN TO METHODOLOGY

When we turn our attention back to generalist courts, we find that here, too, the system has implicitly recognized and provided mechanisms to account for the likelihood of gaps in judges' expertise and the epistemic trespassing that necessarily

[22] Judge Posner suggested as much about constitutional law: "We think of a specialist not just as someone who knows a lot about a subject, but as someone to whom we are willing to entrust important decisions about it that affect us. This willingness depends on a belief that the specialist is objective, in the sense that his judgment is independent of personal values that we may not share, and that is not a sense that most people have about experts in constitutional law." Richard A. Posner, 'Will the Federal Courts of Appeals Survive Until 1984? An Essay on Delegation and Specialization of the Judicial Function,' (1983) 56 *Southern California Law Review* 761, 780.

follows. Because law concerns nearly all aspects of human affairs, judges will often find themselves required to preside over disputes in which they lack even basic familiarity with, to say nothing of expertise about, the contexts in which they arose. And given the scope and complexity of the law, today's judges can be expected to confront legal materials and factual settings in which they lack a deep understanding. In short, judges are often required to make decisions outside their core areas of competence.

Some of the system's features that we have already considered help address this concern. The adversarial process, for one, creates a powerful incentive for litigants to provide a judge with the reading of the applicable legal materials that is most hospitable to their case, and when the process functions well, the two sides' contrasting positions expose the judge to all pertinent authority and provide the raw materials that allow the judge to situate the case within the appropriate legal framework. The mechanism is imperfect because the litigants' incentive is to win rather than to provide the court with the information necessary to reach the best overall conclusion, but it provides some assurance that a judge will approach the dispute in a basically informed manner. Trial judges also have the ability to make use of expert witnesses and special masters to assist in understanding technical or specialized aspects of a case. The system also equips judges with tools by which to make sense of and implement legal materials. Stare decisis creates a strong presumption of continuity with past decisions.

Ballantyne's recommended response to the ubiquity of epistemic trespassing is to identify principles that can help guide us in forming our beliefs. He undertakes the task with skepticism about their ability to do so. "We are opinionated, busy, distractible, and animated by the subterranean forces of our nature."[23] Someone aiming to change another person's mind, he suggests, would likely be better served by focusing on social incentives – the sorts of constraints provided by the judicial audiences and media coverage discussed in Chapter 5. "Intellectual hypocrisy and *akrasia* ['believing one thing ought to be done, yet doing another'] are the norm, not the exception. Our human nature is not easily reasoned with."[24] As Ballantyne candidly admits, "I tend to doubt that our powers of reflection, self-knowledge, and self-control will allow us to reliably follow our principles when we need them – and, regrettably, I don't know of a proven plan, regimen, or twelve-step program for becoming the sort of thinker who can reliably follow epistemic principles."[25] Still, he concludes that principles can help. They can force us to pause, remind us to set aside our first-order preferences, help us focus our attention properly in situations where we lack prior opinions, and sometimes help us resolve tensions or conflicts in our beliefs. "In general, good epistemic principles bring us clarity about which epistemic judgments are correct. They promise us a measure of impartiality."[26]

23 Ballantyne, 'Knowing Our Limits', 63.
24 Id., 64.
25 Id., 64.
26 Id., 66–67.

Interpretive methodologies represent something akin to the principles Ballantyne advocates. Judges must frequently make sense of words as they are used in contracts, constitutions, statutes, and the like. Recall, for example, the discussion of "from the person of another" in Chapter 1. James Madison recognized the point in *The Federalist* No. 37, observing that "no language is so copious as to supply words and phrases for every complex idea, or so correct as not to include many equivocally denoting different ideas." This is not to deny that most cases will be easy. In the case of Professor H. L. A. Hart's famous example of a rule prohibiting "vehicles" in a park,[27] it is clear that a picnicking family's minivan is prohibited. It's just as clear that their picnic blanket and camping chairs are not. There are, in other words, plenty of situations that fall within the core of the rule, and plenty that it obviously does not extend to, just as theft of a wallet out of someone's hand will clearly be "from the person of another." But there are also what Hart characterized as penumbral cases. Does a prohibition on vehicles extend to bicycles, airplanes, and motorized scooters? Toy cars? A decommissioned jeep placed in the park as part of a memorial? How about the showing of a movie of the sort often characterized as a "star vehicle" – one designed to feature and capitalize on the popularity of a particular performer?

The point of the example, of course, is not to generate answers to the question but rather to illustrate the idea that text alone will often not lead to a clear resolution. Every rule will have its penumbral cases, and application of a rule's plain meaning will sometimes produce a result that is clearly contrary to the rule's purpose.[28] It is in these situations where disputes, and thus lawsuits, are most likely to arise. Judges must necessarily go beyond the text to resolve them and the question thus becomes how they should go about doing so. Is it to be an ad hoc process, or is there a recipe – a methodology – that judges should consistently follow? If so, what should it include? And just how precise should it purport to be? The academic literature addressing the question of how courts should go about interpreting statutes is vast and has proliferated, especially over the past four decades. Yet an assertion made by Professors Henry Hart and Albert Sacks in the middle of the twentieth century remains basically true: "American courts have no intelligible, generally accepted, and consistently applied theory of statutory interpretation."[29]

Judges are, of course, humans, and humans, as we have seen, routinely fall prey to motivated reasoning and cognitive biases. Humans have blind spots, and the ability to reason away conflicting evidence and other information suggesting that our thinking might be flawed. Our bases of true knowledge are thin, and our lack of awareness of and appreciation for the significance of what we do not know is vast.

27 H.L.A. Hart, 'Positivism and the Separation of Law and Morals,' (1958) 71 *Harvard Law Review* 593, 606–15.

28 Frederick Schauer, *Thinking Like a Lawyer: A New Introduction to Legal Reasoning* (Cambridge: Harvard University Press, 2009) 151–67.

29 Henry M. Hart, Jr., and Albert Sacks, *The Legal Process: Basic Problems in the Making and Application of Law* (Westbury, NY: Foundation Press, 1994) (William N. Eskridge and Philip P. Frickey, eds.) 116.

Interpretive methodologies thus promise to guide the judge and keep the judge from being misled by information of dubious validity. In a sense, methodologies do what all legal rules do, which is to identify the features of a situation to take into account in making a decision about that situation. Did the defendant commit a tort, or a crime? The applicable rules specify what matters. *These* are the things that determine whether someone committed fraud, or whether a defendant's conduct amounted to a crime and if so how serious a crime, and so on. Other things are of no legal consequence. The fact that a victim might have been partially responsible for the situation will often matter in tort law, and much less so in criminal law. That the defendant is in some sense a "bad person" will typically be out of bounds. And so on, all encapsulated in statutes, constitutions, and doctrine.

Methodologies perform an analogous function, but at a meta level. They are in a sense akin to the rules of evidence, which regulate the admissibility of some forms of evidence and categorically prohibit the use of others, usually because of concerns that the potential of a certain type of evidence to mislead outweighs probative value, but sometimes in order to further other goals. The parallel works like this: Rules 401 and 402 of the Federal Rules of Evidence provide that relevant evidence is presumptively admissible. Relevance is a very low bar, satisfied if a piece of evidence "has any tendency to make a fact [of consequence to the determination of the action] more or less probable" than it otherwise would be. The question, stated differently, is whether, given what's at stake in the case, the evidence could logically make even the tiniest bit of difference to the factfinder. If the answer is yes, it is presumed admissible.

But there are limits. The rules give judges a general power to exclude evidence that will mislead the jury, confuse it, or tempt it to reach conclusions based on prejudice or emotion. Certain types of evidence are presumptively excluded as a categorical matter. For example, a party's character – whether they are in some sense a good or bad person – undoubtedly has some value in answering questions about how they behaved on a given occasion. But it's not terribly reliable. Good people sometimes do bad things and bad people often refrain from doing bad things, and we worry that a jury will be misled. And while we could rely on trial judges to make those determinations on a case-by-case basis, we do not. The rules ensure equality of treatment from one judge to the next. And they also help the judge. A blanket exclusion of the evidence means the question doesn't have to be litigated in every case and allows the judge to offload responsibility for exclusion onto the rule – "my hands were tied" – rather than having to confront the various pressures that would tempt the judge to bend the rule in difficult or high-profile cases.

TEXTUALISM AND STATUTORY INTERPRETATION

That a parallel set of rules is appropriate to guide judges in making sense of statutes is uncontroversial. American judges have long relied on a large array of "canons of construction" to guide the process of interpretation. As Professor William Eskridge characterizes them, "the canons reflect the methodological pluralism of American statutory interpretation – the variety of sources that judges do consider and ought to consider when they interpret statutes."[30] The *ejusdem generis* canon, for example, provides that when a statute includes a list of items and ends with a general term – say, for example, a statute that listed pistols, revolvers, rifles, shotguns, tasers, swords, knives and then concluded with "or any other dangerous weapon" – that general term should be interpreted to include only items of the same kind or nature as those specifically listed. The *expressio unius est exclusio alterius* canon stands for the proposition that the expression of one thing – say, a statute that refers to "personal property" – implies the exclusion of others, such as, in this example, "real property." The list of canons is long, conflicting, and contested,[31] but their existence supports the idea that judges do not, and have not, understood themselves to be able to do as they wish without regard for statutory text and moreover that the system as a whole values and works toward uniformity and consistency.

Disputes over interpretive methodology have more dimensions to them than the analogy to the rules of evidence suggests. A basic question concerns the allocation and balance of power between the legislative and judicial branches. Contemporary discussions tend to take it as given that courts are to occupy a subservient role, that their job is to be a mere conduit – a "faithful agent" – through which the legislature's will is put to work. But the point is debatable at the federal level both as a matter of institutional design and of the original understanding of the judicial power in Article III of the Constitution,[32] and an alternative conception of courts' role is as "partners in the ongoing process of law-making." At the state level, the question is complicated by differing constitutional structures and the fact that many states' judges are elected and consequently have a claim to democratic legitimacy vis-à-vis the legislature that their federal counterparts do not. To say this, too, is not to suggest that judges should have free rein to do as they please. The obligations that partners owe to one another are different than those that agents owe to principals, but they are obligations nonetheless. Judges-as-partners will have a greater range of discretion than judges-as-agents, but neither is unbounded, either in general or from the text. Partnerships exist to accomplish something, and in the case of the legislature

30 William N. Eskridge Jr., *Interpreting Law: A Primer on How to Read Statutes and the Constitution* (St. Paul, MN: West Academic Publishing, 2016) 23.

31 Karl N. Llewellyn, 'Remarks on the Theory of Appellate Decision and the Rules or Canons About How Statutes Are to Be Construed,' (1950) 3 *Vanderbilt Law Review* 395, 401–06 (arguing that there are countervailing canons available for a judge to justify conclusions in either direction); Antonin Scalia and Bryan A. Garner, *Reading Law: The Interpretation of Legal Texts* (St. Paul: West Publishing, 2011) 9 (characterizing theirs as an effort "to collect and arrange only the valid canons (perhaps a third of the possible candidates)").

32 William N. Eskridge, Jr., 'All About Words: Early Understandings of the "Judicial Power" in Statutory Interpretation, 1776–1806,' (2001) 101 *Columbia Law Review* 990.

and the judiciary, the claim is that the partnership exists to further the project of democratic governance.[33]

Especially if the judiciary's role is to be a faithful agent, a question arises about what we might call the ontological status of legislation – what is it, exactly, that a legislature does when it passes a law? One view, that of the textualists, holds that what legislatures enact should be regarded, in effect, as no more or less than a basket of words, such that the interpreter's role is to make sense of those words on their own terms and without regard to some broader conception of what the legislature meant to do. The reasoning is simply that the words are the only thing the legislature voted on. Different legislators likely had different understandings of precisely what they hoped to accomplish with those words, and different conceptions of why what they passed makes sense as a matter of policy. Those who voted in favor of excluding vehicles from the park might have been variously concerned about noise, safety, or aesthetics. Thus, there is no single, collective view of the law's purpose or effect, and even if there were the fact that legislators need not provide reasons for their votes means the raw materials for discerning it will not exist even if it did.

Proponents of this view do not believe it to be impossible or unwise for judges to attribute purpose to statutes. Instead, they purport to restrict the process of ascertaining that purpose to consulting the basket of words. Consider, for example, the approach to Hart's "no vehicles in the park" offered by Justice Antonin Scalia and Bryan Garner in their influential treatise on interpretation.[34] They begin by consulting dictionaries and considering and quickly dismissing yet another definition of vehicle – "a substance, esp. a liquid, serving as a means for the readier application or use of another substance mixed with or dissolved in it."[35] They no doubt correctly conclude that this is outside the scope of what the rule is designed to prohibit, though their reasoning is incomplete at best. "The context of the sign here at issue, which includes its *purpose* of excluding certain things from the park – presumably things that would otherwise commonly be introduced – makes clear that this is not the sense that the sign bears."[36] (But the possibility of common introduction cannot, in itself, be doing the work Scalia and Garner suggest. One can easily imagine things like suntan lotion, barbecue sauce, and ranch dressing, each of which involves a vehicle in just this sense, being commonly introduced at a park.) Other dictionary definitions, which incorporate the notion of vehicles as means of conveyance or transport, are closer to the mark but imperfect. It's "common usage" they're after, and no dictionary definition quite hits the mark. "The proper colloquial meaning in our view (not all of them are to be found in dictionaries) is simply

33 Eskridge, 'Interpreting Law', 11 (describing judges as "partners in governance and fiduciaries of We the People").

34 Scalia and Garner, 'Reading Law', 36–39.

35 The Oxford Universal Dictionary 2339 (1955).

36 Scalia and Garner, 'Reading Law', 37.

a *sizable* wheeled conveyance (as opposed to one of any size that is motorized)."[37] But they do not show us this so much as tell us that it is the best expression of "the one purpose unquestionably demonstrated from reading the text in context."[38]

A second view, that of the purposivists, regards statutes differently. What the legislature passed is not merely a collection of words. Instead, "legislation is a purposive act, and judges should construe statutes to execute that legislative purpose."[39] From this perspective, the judge's job is not merely to make sense of the basket of words, because truly giving them meaning involves understanding them as human communication (which depends on all manner of nontextual cues to convey its full meaning) produced by a collective human process that can often move forward only by leaving some things unsaid. Doing so requires drawing on the available evidence to determine what it was that the legislature was trying to accomplish.[40] The court as the faithful legislative agent on this view is oriented toward discerning the principal's true purpose. A good agent appreciates that it is sometimes necessary to fill in the blanks and read between the lines to accomplish the desired end. That entails resorting to a broader landscape of information, including legislative history – the record of a law's creation, such as things like legislative debates and committee reports. The purposivist understands that this can be an elusive quest and that there may often be no singular purpose behind a collective enactment. But the fact that such an inquiry is not always possible does not mean that it is never possible. As Judge Robert Katzmann put the point, "to jettison the inquiry altogether, because of the difficulty in particular cases, means that judges will interpret statutes unmoored from the reality of the legislative process and what the legislators were seeking to do."[41]

A different level of the debate returns us to the analogy to the rules of evidence. The textualist's next objection to judicial resort to information outside the text is that their colleagues cannot be trusted with it. Even if a faithful agent would go beyond the text, textualists doubt that judges can go beyond the text and remain faithful. Scalia and Garner assert that judges like "liberation from text" because "[i]t increases their ability to do what they think is good."[42] As Justice Amy Coney Barrett put the point, they believe that "the dangers of judicial willfulness exceed the dangers of judicial woodenness."[43] Part of their argument is that because any

[37] Id., 37.

[38] Id., 38.

[39] Robert A. Katzmann, *Judging Statutes* (Oxford: Oxford University Press, 2014) 31.

[40] As Frederick Schauer puts the point, "[A]lthough reason, intention, and purpose are three different things, they all coalesce around the view that it is the job of a judge to try to make sense out of a statute rather than just slavishly follow its words down a ridiculous path." Schauer, 'Thinking Like a Lawyer', 165–66.

[41] Katzmann, 'Judging Statutes', 35.

[42] Scalia and Garner, 'Reading Law', 10.

[43] Amy Coney Barrett, *Notre Dame Law Review* 2022 Symposium Keynote Address, February 14, 2022, available at www.youtube.com/watch?v=noLA-z-SW5w. Scalia and Garner make the point in an even

statute will have multiple purposes, a judge can emphasize one or another as they see fit to achieve a desired result.[44] And part arises out of the increased range of evidence available to the judge whose mandate is to discern a statute's purpose rather than working only with its text, and in particular legislative history. Legislators will say many conflicting things in debates and in committee reports, and little or none of it will be said with the precision of statutory language.[45] As the notion is often described, the concern is that using legislative history is like "looking out over a crowd and picking out your friends."[46] Whether legislative history influences the decision-making process or instead simply provides a greater array of window dressing for decisions departing from text, the argument runs, its availability as an authoritative source makes it too easy for judges to impose their own preferences.

There is a strong sense in which the textualist position has prevailed. The literature repeatedly cites Justice Elana Kagan's apparent concession that "we're all textualists."[47] Nearly two decades ago, Professor Jonathan Molot argued that textualism had been so successful that its proponents had outrun their project, that by continuing to wage methodological war, they were forced to both misrepresent the views of their perceived opponents and adopt increasingly radical positions for themselves.[48] And indeed, there is widespread agreement that text is the necessary starting point for and key ingredient of statutory analysis.

What there is not, however, is consensus as to precisely what that means. Professor Tara Leigh Grove identifies a distinction between "formalistic" and "flexible" textualism.[49] The former "instructs interpreters to carefully parse the statutory language, focusing on semantic content and downplaying policy concerns or the practical (even monumental) consequences of the case." The latter "attends to text but permits interpreters to make sense of that text by considering policy and social context as well as practical consequences." "[J]udges apply not simply textualism but *textualisms*."[50]

more overstated way, apparently seeing the only available options as an imperfect constraint and total anarchy: "[T]here is a world of difference between an objective test (the text) – which sometimes provides no clear answer, thus leaving the door open to judicial self-gratification – and tests that invite judges to say that the law is what they think it ought to be." Scalia & Garner, 'Reading Law', 22.

44 Scalia and Garner, 'Reading Law', 18–19.

45 Frank H. Easterbook, 'Foreword', in Scalia and Garner, 'Reading Law', at xxii.

46 Adam Samaha, 'Looking Over a Crowd – Do More Interpretive Sources Mean More Discretion?,' (2017) 92 *New York University Law Review* 554. Samaha argues that the logic behind the claim that increasing the number of sources increases decision-maker discretion is questionable at best.

47 Harvard Law School, The 2015 Scalia Lecture Series: A Dialogue with Justice Elena Kagan on the Reading of Statutes, YouTube, at 08:29 (November 25, 2015), www.youtu.be/dpEtszFToTg [perma.cc/L65V-9AET]. For a general overview, Justice Kagan's statement, her subsequent recantation, and the ways in which others have used it, see Kevin Tobia, 'We're Not All Textualists Now,' (2023) 78 *NYU Annual Survey of American Law* 243.

48 Jonathan T. Molot, 'The Rise and Fall of Textualism,' (2006) 106 *Columbia Law Review* 1.

49 Tara Leigh Grove, 'Which Textualism?,' (2020) 134 *Harvard Law Review* 265, 267.

50 Id., at 271. For a thoughtful historical analysis of the development of textualism, see Tara Leigh Grove, 'The Misunderstood History of Textualism,' (2023) 117 *Northwestern University Law Review* 1033.

A small sampling of examples follows. Writing in 1994, Judge Frank Easterbrook offered this description of

> what is coming to be called "textualism": sticking to lower levels of generality, preferring the language and structure of the law whenever possible over its legislative history and imputed values. Searching for meaning, to be found in structure and appeals to the objective legal culture, rather than in "intent"—for references to intent are just another way to shift the level of generality and scoot off in a new direction.[51]

Scalia and Garner advance what they call the "fair reading method." They describe it as follows:

> [D]etermining the application of a governing text to given facts on the basis of how a reasonable reader, fully competent in the language, would have understood the text at the time it was issued. The endeavor requires aptitude in language, sound judgment, the suppression of personal preferences regarding the outcome, and, with older texts, historical linguistic research. It also requires an ability to comprehend the *purpose* of the text, which is a vital part of its context. But the purpose is to be gathered only from the text itself, consistently with the other aspects of its context. This critical word *context* embraces not just textual purpose but also (1) a word's historical associations acquired from recurrent patterns of past usage, and (2) a word's immediate syntactic setting—that is, the words that surround it in a specific utterance.[52]

Professor Adrian Vermeule, emphasizing judges' bounded rationality and the complexity and uncertainty of the empirical intuitions (such as those relating to legislators' incentives) on which the various interpretive methods are premised, offers a different prescription:

> When the statutory text at hand is clear and specific, judges should stick close to its surface or apparent meaning, eschewing the use of other tools to enrich their sense of meaning, intentions, or purposes. When the statutory text at hand is ambiguous or vague, judges should defer to the interpretations of administrative agencies or executive agents rather than attempting to fill in gaps or ambiguities by reference to other sources. In either type of case the tools that should be excluded from the judicial kit-bag include legislative history, many of the canons of construction, and holistic textual comparison, which supplements or overrides the provisions at hand by reference to other provisions of the same or other statutes.[53]

As a recipe for decision-making, textualism is not an agreed-upon thing. Or rather, those who fall in the textualist camp agree at the level of vibe but not in their particulars. As Grove puts it, "modern textualism has become a big tent."[54]

[51] Frank H. Easterbrook, 'Text, History, and Structure in Statutory Interpretation,' (1994) 17 *Harvard Journal of Law and Public Policy* 61, 64.

[52] Scalia and Garner, 'Reading Law', 33.

[53] Adrian Vermeule, *Judging under Uncertainty: An Institutional Theory of Legal Interpretation* (Cambridge: Harvard University Press, 2006) 183.

[54] Grove, 'Misunderstood History', 1084.

Moreover, as is perhaps often the case with these sorts of debates, especially when academic careers are involved, the differences between the approaches are exaggerated. The competing schools' approaches lead to differing results, but, Professor Caleb Nelson suggests, they "are less categorical than either textualists or their critics generally acknowledge, and they are correspondingly harder to describe."[55] "What *is* clear," in Nelson's view, "is that judges whom we think of as textualists have a greater affinity for 'rules' [as contrasted with 'standards'] than judges whom we think of as intentionalists."[56] Professor Richard Re concludes that, "while individual cases may be textualist or originalist, the overall practice of interpretation remains flexible and multifaceted."[57] The inconsistency exists even when one examines the practices of individual judges. As Grove notes, "no self-proclaimed textualist on the Supreme Court seems to have adopted a consistent approach; the Justices vacillate between a more formal and a more flexible textualism."[58]

Even so, Professor Aaron Bruhl, having surveyed the actual statements and practices of courts, found "quite a bit" of methodological consistency in the federal courts.[59] But that consistency covers only a portion of the endeavor. Courts agree on certain aspects of the resort to and use of canons of construction, for example. But the agreement is not comprehensive, and Bruhl found a "surprising lack of consistency when it comes to which tools are even employed."[60] Bruhl has also found considerable differences between interpretive practice in the Supreme Court and in the lower federal courts.[61] The courts at the different levels differ from one another in terms of which tools they resort to and how those tools are implemented, even within the same case: "There are many cases in which the Supreme Court's analytical tools did not appear at all in the opinions of the court of appeals or the district court."[62] The entire apparatus has become more textualism-inflected – which is not at all to say that it has become thoroughly textualist.

55 Caleb Nelson, 'What is Textualism?,' (2005) 91 *Virginia Law Review* 347, 249.

56 Nelson, 'Textualism', 416. "Within certain constraints, all mainstream interpreters seek the meaning intended by the enacting legislature. As a methodological matter, however, textualists may believe that a relatively rule-based approach to statutory interpretation is likely to bring judges closer to that goal than the more holistic techniques favored by intentionalists. As a normative matter, moreover, textualists are more likely than intentionalists to resolve uncertainties in favor of 'ruleness'; when the meaning intended by the enacting legislature is concededly unclear, it is unusual for intentionalists to settle upon a more rule-like interpretation than textualists." Nelson, 'Textualism', 417.

57 Richard M. Re, 'Permissive Interpretation,' (2023) 171 *University of Pennsylvania Law Review* 1651, 1652.

58 Grove, 'Misunderstood History', 1085.

59 Aaron-Andrew P. Bruhl, 'Eager to Follow: Methodological Precedent in Statutory Interpretation,' (2020) 99 *North Carolina Law Review* 101, 159.

60 Bruhl, 'Eager to Follow', 163.

61 Aaron-Andrew P. Bruhl, 'Statutory Interpretation and the Rest of the Iceberg: Divergences Between Lower Federal Courts and the Supreme Court,' (2018) 68 *Duke Law Journal* 1.

62 Bruhl, 'Rest of the Iceberg', 7.

The reality that Bruhl describes is one in which change from past practice is real and observable, but of the more diffuse sort that results from shifts in norms rather than from the more categorical change that the more strident advocates of textualism demand. It results from what he characterizes as "environmental conditions."[63] Courts are more aware of the significance of methodology, there has been "a longer-term shift toward expansive notions of precedent,"[64] and a renewed emphasis on method in law schools has produced a generation of law clerks and, increasingly, judges who are primed to think about interpretation in this way.

And yet Bruhl remains skeptical about the possibility that methodological precedent can attain comprehensiveness and generate the predictability that its proponents claim. One reason is simply that some of the underlying disagreement is too strong to allow for settlement of the issue. Another is simply that the problems of interpretation cannot be mapped out in complete detail. Thus, while it is possible, at least in theory, to resolve questions such as the order of priority among competing canons and whether a given canon is valid at all, there are other matters such as "questions of a source's *weight* (how powerfully does the source contribute to meaning) and *noncategorical matters of scope* (for example, how ambiguous does text have to be before canon X applies?), neither of which is susceptible of precise specification,"[65] that cannot be specified in advance.

The conclusion to which all of this leads is this: the need for judgment is ineradicable. As emphasized earlier, Scalia and Garner expressly include "sound judgment" in their preferred recipe for textualism. Their decree as to the common meaning of "vehicle" is no more based on something tangible than would be a conclusion – whether consistent or inconsistent with theirs – based on the legislative history of the statute. Just as they pick and choose from among dictionary definitions and ultimately conclude that none of them is quite right, so, too, must a purposivist make judgments about which evidence provides the best fit. As Scalia and Garner acknowledge, words have no inherent meaning: "Nothing but conventions and contexts cause a symbol or sound to convey a particular idea."[66] Judges necessarily draw upon their sense of a collective understanding to make sense of language, and they necessarily exercise judgment and discernment in doing so. Re makes the point that actual practice demonstrates that interpretive freedom is inescapable. Text, purpose, and consequences will often pull in different directions. "Judges sometimes claim to be governed by mandatory interpretive principles and even criticize one another on that basis. But both formal law and actual practice allow jurists to choose among a wide range of interpretive theories."[67]

63 Bruhl, 'Eager to Follow', 159.
64 Id., 160.
65 Id., 161.
66 Scalia and Garner, 'Reading Law', xxvii.
67 Re, 'Permissive Interpretation', 1654.

Yet the fact that there is no single, unified "textualism" has not prevented the methodology's more vocal proponents from using aggressive rhetoric. Advocates of textualism often insist not only that textualism is an appropriate way to interpret statutes but also that it is *the only* appropriate way. As we have seen, the literature on statutory interpretation is vast, and textualism comes in many varieties.[68] Yet Professor Glen Staszewski identifies a consistent theme among these proposals – a trend toward simplification – which he characterizes as "the dumbing down of statutory interpretation."[69] Staszewski draws on political theory to reject the push toward these simplified approaches and to contend "that the resolution of disputes regarding the permissible scope of governmental authority in difficult statutory cases requires the use of practical reasoning, and that the quality of statutory law and its democratic legitimacy benefit from an ongoing, multi-institutional, systemic dialogue on those questions."[70]

But as the textualist position is often presented, all other approaches are by implication illegitimate.[71] As Professors Anya Bernstein and Glen Staszewski argue, the rhetoric has a populist dimension: it "presents *legal text* as the authoritative embodiment of the people's will, and purports to provide the only legitimate interpretive methods to do *the people's* bidding."[72] Stated someone colloquially, the appeal of the approach is clear: it's the legislature's job to pass laws, and it's the court's job to apply those laws according to their common and ordinary meaning. The role of the faithful agent is simple, obvious, and intuitive. Anyone advocating something to the contrary must be up to no good. The version of textualism that features in campaign ads, confirmation hearings, and promises to nominate "strict constructionists" is one in which the method appears as a form of mechanical jurisprudence.[73] The complexity and nuance, and the need for judgment, are left for the fine print.

The textualists' more provocative statements of their position, such as Scalia and Garner's claim that nontextualism "frees the judge from interpretive scruple,"[74] are surely overstated. Again, Scalia and Garner's own depiction of their preferred

[68] For an overview, see Glen Staszewski, 'The Dumbing Down of Statutory Interpretation,' (2015) 95 *Boston University Law Review* 209.

[69] "The trend is for commentators to advocate relatively simple and uniform formulas for ascertaining the meaning of the law in any particular case, which typically include some combination of (1) simple, clear, and consistent rules for identifying and enforcing unambiguous statutory mandates; (2) simple, clear, and consistent rules for resolving statutory ambiguity; and (3) simple, clear, and consistent hierarchical frameworks for proceeding through the various stages of the analysis in statutory cases." Staszewski, 'Dumbing Down', 242.

[70] Id., 243.

[71] Charlie D. Stewart, 'The Rhetorical Canons of Construction: New Textualism's Rhetoric Problem,' (2018) 116 *Michigan Law Review* 1485.

[72] Anya Bernstein and Glen Staszewski, 'Judicial Populism,' (2021) 106 *Minnesota Law Review* 283, 309.

[73] Ryan D. Doerfler, 'Late-Stage Textualism,' (2021) *Supreme Court Review* 267, 269 ("modern textualists did continue to promise, at least implicitly, something like a mechanical jurisprudence despite its having explicitly been disavowed.").

[74] Scalia and Garner, 'Reading Law', 18.

methodology, quoted earlier, includes "sound judgment" and "the suppression of personal preferences regarding the outcome" as necessary ingredients, and if that is so, then it may be these ingredients, rather than a text-centered recipe, that provide textualism's restraint – and those ingredients form the core of nontextualist methods as well. But even if the more pluralistic approach of purposivism leaves incrementally more room for the operation of improper factors, the purposivist in response is likely to invoke Justice Joseph Story's warning: "It is always a doubtful course, to argue against the use or existence of a power, from the possibility of its abuse."[75] That nontextualism entails freedom for judges to do whatever they want is more of a charge that some textualists lob, sometimes perhaps even unscrupulously, rather than a power that mainstream nontextualists claim for themselves.[76] As we have seen, the fact that the disciplining forces are less apparently tangible than words on the page, or include a larger collection of words than just those included in a statute, does not mean that those forces do not exist or that they cannot provide adequate constraint.

ORIGINALISM AND CONSTITUTIONAL INTERPRETATION

There's a parallel story to be told about methodological claims concerning constitutional interpretation. Textualism is an option here, too. But contemporary discussions of interpretive methodology are dominated by originalism, which is a distinct thing holding that the Constitution must be interpreted in accordance with its original meaning.[77] And here, as we have seen with statutory interpretation, there are both ontological and pragmatic justifications for the methodology.

The ontological case for originalism has an undoubted, albeit superficial, rhetorical appeal. As I often explain it to my students, the popular logic of originalism goes like this: (1) The Constitution is law, just like any other law. (2) One characteristic of law is that it has meaning at the moment of its enactment. (3) That meaning doesn't change until the law is changed via the appropriate mechanisms, which in the case of the Constitution is by amendment. (4) Therefore, the only appropriate judicial approach to interpreting the Constitution is to figure out what it meant at the time of its enactment. As Professor Lawrence Solum puts it, "The meaning of the constitutional text is fixed when each provision is framed and ratified: this claim can be called the *Fixation Thesis*. This thesis is one of two core ideas of

[75] *Martin* v. *Hunter's Lessee*, 14 US (1 Wheat.) 304 (1816).

[76] For example, Professor Jonathan Molot characterizes the prevailing view as being "that courts should be faithful to legislative instructions and follow laws enacted through bicameralism and presentment, rather than make new laws themselves." Jonathan T. Molot, 'Ambivalence About Formalism,' (2007) 93 *Virginia Law Review* 1, 11–12.

[77] Katie Eyer, 'Distentangling Textualism and Originalism,' (2021) 13 *ConLawNOW* 1115. As Stephen Sachs points out, originalism could exist even in the absence of a text to apply it to. Stephen E. Sachs, 'Originalism Without Text,' (2017) 127 *Yale Law Journal* 156.

originalist constitutional theory: the other is the *Constraint Principle*, which holds that the original meaning of the constitutional text should constrain constitutional practice."[78]

Originalism may be, or may be on the verge of becoming, "our law,"[79] but the ontological case for originalism is not airtight. Surely it is correct to regard the Constitution as law. But it does not follow that it has the same characteristics as, say, statutory law. The idea can be expressed in a couple ways. One is to think about it in terms of what Professor H. L. A. Hart called a "rule of recognition" – roughly speaking, a master rule by which it is possible to assess the authority and legality of subordinate legal rules.[80] For statutory law, this is relatively straightforward. When presented with text that someone claims is a portion of the United States Code, there is a reliable way to determine whether that is so, which is to ask whether that text was validly enacted according to the procedures set forth in the Constitution. We can assess changes to statutory meaning in this way as well. Unless a statute is amended via the process of bicameralism and presentment, it remains unchanged – at least unless the proper understanding of the judicial power as allocated in the Constitution includes the authority to alter statutory meaning to some greater or lesser degree. Indeed, as we have seen, a portion of the debate over statutory interpretation concerns whether the Constitution envisions courts as "faithful agents" of Congress or rather as "partners" with some authority to update or otherwise revise statutory meaning. Put differently, we know that in order to answer questions about statutory validity, we can and must ultimately look to the Constitution.

But no such rule or set of rules exists by which to assess the validity of the Constitution itself. Consider, for example, the fact that the Constitution was, in some sense, an illegal document.[81] The delegates to the Constitutional Convention were authorized only to consider amendments to the Articles of Confederation, which by their terms could be validly amended only with the approval of all of the states. The Framers thus acted outside their mandate in proposing the Constitution. And by providing that the document would become effective upon the ratification of nine states rather than by all thirteen, as the Articles required, the Constitution simply asserted its own validity, which alone cannot be enough. (As Professor Frederick Schauer has pointed out, any group of people could draft a document entitled "Constitution of the United States of America," which provides that it supersedes the existing Constitution and that it becomes valid upon the approval of

78 Lawrence B. Solum, 'The Fixation Thesis: The Role of Historical Fact in Original Meaning,' (2015) 91 *Notre Dame Law Review* 1.

79 William Baude, 'Is Originalism Our Law?,' (2015) 115 *Columbia Law Review* 2349.

80 There is, of course, considerably more complexity here than this brief discussion reflects. See, for example, Kent Greenawalt, 'The Rule of Recognition and the Constitution,' (1987) 85 *Michigan Law Review* 621.

81 Richard S. Kay, 'The Illegality of the Constitution,' (1987) 4 *Constitutional Commentary* 57.

some designated set of people.[82] That document would be valid according to its own terms. It would also rightfully be ignored.) Even so, the people quickly accepted the Constitution as having taken the place of the Articles of Confederation. Its validity stemmed not from any sort of technical compliance with the Articles or any other rule, but simply by virtue of having been generally accepted as the law of the land. Professor Stephen Griffin comes at the point from a different direction by observing that, in contrast to ordinary laws, there is no external agency available to remedy constitutional violations. As a result, "constitutions must ultimately be enforced by the operation of the entire political system, or, one might say, by the people as a whole."[83] If the people as a whole accept a certain meaning of a constitutional provision – as by, for example, electing a President who was born in the Panama Canal Zone, or in Canada to parents who were not both US citizens – then that will become its meaning regardless of whether the "natural born citizen" clause was originally understood in that way.

There is also a sense in which originalism might be self-refuting. It's far from clear that the framers and ratifiers of the Constitution intended or imagined that it would be interpreted in an originalist way. Dean Erwin Chemerinsky argues that "the Framers likely did not want their views to control constitutional interpretation."[84] They sought not to create a document to be regarded in the same manner as a statute, but rather, as Justice Stone put it in *United States* v. *Classic*, "an enduring framework of government" designed "to carry out for the indefinite future and in all the vicissitudes of the changing affairs of men, those fundamental purposes which the instrument itself discloses."[85] Noah Webster – more famous for his dictionary but also on the scene for the early debates over the Constitution – put the point more strongly: "We have no right to say that our posterity shall not be judges of their own circumstances. The very attempt to make perpetual constitutions, is the assumption of the right to control the opinions of future generations; and to legislate for those over whom we have as little authority as we have over a nation in Asia."[86]

The problem has a more general dimension as well. The notion of a written constitution was an unfamiliar one to the Framers, such that they wrote on an intellectual slate that was in important respects blank. As inheritors of the British legal tradition, the constitution with which the Framers were familiar was not a written document. As Professor Jonathan Gienapp has demonstrated, they were not entirely sure what it was they had created: "When it first appeared, the new Constitution was

[82] Frederick Schauer, 'Amending the Presuppositions of a Constitution,' in Sanford Levinson, ed., *Responding to Imperfection: The Theory and Practice of Constitutional Amendment* (Princeton: Princeton University Press, 1995) 145, 150.

[83] Stephen M. Griffin, 'Rebooting Originalism,' (2008) *University of Illinois Law Review* 1185.

[84] Erwin Chemerinsky, *Worse Than Nothing: The Dangerous Fallacy of Originalism* (New Haven: Yale University Press, 2022) 75.

[85] 313 US 299, 316 (1941).

[86] Noah Webster, 'On Bills of Rights,' 1 *American Magazine*, December 1787, at 13–14.

a completely unprecedented kind of object; as a result, describing and interpreting it was an entirely novel exercise."[87] Was it to be regarded as comprehensive and complete, or subject to further additions and refinements? Was it analogous to familiar legal instruments, or was it some entirely new type of creature? The Framers' mindset, as Gienapp depicts it, was very different from our own: "In 1787, the Constitution was more often imagined as a system that needed to be brought to equilibrium than as words on parchment that meted out judgments. The written constitution was not a discrete, self-sufficient thing; embedded within a wider, dynamic, indivisible field of action, it was a script awaiting enactment."[88] Ascertaining precisely what the Constitution is turns out to be more difficult than first meets the eye.

As is the case with statutory interpretation, there is a pragmatic justification for originalism as well: it provides judges with a fixed target. Judges will often miss that target – they will err in divining a provision's original meaning – but they will have a goal toward which to orient themselves, and they will understand that their mission is to look to something outside themselves and their own preferences in answering constitutional questions. As Justice Scalia put it, "the main danger in judicial interpretation of the Constitution … is that the judges will mistake their own predilections for the law."[89] Originalism "establishes a historical criterion that is conceptually quite separate from the preferences of the judge himself."

Here, too, competing theorists offer differing formulas for how to carry out the originalist project.[90] There are views that have been largely discredited. One such is what we might call Originalism Version 1.0, often associated with Reagan administration Attorney General Edwin Meese, which called for an inquiry into the Framers' "original intent."[91] The crucial objection to this approach mirrors one covered earlier in the discussion of statutory interpretive method: it is impossible to ascribe a single intent to a collective body. For any of the Constitution's many general or imprecise words and phrases, it was possible and indeed likely that the document's drafters held differing conceptions of what was at stake and how the provision in question addressed it. Another is that the search should be for "original expected applications," a position that holds that a provision should be applied in the precise manner that those who drafted and ratified it would have applied it.[92]

87 Jonathan Gienapp, *The Second Creation: Fixing the American Constitution in the Founding Era* (Cambridge: Harvard University Press, 2018) 5.

88 Gienapp, 'Second Creation', 7.

89 Antonin Scalia, 'Originalism: The Lesser Evil,' (1989) 57 *University of Cincinnati Law Review* 849.

90 For an overview of the history of the development of originalism, see Lawrence B. Solum, 'What Is Originalism?,' in Grant Huscroft and Bradley W. Miller, eds., *The Challenge of Originalism: Essays in Constitutional Theory* (Cambridge: Cambridge University Press, 2011) 12.

91 For an overview, see Jonathan K. Van Patten, 'The Partisan Battle Over the Constitution: Meese's Jurisprudence of Original Intention and Brennan's Theory of Contemporary Ratification,' (1987) 70 *Marquette Law Review* 389.

92 For example, Professor Michael McConnell contended that "no reputable originalist … takes the view that the Framers' 'assumptions and expectations about the correct application' of their principles is

Under this approach, the task is not merely to identify the outlines of the concept of, say, a "natural born citizen," but also to determine how the Framers would have applied it were they confronted with a specific factual situation.

The currently prevailing view among originalists is that the core idea is to search for the original public meaning of the applicable word or phrase.[93] That meaning "is either (1) what a reasonable person who knew the publicly available facts about the context of its drafting would have taken it to mean or (2) what literate and informed members of the public actually understood it to be, at the time of its promulgation."[94] A recent innovation is the rise of "corpus linguistics" – "the use of large, searchable databases, or corpora, of computer-annotated texts to ascertain evolving patterns of word use over time."[95] The rise of, and debates over, corpus linguistics recapitulate many of the claims and critiques concerning originalism and textualism in general.[96] The primary argument in favor of its use is that it reduces the subjectivity involved in ascertaining a text's original meaning. Not even its strongest advocates claim that it makes the process mechanical; judgment is required. Critics claim that it provides only the illusion of objectivity and point out that the judges who rely on corpus linguistics tend to do so opportunistically, departing from best practices when they generate undesired results.

Once discerned, a word or phrase's meaning may then need to be "constructed" – given legal effect through implementing rules.[97] Take for example the Fourth Amendment's prohibition of "unreasonable searches and seizures." Determining what the original public meaning of that phrase was does not answer the question of whether or when the use of drones or infrared cameras is unconstitutional. But precisely how constitutional construction takes place is a matter of disagreement, and will be driven not by the text or by originalism itself, but by judges' or theorists' other normative commitments. For example, "[o]riginalists who ground their commitment to originalism in notions of popular sovereignty can be expected to favor principles of construction that reflect this normative commitment. Likewise, those who favor originalism as a means to protect the background rights retained by the people will likely favor rules of construction that are rights protective."[98] The bottom line

controlling." Michael W. McConnell, 'The Importance of Humility in Judicial Review: A Comment on Ronald Dworkin's "Moral Reading" of the Constitution,' (1997) 65 *Fordham Law Review* 1269, 1284.

93 Professor Richard Kay provides a thoughtful history of the evolution of originalism, including the observation that searches for original intent and original public meaning will typically converge on the same result. Richard S. Kay, 'Original Intention and Public Meaning in Constitutional Interpretation,' (2009) 103 *Northwestern University Law Review* 703.

94 Richard H. Fallon, Jr., 'The Chimerical Concept of Original Public Meaning,' (2021) 107 *Virginia Law Review* 1421, 1425–26.

95 John S. Ehrett, 'Against Corpus Linguistics,' (2019) 108 *Georgetown Law Journal Online* 50, 51.

96 For a good overview of the debate, including a survey of the relevant literature, see Kevin Tobia, 'The Corpus and the Courts,' (2021) *University of Chicago Law Review Online*.

97 Lawrence B. Solum, 'Originalism and Constitutional Construction,' (2013) 82 *Fordham Law Review* 453.

98 Randy E. Barnett, 'Interpretation and Construction,' (2011) 34 *Harvard Journal of Law and Public Policy* 65.

for originalism ends up being similar to that for textualism: there is agreement at a certain level of generality about what it entails, but viewed in terms of specifics, it becomes less of a unified approach and more of a family of theories. In Professor Andrei Marmor's phrasing, "'[O]riginalism' is not the title of one particular theory of constitutional interpretation but rather the name of a family of diverse ideas, some of which are actually at odds with each other."[99]

Even assuming a set understanding of how the method works, figuring out what the Constitution meant to the people who wrote and ratified it is difficult. Sometimes the evidence is either nonexistent or inconclusive. The Framers could not possibly have thought of everything. Even as to those things they did think of, there may not be a clear original meaning, as noted earlier. Just as the various members of a legislative body might have different motivations for prohibiting vehicles in a park, and different views of what the concept of "vehicle" entails, so, too, did the framers and ratifiers of the Constitution likely have different conceptions of the contours of and justifications for provisions such as the "natural born citizen" requirement. In Chemerinsky's estimation, "[t]he reality is that for most provisions, this single understanding did not exist. Almost always, there were different views as to what the words of the Constitution meant."[100] The target is less fixed than first meets the eye.

Today's problems are often not ones that the Framers could have anticipated, and even issues that were familiar to them can be regarded as meaningfully different now simply because ours is a larger, more urban, and more connected world. We communicate instantaneously around the globe, and we speak in terms of hours about journeys that for them took days, weeks, or even months. They could hardly have dreamed of the scale of our cities and the nature of our technology. Professor Mike Klarman presses the point, noting that "the Framers are not us. Indeed, in most ways the Framers do not even remotely resemble us, and it is not clear that they have a great deal of relevance to say about how we should govern ourselves today."[101] If we decide that we must account for changed circumstances in implementing the ideas in the Constitution, then we have to decide which changes matter, and what the Framers would have done in light of them, and once we reach a certain level of making adjustments, we risk simply turning the Framers into ourselves: "If we treat all of these changed circumstances as relevant variables, and ask how the Framers would have solved today's problems in light of today's circumstances, surely the answer is that they would have behaved pretty much as we do, which is to say that they would have disagreed among themselves about how to weigh the competing virtues and virtues and vices …."

Originalism's intuitive appeal is undeniable. It, like textualism, offers a seemingly straightforward and effective recipe for fulfilling the judicial role. Under their pragmatic justifications, both methods represent efforts to prevent judges from misusing

99 Andrei Marmor, *Interpretation and Legal Theory* (Oxford: Oxford University Press, 2nd ed., 2005) 155.
100 Chemerinsky, 'Worse Than Nothing', 56.
101 Michael J. Klarman, 'Antifidelity,' (1997) 70 *Southern California Law Review* 381.

information, or from failing to give appropriate weight to certain types of information, in ways that open judges to improper influences. At first blush, originalism thus seems obviously desirable, and, when coupled with the syllogistic account of the methodology's justification outlined earlier, no doubt accounts in large part for its influence. And one can further appreciate that it holds a particular appeal for law students first encountering constitutional law. One of the subject's difficulties, especially when contrasted with the other standard fare of first-year classes such as torts, contracts, and property, is that there are few shared premises. Majority and dissenting opinions in those classes will usually be arguing over the same thing. In constitutional law, by contrast, the justices' opinions often proceed from different assumptions about what the Constitution is, what the courts' role in interpreting it is, and so on. The opinions often talk past one another, and the result can seem like a trip through a house of mirrors in which majority, concurring, and dissenting opinions all make compelling cases for their respective positions. To one unfamiliar with the landscape of constitutional argumentation, and thus with the many levels and locations at which disagreement might take place, the attitudinalist depiction of a purely political process unbounded by rules can easily appear to be descriptively accurate. Originalism and its superficially clean logic offer a seemingly sensible and firm foothold, and the promise of what first-years crave but often cannot find in constitutional law: rules with relatively hard edges, and a set of tools with which to find them.

As we have seen, of course, things are not so simple as they first appear. Even a cursory review of the work produced by serious originalist scholars reveals recognition of the nuance and difficulty inherent in both the theory and practice of originalism when it is done well. To read this work is to come to understand that the application of judgment is unavoidable. The problem is that there is a disconnect between the work done by those who take originalism seriously in an intellectual way and those who are parasitic on the veneer of legitimacy that those scholars provide.

I have contended that ours is a world that distrusts judgment and that privileges the tangible and seemingly quantifiable. Ours is a society conducive to the flourishing of methodologies that purport, especially in their popular versions, to provide a step-by-step recipe for judicial decision-making. Both textualism and originalism play to the idea that judges are simply to apply, and not to make, law. And both, as popularized, seem to offer a formula that is both simple and algorithmic. "Just do this," proponents claim, "and you will eliminate subjectivity from the process." The approaches make for easy marketing, and the fact that they tend to facilitate the justification of conservative results means that one side in our polarized world has especially had an interest in marketing them. As Professor Mitch Berman contends, originalism "is not merely false but pernicious as well. It is pernicious because of its tendency to be deployed in the public square – on the campaign trail, on talk radio, in Senate confirmation hearings, even in Supreme Court opinions – to bolster the popular fable that constitutional adjudication can be practiced in something close to an objective and mechanical fashion."[102]

It is also pernicious when portrayed as the single, correct way to engage in interpretation, with all others left, either expressly or by implication, as illegitimate. Professor Carolyn Shapiro identifies a meaningful distinction between calling a judicial decision wrong and calling it illegitimate.[103] The rhetoric is not simply misguided, but potentially harmful. As Professor Dan Kahan has observed, "Studies of motivated cognition and related dynamics show that pronouncements of *certitude* deepen group-based conflict."[104] At the same time, originalism, like any interpretive theory that aspires to broad application, is unlikely to gain broad enough acceptance to be truly characterized as the single, correct approach.[105] These debates have been going on for a long time, and the parties to them seem no closer to reaching shared conclusions than ever. What has changed is not so much the attaining of consensus – though it seems understood that contemporary judges give greater primacy to text and original meaning as contrasted with some of their predecessors – but the stridency of the debate.

At the same time, originalism does not provide the constraint that its proponents claim. Judge Posner insists that it cannot, and that "[t]he claim that judicial interpretation is a rigorous analytical process, comparable to syllogistic deduction [that] really does generate demonstrably correct answers to even the most difficult-seeming questions that arise in litigation, is fatuous."[106] Jurists who imagine otherwise – who regard originalism as a form of constitutional arithmetic – increase their susceptibility to bias. If the logic of one's methodology is rooted in a mistrust of judgment, and a belief that the true work of decision-making can be offloaded onto a formula, then one is tempted to imagine the enterprise as mechanical. If one is simply following a recipe, then there is no need to be on the lookout for the influence of biases, which in turn makes noticing them less likely.

And if the recipe does not provide the right results, a different one surely will. As several scholars have pointed out, originalist justices on the Supreme Court are opportunistic in their reliance on the methodology. Chemerinsky contends that "originalists often abandon the method when it fails to give them the results they want. Conservative justices use originalism when it justifies conservative decisions,

102 Mitch Berman, 'Originalism is Bunk,' (2009) 84 *New York University Law Review* 1, 8.

103 Carolyn Shapiro, Remarks at the Law Day Lunch held by the McLean County (Illinois) Bar Association (May 2, 2018) (transcript on file with author).

104 Dan M. Kahan, 'The Supreme Court 2010 Term – Foreword: Neutral Principles, Motivated Cognition, and Some Problems for Constitutional Law,' (2011) 125 *Harvard Law Review* 1, 60.

105 H. Jefferson Powell, *Constitutional Conscience: The Moral Dimension of Judicial Decision* 13 (Chicago: University of Chicago Press, 2008).

106 Richard A. Posner, *Divergent Paths: The Academy and the Judiciary* (Cambridge: Harvard University Press, 2016) 101. In Posner's view, the judge who is an honest formalist is deceived, "[b]ut for many judges formalism appears to be a fig leaf covering politically motivated conservative decisions, whether or not the judges have sufficient self-awareness to be conscious of their motivations. The most conservative judges deny that they exercise any discretion in deciding cases. The least political judges acknowledge that they do." Posner, 'Divergent Paths', 92.

but they become non-originalist when doing so serves their ideological agenda."[107] Fallon notes that "it takes only realism, not cynicism, to recognize that the modern Justices who are regularly identified as originalist are also conservative and that they seldom rely on originalist premises to support conclusions that they would find ideologically uncongenial."[108] If such a state of affairs exists at the Supreme Court, where the justices know their output will be subject to intense scrutiny, similar departures in the comparatively anonymous worlds of state and lower federal courts seem inevitable.

Even mildly sophisticated advocates understand that these methodologies can be hacked. Lawyers have long understood that presenting an appealing case on the equities is a useful predicate to making an effective legal argument, and legal writing instructors emphasize the importance of a well-crafted statement of facts. As a wise senior lawyer once told me, the key to presenting a strong case on appeal is using the statement of facts to demonstrate "that your client got screwed." A lawyer arguing a statutory interpretation case will find a way to emphasize, or at least make known, favorable legislative history even to a court that purports to be textualist. One in a constitutional case will point out the undesirable consequences of following originalism. As we saw in Chapter 3, judges often struggle with ignoring inadmissible information. We should imagine nothing different when it comes to material deemed out-of-bounds by methodology. The skilled advocate will draw attention to it in the hopes that it will trigger motivated reasoning. The evidence surveyed in this book suggests that they are not wrong to do so.

Interpretive methodologies are not, in themselves, the problem. As noted at the outset of this chapter, they work in much the same manner that law in general does, by circumscribing the universe of things that matter in making a decision, and in doing so by discouraging or even prohibiting reliance on unreliable information. That is a useful function because, as we have seen, the law itself leaves room for the influence of nonlegal factors. But methodologies cannot live up to the promises their most strident adherents make. No methodology can constrain a judge consciously seeking to reach a desired result. A judge acting in bad faith will always be able to manipulate doctrine, facts, or both to provide adequate cover. And unconscious influences present a danger even for judges acting in good faith. The potential for motivated reasoning is ever-present. The problem with foundationalist methodology is not that it offers guidance where none is needed or that its guidance is in some absolute sense wrong. It is rather that it provides, or purports to provide, too much guidance by making the perfect the enemy of the good,[109] by

[107] Chemerinsky, 'Worse Than Nothing', 139.

[108] Richard H. Fallon, Jr., 'Selective Originalism and Judicial Role Morality,' (2023) 102 *Texas Law Review* 221, 231.

[109] Professors Dan Farber and Suzanna Sherry develop broadly similar arguments in Daniel A. Farber and Suzanna Sherry, *Desperately Seeking Certainty: The Misguided Quest for Constitutional Foundations* (Chicago: University of Chicago Press, 2002); Daniel A. Farber and Suzanna Sherry, *Judgment Calls: Principle and Politics in Constitutional Law* (New York: Oxford University Press, 2009).

playing to the intuition that the absence of complete constraint entails the absence of all constraint.

As we have seen, however, constraint has historically had many sources. Interpretive methodology is among them, but it hardly stands alone. It comes from process, from the influence of the various external forces that operate on the judiciary, and from the professional norms and knowhow that judges have internalized over the course of their education and careers.[110] And it involves the exercise of judgment. It comes from the person.

[110] Professor Jack Balkin makes the point thusly: "Constraining judges in a democracy is important. But in practice most of that constraint does not come from theories of constitutional interpretation. It comes from institutional features of the political and legal system. Some of these are internal to law and legal culture, like the various sources and modalities of legal argument .... Others are external to legal reasoning but nevertheless strongly influence what judges produce as a group." Jack M. Balkin, 'Abortion and Original Meaning,' (2007) 24 *Constitutional Commentary* 291, 310.

8

Character, Wisdom, and Humility

The standard model of judging – featuring independent judges applying preexisting rules via a process that gives disputants a full opportunity to present the law and the facts in what they regard as their best light – is an appealing ideal. It was what Chief Justice Roberts had in mind when invoking the "justice-as-umpire" metaphor at his confirmation hearing, and it provides the assumptions underlying the Supreme Court's analysis in cases such as *Rucho* v. *Common Cause*. And in a great many cases, those in which the law is clear and the facts are straightforward, it works as a depiction of how courts function.

But in situations where things are not so clear, where the law runs out, has fuzzy contours, or seems in conflict with itself, or where the facts or their implications are disputed, the model cannot get us all the way to our destination. Language is inherently imprecise, lawmakers have limited foresight, and judges are humans and accordingly susceptible to the same limitations and forces that sway the thinking of humans more generally. Yet the judge must still decide. The legal system has developed mechanisms to mitigate these limitations and counteract these forces, but many have weakened. Even when those mechanisms are at their strongest, it has always been the case that the exercise of judgment is necessary and inevitable. And if judgment is inevitable, then surely we want our judges to have the capacity for and to exercise *good* judgment.

This, of course, raises questions. The first concerns how we are to know whether judgment is good. Roughly stated, I regard the correctness of a judicial decision as measured by reference to law, which consists not merely of positive law in the sense of statutes, regulations, and past judicial decisions but also of norms, know-how, and tacit knowledge, all as situated in the facts of a particular case as well as a larger institutional and sociopolitical context. On this view, some legal questions will have clearly correct answers, and others will have multiple answers that all fall within some zone of correctness. Occasionally the correct product of this all-in consideration will diverge from, and even contradict, what an analysis limited to the positive law would yield. In the context of a given case, this will entail exercise of courts' equitable powers, and when courts are engaged in the prospective task of law-creation, it can involve updating or changing the law, perhaps even dramatically. Good judgment is no guarantee of a correct result in any given situation, and it bears no necessary connection to the rightness of an answer in a specific case. It is a tendency. Stated somewhat differently, judges with good judgment will sometimes get the answers wrong, and those lacking good judgment will nonetheless often – indeed, one hopes, most of the time – get the answers right. The reason for emphasizing good judgment is thus at bottom practical: it serves the purpose of making it more likely that a judge will reach the (or "a") correct conclusion in any given situation.[1]

This of course assumes that there are people who have consistently good judgment, which raises the question of whether that is so and if it is whether we can reliably identify them. I believe the answer to both questions is yes, though imperfectly, and I'll begin anecdotally. It has been my experience, over the course of more than three decades in the law, that some lawyers have good professional judgment and others do not. Or, to state things more precisely, that "good judgment," like other characteristics, is not evenly distributed throughout the population. There are those who have near-impeccable judgment, whose advice I would not hesitate to seek concerning any problem I were to encounter, and there are those whose judgment I would not trust with respect to any significant matter. The presence of the characteristic seems to follow a statistically normal distribution – the vast majority of people have average or average-ish judgment, a smaller number have notably good or bad judgment, and there are outliers on either end. The characteristic is distinct from other salient traits such as intelligence or ideology and is certainly distinct from an eagerness to offer advice.

There is, no doubt, a definitional fuzziness here, and perhaps inevitably an "I know it when I see it" aspect to the notion of good judgment. Yet that is not all there is. My experience further suggests that my personal assessments of who has good judgment are not idiosyncratic. At least at a certain level of generality, it seems possible to identify a context- and observer-independent conception of the features of good judgment, and the idea that there is such a thing seems uncontroversial both within and outside of the legal profession. For example, Professors David Luban and Michael Millemann contend both that "good judgment is the most valuable thing a lawyer has to offer clients" and that it can be cultivated in students and lawyers.[2] Or consider a recent essay entitled "The Elements of Good Judgment," by Sir Andrew

[1] There is an affinity between my approach and one widely accepted among social scientists and philosophers, who "often evaluate judgments against two gold standards: correspondence and coherence. Measures of correspondence capture the degree to which judgments agree with empirical observations, and coherence criteria assess the degree to which judgments are consistent with logical or axiomatic principles." Barbara A. Mellers, Joshua D. Baker, Eva Chen, David R. Mandel, and Philip E. Tetlock, 'How Generalizable Is Good Judgment? A Multi-Task, Multi-Benchmark Study,' (2017) 12 *Judgment and Decision Making* 369–81.

[2] David Luban and Michael Milleman, 'Good Judgment: Ethics Teaching in Dark Times,' (1995) 9 *Georgetown Journal of Legal Ethics* 31–87.

Likierman, former dean of the London Business School, which appeared in the *Harvard Business Review*.[3] Likierman defines judgment as "the ability to combine personal qualities with relevant knowledge and experience to form opinions and make decisions," and *good* judgment as what "enables a sound choice in the absence of clear-cut, relevant data or an obvious path." His effort to identify the ingredients of good judgment involved surveying leaders across a range of endeavors and professions. He landed on a list of characteristics that included tendencies to draw upon a wide range of information, to be attentive to its quality, to recognize the gaps in one's knowledge, to be vigilant in monitoring one's thought for the influence of biases and motivated cognition, and to maintain an appropriate level of intellectual and emotional detachment.

I am hardly the first to suggest that having judges with the right characteristics is the appropriate response to the reality that the more tangible tools of legal argumentation and analysis often cannot provide guidance on the last leg of the journey from legal authorities to appropriate conclusions. Professor Mark Tushnet asked, "If personal judgment replaces constitutional theory as the primary force behind judicial review, how are we as citizens to be confident that the Justices' judgments are indeed sound?"[4] His answer was "character:" "the deeper sense of public and private lives being inseparably intertwined, such that the exercise of bad judgment in the Justice's public capacity becomes as unthinkable as exercising bad judgment in his or her personal life."[5] As Professor Paul Horwitz put the point, "Because [character] cannot be avoided, it must not be neglected."[6] Professor Suzanna Sherry contends that "[h]owever daunting the task may seem, in the end, describing (and finding) individuals well-suited to the task of judging is likely to prove more useful than seeking artificial mechanisms to constrain poor judgment …."[7]

To conclude that judicial character is important is one thing. To identify its specific contours is quite another. Good judging, in Sherry's estimation, is like good writing in that beyond a certain point rules tend to diminish it rather than enhance it. "[A]t best, we can provide exemplars, we can rely on experience to guide judges, and we can look for character traits—akin to an inborn ear for language in good

3 Sir Andrew Likierman, 'The Elements of Good Judgment,' *Harvard Business Review*, January–February 2020, available at https://hbr.org/2020/01/the-elements-of-good-judgment.

4 Mark Tushnet, 'Constitutional Interpretation, Character, and Experience,' (1992) 72 *Boston University Law Review* 747.

5 Tushnet, 'Constitutional Interpretation', 762.

6 Paul Horwitz, 'Judicial Character (And Does It Matter),' (2009) 26 *Constitutional Commentary* 97, 146.

7 Suzanna Sherry, 'Judges of Character,' (2003) 38 *Wake Forest Law Review* 793, 812. See also Brett Scharffs, 'The Role of Humility in Exercising Practical Wisdom,' (1998) 32 *UC Davis Law Review* 127; Zachary K. German and Robert J. Burton, 'Constitutional Humility: The Contested Meaning of a Judicial Virtue,' (2021) 10 *American Political Thought* 2, 238–70. Kronman's effort can be regarded as directored toward the profession as a whole. Anthony T. Kronman, *The Lost Lawyer: Failing Ideals of the Legal Profession* (Cambridge: Harvard University Press, 1993).

writers—that lend themselves to good judgment."[8] Good judgment, the suggestion runs, is the product of good character.

Can we further refine the matter? Is it possible to achieve consensus on what the attributes of good judicial character are or on the particulars of how a given trait should be defined? Kronman argued that the lawyer-statesman ideal once provided the template, but that it has vanished as a professional norm, and that there is no going back because we no longer inhabit a world hospitable to it. On that view, it is not realistic to imagine that the profession will reconverge around its vision of what the judicial role ought to look like. Disagreement is a permanent fixture of our social and political lives, especially the more into particulars one gets. The breadth and depth of that disagreement are significant and growing. No effort to secure robust consensus on the nature of legal argument or methodology is ultimately anything but a fool's errand, and one could reasonably be skeptical of the proposition that changing the question to the attributes of judicial character will change that answer.

The remainder of this chapter seeks to do three things. The first is to bolster the claim that judicial character matters and that, while it may not be possible to achieve general agreement on a robust conception of good judicial character, the task is not out of reach with respect to a more limited set of attributes. The second is to explore two such attributes – practical wisdom and intellectual humility. The third is to briefly explore ways in which we might foster the development and identification of such judges.

Within the legal academy, the primary contemporary advocate for emphasizing judicial character is Professor Lawrence Solum. Solum draws on virtue ethics to offer a "virtue-centered theory of judging." He contends that, while virtue is not the only component of good judging, it is a necessary component.[9] On this account, which like Kronman's lawyer-statesman ideal is rooted in the work of Aristotle, and primarily *Nicomachean Ethics*,[10] "[a] *judicial virtue* is a naturally possible disposition of mind or will that when present with the other judicial virtues reliably disposes its possessor to make just decisions."[11] Virtuous decisions are those made by virtuous judges who are "acting from the judicial virtues in the circumstances that are relevant to the decision."[12] In stronger versions of virtue theory, there is a necessary connection between the evaluation of a decision and the character of the judge(s) who made it, such that just decisions are and can only be decisions made by virtuous judges.[13] Weaker versions rest on a connection similar to what I have sketched out earlier, in

[8] Sherry, 'Judges of Character', 797–98.

[9] Lawrence B. Solum, 'Virtue Jurisprudence: A Virtue-Centered Theory of Judging,' (2003) 34 *Metaphilosophy* 178, 184.

[10] For a more developed account of the connection to Aristotle and to virtue ethics more generally, see Horwitz, 'Judicial Character', 146–51.

[11] Solum, 'Virtue Jurisprudence', 198.

[12] Id.

[13] Katharina Stevens, 'Humility as a Necessary Virtue in Common-Law Decision Making,' (2023) 14 *Jurisprudence* 443, 444.

which "the virtuous legal decision-maker has a privileged standpoint to access the relevant reasons, thereby providing the best criterion to determine which decisions are right—where their rightness is a function of virtue-independent reasons."[14]

Crucially, virtue-centered accounts of judging – consistent with Aristotle's injunction, as phrased in one translation, that "[n]othing connected with human action is hard and fast"[15] – reject "the assumption that there is a single 'decision procedure for judging' – some rule that would guarantee the correct outcome in every single case. Just as the world is more complex than any set of moral rules, so too, the complex facts of particular cases can outrun the capacities of any single uniform decision procedure for judging."[16] This is not to deny a role for rules or methodologies. The virtuous judge values fidelity to law, as law is typically (and narrowly) conceived, but also has the capacity to recognize when the situation calls for something other than the inflexible application of the rules.[17] As Aristotle observed, claims about what people should do, or ought to have done, can be stated in outline form only.[18] The details must be filled in as the situation demands.

It is of course one thing to accept the proposition that decision-makers with the right attributes will make better decisions and quite another to establish consensus as to what those characteristics are. We can begin with those identified by virtue epistemologists focused on thought more generally. For example, Professor Jason Baehr's list of intellectual virtues drills deeply into cognitive processes and includes "inquisitiveness, reflectiveness, contemplativeness, curiosity, and wonder" as well as "intellectual fairness, consistency, and objectivity" and "impartiality and open-mindedness."[19] He further contends that successful inquiry requires "a kind of cognitive integrity" – an ability to accurately assess the reliability of sources, to pursue a thorough analysis rather than reaching premature conclusions, and to resist attractive-but-implausible hypotheses. At times, it becomes necessary to transcend existing categories, thus making virtues of "imaginativeness, creativity, intellectual adaptability, flexibility, [and] agility."[20] Other times, what's required is sheer effort, "a willingness to persist or perseverance [that] might take the form of virtues like intellectual courage, determination, patience, diligence, or tenacity."[21]

Some theorists focused specifically on judicial virtue offer a similarly lengthy list of attributes. Professor Amalia Amaya, for example, categorizes the virtuous

[14] Amalia Amaya, 'Reasoning in Character: Virtue, Legal Argumentation, and Judicial Ethics,' (2023) *Ethical Theory and Moral Practice*, DOI: 10.1007/s10677-023-10414-z.

[15] Aristotle, *Nicomachean Ethics* (London: Penguin Classics, 2020) (Adam Beresford, ed.) 1104a1-5, at 30.

[16] Lawrence B. Solum, 'The Aretaic Turn in Constitutional Theory,' (2004) 70 *Brooklyn Law Review* 475, 498.

[17] Amaya, 'Reasoning in Character', 4.

[18] Nicomachean Ethics, Beresford ed., 30.

[19] Jason Baehr, *The Inquiring Mind: On Intellectual Virtues and Virtue Epistemology* (Oxford: Oxford University Press, 2011) 19–20.

[20] Baehr, 'Inquiring Mind', 21.

[21] Id.

judge as possessing sets of moral virtues ("temperance, courage, impartiality, magnanimity, and humility"), intellectual or epistemic virtues (including open-mindedness, perseverance, autonomy, sobriety, humility, patience, and vitality), argumentative virtues (a willingness to question premises, to pursue that questioning to its conclusion, and to modify one's beliefs as appropriate), communicative virtues (including not simply the ability to convey information clearly, but to do so candidly in a manner that is, among other things, accurate and tactful), judicial virtues (including an inclination to appeal to the virtue of justice, as well as loyalty in the sense of affording "proper weight to authoritative reasons"), and group-deliberative virtues (the skills necessary to effective participation in a collective decision-making effort).[22] Amaya concludes by identifying practical wisdom "as a particularly important virtue for successful judicial decision-making." It's a "meta-virtue," which "is necessary to arbitrate between the demands imposed by the specific virtues."[23]

Solum takes a different approach, one designed to formulate a menu of virtues more likely to generate consensus. He begins by offering a "thin theory of judicial virtues" formulated via a focus on traits generally regarded as undesirable in judges.[24] Because we clearly do not want judges who are stupid or foolish, it must be that intelligence and practical judgment are desirable characteristics. Because we do not want judges who are corrupt, who are influenced by the potential implications of their decisions for their social standing or opportunities for retention or promotion, or who are hot-tempered, we must value judges who are incorruptible, who possess civic courage, and who have an appropriate temperament.[25] Beyond that, in Solum's estimation, it becomes difficult to identify the characteristics necessary to the formulation of a thicker theory of virtues, simply because what counts as virtuous will vary depending on one's conception of the judicial role. For example, we might imagine that excellence in implementing an originalist approach to constitutional interpretation requires a different skillset than does excellence in deploying common-law constitutionalism. As a result, what would be a virtue in one regime will not necessarily count as one in the other. Even so, Solum has elsewhere offered slightly more expansive versions of the list, which include impartiality, diligence, carefulness, and communicative skill.[26]

22 Amaya, 'Reasoning in Character', 9–11.

23 Id., 11.

24 Solum's preferred label for this approach is "aretaic," which is tied to the ancient Greek word for "excellence." I avoid the label based on the instinct that it is, to put the point accurately but imprecisely, not likely to be effective in any campaign to get the bar or the general public to buy in to the approach.

25 Solum's list of "uncontested" virtues includes incorruptibility, courage, sobriety, good temper, impartiality, diligence, carefulness, intelligence, learnedness, and oral and written communication skills. Lawrence B. Solum, 'A Tournament of Virtue,' (2005) 32 *Florida State Law Review* 1365, 1368–76.

26 See, for example, Colin Farrelly and Lawrence B. Solum, eds., 'An Introduction to Aretaic Theories of Law,' in *Virtue Jurisprudence* (London: Palgrave Macmillan, 2008) 1–23.

Virtue-centered accounts have not gained much traction within the legal academy. Some of the objections are practical in nature. As I suggested earlier, there are reasons to greet the idea of a character-focused approach with at least mild skepticism. It assumes that people, or at least some of them, possess traits of character that are relatively stable across contexts, as opposed to more situationally contingent tendencies.[27] A skeptic would maintain that rather than, for example, courage and temperance, "[t]here are only such traits as sailing-in-rough-weather-with-friends-courage and office-party-temperance, which are perfectly compatible with acting in a cowardly fashion when sailing in rough weather with new acquaintances and drinking excessively at family gatherings."[28] Even if we accept that there are such traits, we should understand them as tendencies rather than absolutes. Character is not binary. It will manifest itself to a greater degree in some than in others, and more consistently in some than in others.

Another objection is that a character-based approach provides no useful direction when it comes to deciding particular cases.[29] "Do what a virtuous judge would do" is imprecise and therefore presumptively unpalatable to a society with a taste for the left-brained and quantifiable. What's more, a focus on character entails reliance on a set of traits likely to present as expertise in a world that is skeptical of expert judgment.[30] Such an approach locates the attributes of a good decision in the nature of the person who made it rather than in some independently assessable aspect of the decision itself. In that sense, the approach is open to charges of elitism, in that it can be characterized as an effort to return to a version of the triad in which the decision-maker's legitimacy is derived from their status as a wise elder, but in a world in which there's no consensus among those who will be parties to disputes concerning what a wise elder looks like. Moreover, given the Cassandra Quandary, the idea of following the lead of a virtuous judge will be partially or entirely inaccessible to someone who lacks virtue (or at least the capacity for it). Put differently, if lacking good judicial character is at least partly a product of lacking the capacity to appreciate the nature of good character, then many of those without the requisite traits will not recognize good character when they see it in others. Indeed, to return briefly to anecdote, it has been my experience that many who have poor judgment lack awareness of that fact and that others perceive them in that way. They similarly struggle to recognize good judgment in others.

27 Rachana Kamtekar, 'Situationism and Virtue Ethics on the Content of Our Character,' (2004) 114 *Ethics* 458.

28 Jonathan Webber, 'Virtue, Character, and Situation,' (2006) 3 *Journal of Moral Philosophy* 193.

29 Horwitz, 'Judicial Character', 151.

30 Indeed, Amaya has described aspects of the exercise of virtue as involving expertise. Amaya, 'Reasoning in Character', 5. See also Amalia Amaya, 'Ambivalence, Judicial Craftmanship, and the Development of the Law: Variations on a Theme of Benjamin Cardozo,' (2023) 34 *Yale Journal of Law and the Humanities* 190.

The argument in favor of a character-based approach, and the implementation of such an approach, thus cannot simply be rooted in an appeal to authority – we're the experts, therefore you should trust us as to what's best. "Trust us" is too easily mistaken for an effort to smuggle in judges actually selected for other reasons. And there's a danger that it could become so – that the selectors, whoever they might be, will fall prey to the same sorts of biases and blind spots that accompany the exercise of judgment more generally. That is, that they will too readily confuse "that person sees things the way I do" for "that person has good judgment." All the flaws that lead to motivated reasoning when it comes to the resolution of disputes can also apply to the recognition of characteristics in people. The criteria must instead be connected to the functions of the judiciary and the notion of the rule of law.[31]

Another theoretical objection concerns the basic assumptions underlying the entire project. To the extent that virtue jurisprudence is tied to a virtue ethics rooted in Aristotle, and thus grounded on a vision of law as designed to promote virtue among the citizenry, then it is the product of assumptions that aren't widely shared.[32] And there is, relatedly, what might be called a public relations concern. Appeals to virtue seem passé and unlikely to gain traction in a social and political world in which playground-level dialogue (and behavior) predominates.

But a substantial connection to virtue ethics is unnecessary. Similar lists of characteristics feature in the ideal conceptions of judges offered by legal scholars not deep in the Aristotelian tradition. Sherry, for example, lists "traits such as honesty, impartiality, and integrity" as well as "empathy, imagination, candor, and self-awareness."[33] She adds humility and courage and emphasizes them as being among the most critical. By courage, she means "confronting one's fears and acting despite them." "A good judge, because she is humble about her own role and abilities, is especially likely to fear being wrong. In the face of such a fear, it is easier not to act than to act: sins of omission never seem as frightening when the alternative is to take a bold step that might be mistaken. Thus, judicial courage entails acting despite the uncertainty, born of humility, about the correctness of one's actions."[34] There is, undoubtedly, tension to be resolved. "In the end, humility and courage are like other constitutional dualities: there is no mechanical device that can mediate between them. But judges who are inclined both to doubt themselves and to risk being wrong are more likely to reach a happy medium than are judges who are too strongly inclined toward arrogance or timidity."[35]

31 In this sense, I agree with Solum, though like Paul Horwitz, I do not agree with him that acknowledging the point necessarily leads to formalism.

32 Professor R. A. Duff suggests that "[t]he antennae of traditional liberals will quiver at the suggestion that this is any part of the law's proper aim." R. A. Duff, 'The Limits of Virtue Jurisprudence,' (2003) 34 *Metaphilosophy* 214, 215. See also Gregory Bassham and Olivia Ostrowski, 'A Pluralistic Virtue-Centered Theory of Judging,' (2022) 35 *Ratio Juris* 3.

33 Sherry, 'Judges of Character', 797–98.

34 Id., 798.

35 Id., 810.

Some, of course, will suggest that the exercise of proper judicial character entails resorting to certain methodologies. Sherry's argument, for example, at least implicitly equates good character with a pragmatic approach, and Horwitz agrees.[36] Solum, on the other hand, has argued for a thicker conception of virtue jurisprudence that leads to formalism. Good judges, he suggests, have the virtue of justice in addition to the virtues he includes within his thin account. It is not just that they reliably follow a vision of law – that a judge who professes to regard, say, originalism or economically driven decision-making as the proper way to "do law" does so well and consistently. But it is that they have the right vision of doing law. For Solum, given the rule of law as an overarching ideal, formalist judges best exhibit the virtue of justice. The arguments he offers, though, pit "decision according to law" against "decision according to political ideology," thus overlooking that there is a middle ground between hard formalism and pure politics. To a substantial degree, placing detachment on the list of desirable characteristics would appear to do much of the same work. On this view, a judge won't have or choose a side in an ideological sense, and those who are external to the legal system and who are on an ideological side will understand that a crucial component of the rule of law is that their side will not always prevail.

Consideration of those who have previously advocated an emphasis on character provides further support for the suggestion that character-based approaches entail no necessary methodological or ideological commitments. Sherry is a pragmatist. Tushnet was a pioneering member of the Critical Legal Studies movement. Solum is an originalist. One can certainly imagine a conception of judicial character that is agnostic as to methodology, and there seems to be nothing problematic about an approach that prioritizes good character, with methodological and other preferences taking a secondary position.[37] Indeed, that is the very thing that Solum's thin theory aims to identify. Imagine, for example, someone who, all else equal, prefers pragmatist judges but who prefers judges of good character even more strongly. That person would advocate the selection of an originalist with good character over a pragmatist without it. The logic of the triad suggests as much. The parties to a dispute, looking to a third party to provide resolution, will be interested in knowing that they can trust the third party to strive to faithfully and capably apply a methodology before knowing what that methodology is.

One therefore need not go so far as to accept conclusions about the ends of law or the necessity of a connection between the virtue of a judge and the virtuousness or even legality of that judge's decisions[38] to conclude that judges' professional and

36 Horwitz, 'Judicial Character', 155.

37 Robert Roberts and Jay Wood make a similar point: "Within limits we want to be able to attribute intellectual virtue to a person with a systematically distorted conception of the intellectual goods." Robert C. Roberts and W. Jay Wood, *Intellectual Virtues: An Essay in Regulative Epistemology* (Oxford: Oxford University Press, 2007) 307.

38 For a partially critical take on Solum's articulation of virtue jurisprudence, see Duff, 'The Limits of Virtue Jurisprudence'.

intellectual characteristics matter. The notion that judges should be of good character is a familiar one. Many of the items on these lists appear in codes of judicial ethics, for example, such as requirements of impartiality, competence, diligence, and displaying an appropriate demeanor. Like Sherry and others, I believe there is a strong pragmatic case to be made for emphasizing those characteristics. As I developed at the outset of this book, courts, and therefore judges, exist to serve social functions. The core function, that of resolving disputes, implies the need for maintenance of the triadic structure, which in turn creates the need for judges to engage in the primarily retrospective task of finding (or overseeing the finding of) facts and identifying the applicable legal standards in an attentive and dispassionate manner. Other functions, ranging from the creation and refinement of law to the supervision of defendants in drug courts, require a more prospective and predictive orientation. The intricacies and nuances of a case will often elude the precise reach of existing authorities. There will be hard cases in which judges have to accommodate and mediate among uncertainty and conflict. Having good judicial and intellectual character does not guarantee that a judge will undertake any of these functions flawlessly. But, when coupled with the range of other factors that work to channel judicial behavior, it will make good decisions more likely.

In proceeding from this functionalist understanding of the role, I want to emphasize two character traits that I contend should feature heavily in the list of critical characteristics. The first is practical wisdom, which, as we have seen, regularly appears on lists offered by those who emphasize judicial character.[39] Practical wisdom is typically presented by virtue ethicists as something of a master virtue, one drawn on to coordinate among and mediate the working of the other virtues, which will often pull in different directions in a given situation. Professors Robert Roberts and Jay Wood offer that it "is involved in every virtue, as constituting good judgment without which no human virtue could be exemplified in action, emotion, or judgment."[40] As with ideal characteristics more generally, it's difficult to pin down precisely what practical wisdom entails; it's a right-hemisphere construct that doesn't resonate in our left-hemisphere world.[41] Yet it is evident in concepts such as Kronman's lawyer-statesman and Llewellyn's notion of situation sense. "Practical wisdom is the virtue that enables one to make good choices in particular circumstances. The person of practical wisdom knows which particular ends are worth pursuing and knows which means are best suited to achieve those ends. Judicial wisdom is simply the virtue of practical wisdom as applied to the choices that must be made by judges."[42] For Kronman, the exercise of practical wisdom involves both sympathy and detachment,

39 For a survey of efforts to define the concept of wisdom, see Bridget R. Dunnavant and Heidi M. Leviitt, 'The Development of Wisdom in Judicial Decision-Making,' (2015) 43 *The Humanistic Psychologist* 1, 1–5.

40 Roberts and Wood, 'Intellectual Virtues', 305.

41 Scharffs, at 133–34.

42 Solum, 'Aretaic Turn', 510.

an ability to appreciate others' perspectives – to "have experienced something of the power and appeal of a value and [to] understand why others are drawn to it"[43] while at the same time holding that value at a sufficient emotional and intellectual distance so as to be able to assess it against alternative perspectives viewed in the same way.[44] It involves an ability to reconcile, or to make the best sense of, the conflicting views and values that present themselves in the context of a given dispute, not to impose one's own views of what the situation requires but to extract "the principles imminent in the law"[45] and to bring them to bear on the resolution.

I opened this book with a discussion of the dissenting opinion in *Dobbs* v. *Jackson Women's Health Organization*, its characterization of the joint opinion in *Planned Parenthood* v. *Casey* as having exemplified wisdom, and the parallel between that characterization and Kronman's depiction thirty years earlier of the *Casey* joint opinion as an example of the exercise of the sort of practical wisdom emblematic of his lawyer-statesman ideal. In some respects, *Casey* and *Dobbs* are less-than-ideal illustrations of the concept simply because for many on the opposing sides of the abortion debate the matter is black-and-white and leaves no room for compromise. Viewed from another vantage point, and certainly, one imagines, from that of Justices Kennedy, O'Connor, and Souter, the reasoning process involved precisely the sort of detached approach characteristic of practical wisdom. Each of these justices is generally regarded as personally opposed to abortion, and as someone who would not have favored the recognition of a right had they been on the Court when the question first arose. But they recognized the existence of other, conflicting values, including the force of precedent and the strongly held beliefs and interests of those on the other side of the issue. Yet when an issue is so divisive, many will find such balancing unsatisfactory. One person's wisdom will be another's folly.

Rucho v. *Common Cause*, by contrast, in my estimation did present a situation where the Court passed up an opportunity to exercise practical wisdom in a situation where it would have been appropriate to do so. In a sense, *Rucho* represents a complete triumph of what McGilchrist characterizes as left-hemispheric thought. The highly gerrymandered maps at the center of the case were the product of technology able to slice the electorate with surgical precision. The majority's capitulation to the extreme gerrymandering resulted from its inability to find a comparably precise metric by which to assess whether and when things have gone too far. Because it could not identify the specific point at which the grains of sand – the partisanship that routinely inflects the drawing of electoral districts – became a heap, the majority refused to recognize that there was a heap at all.

43 Kronman, 'Lost Lawyer', 71.

44 Id.

45 Lawrence B. Solum, 'A Virtue-Centered Account of Equity and the Rule of Law,' in Farrelly and Solum, eds., '*Virtue Jurisprudence*', 142, 158. The reader here may be reminded of Ronald Dworkin's hypothetical judge, Hercules. Solum notes the parallel and helpfully explores the distinction between the two approaches.

The Court does not always insist on such precision. For example, it took a very different approach in *Old Chief* v. *United States*.[46] On the surface, the question was very different from in *Rucho*. The defendant was charged with crimes including being a felon in possession of a firearm and assault with a dangerous weapon. His prior conviction was for an assault, and he offered to stipulate to being a felon so that the jury would not be tempted to use his past assault conviction as improper character evidence bearing on the assault charge before it. Justice Souter's majority opinion acknowledged that the prosecution is normally entitled to choose how to prove its case. The reasons for that echo the case for practical wisdom and recognize its importance in the legal system. "Evidence … has force beyond any linear scheme of reasoning,"[47] and "the evidentiary account of what a defendant has thought and done can accomplish what no set of abstract statements ever could."[48] "A syllogism is not a story, and a naked proposition in a courtroom may be no match for the robust evidence that would be used to prove it."[49] There is room for choice, and normally that choice will be left undisturbed. But occasionally, it will be clear that things have gone too far. Where the alternatives are both "propositions of slightly varying abstraction" – the jury hearing simply that the defendant has a felony conviction versus hearing the name of that felony – that choice can be curtailed. Something that is typically acceptable in this case was not.

This recognition – that particulars differ from one situation to the next, sometimes in ways that matter even if the variation has not been, and perhaps cannot be, captured in general rules – is at the heart of practical wisdom. "General propositions do not decide concrete cases,"[50] as Holmes reminds us. "The decision will depend on a judgment or intuition more subtle than any articulate major premise." That judgment requires extrapolation from and interpolation among not only the various purposes and principles embedded in the general proposition but also the various social, institutional, and factual features of the situation to which it is to be applied. The equities of the individual case may run counter to the equally real and important values of decision according to rules, having policy judgments made by legislatures, and the like, and social pressures will exert their pull as well. Practical wisdom represents a distillation of all of these, a determination about which features of the situation to emphasize, which of the important judicial characteristics to bring to the fore.[51]

46 519 US 172 (1997).

47 519 US at 187.

48 Id.

49 519 US at 189.

50 *Lochner* v. *New York*, 198 US 45, 76 (1905) (Holmes, J., dissenting).

51 Put in the language of virtue ethics, it "consists in both the patterns of thought and perception characteristic of the specific virtues … and also the unification of all these patterns, a facility for switching from one to another as occasion requires, for blending the considerations characteristic of one virtue with those of the others, and for adjudicating between the different appeals of virtues when they seem to conflict." Roberts and Wood, 'Intellectual Virtues', 311.

The second trait I want to emphasize – humility – appears less uniformly in discussions of judicial character. But it does appear, and Professor Katharina Stevens contends that "it has been discussed often enough that its importance can be considered generally acknowledged."[52] Sherry, as we saw, regards it as critical. So, too, did judges in medieval England.[53] Stevens argues that humility is a necessary ingredient of a fully justified judicial decision. Yet judicial humility is far from universally acclaimed. As Professor Brett Scharffs lamented in making the case for humility's role in the exercise of practical wisdom, "the virtue of humility is so widely misunderstood and lightly appreciated."[54] This resistance is also of long standing. To take just one example, nearly 1,600 years ago, Saint Augustine, in the preface to *The City of God*, noted the difficulty involved in persuading "the proud of the power and excellence of humility, an excellence which makes it soar above all the summits of this world."[55] It is hardly a surprise that one finds more than a few of "the proud" among the legal community. The message, delivered with some greater or lesser degree of directness, that they ought not be so will not always be well received.

But there is perhaps more to it. At least some of the resistance proceeds from the word's imprecision. There are at least two broad senses of meaning at play. The first sense, and the one that seems most often to come to people's minds when they encounter the suggestion of judicial humility, involves matters on what we might think of as the output side of the judicial process.[56] On that view, humility is primarily a matter of self-presentation at either the individual or institutional level. It conjures up notions of deference, politeness, and timidity. So conceived, a humble judge is mindful of boundaries, and worried about overstepping them. A court filled with such judges will be a restrained court, disinclined to overrule the actions of legislatures and executives. And that, of course, is a long-contested position in debates over the proper contours of the judicial role. Some advocates of judicial humility have that version in mind,[57] but such an institutional posture is not what I envision in invoking the concept.[58]

52 Stevens, 'Humility as a Necessary Virtue', 443.
53 Elizabeth Papp Kamali, *Felony and the Guilty Mind in Medieval England* (Oxford: Oxford University Press, 2019) 292 ("Just as Seneca and his medieval English adapters warned about the perils of anger-fueled judging, so, too, did they offer practical advice to the conscientious judge or juror who wished to take such warnings to heart. Above all, advice centered on the virtue of humility.").
54 Scharffs, 'Role of Humility', 157.
55 Saint Augustine, *City of God, Preface* (London: Penguin Classics, 2003) (Henry Bettenson, ed.).
56 Scharffs, for example, offers a vision of humility that emphasizes (though certainly not exclusively) features on the output side, including having a tendency to resist radical change, to eschew judicial activism, to avoid the abuse of power, and to be respectful of those who appear before them. Scharffs, 'Role of Humility', 185–98. His more input-oriented justifications are that humility will guide judges in mediating between sympathy and detachment when the two conflict, being respectful of courses of legal authority, and being open to the reconsideration of past positions.
57 For a discussion of this view and some of its proponents, see German and Burton, 'Constitutional Humility', 243–45.
58 Amalia Amaya, 'The Virtue of Judicial Humility,' 9 *Jurisprudence* 97 (2018); see also Amalia Amaya, 'Humility in Law,' in Mark Alfano, Michael P. Lynch, and Alessandra Tanesini, eds., *The Routledge*

I seek instead to emphasize a different sense of humility, often referred to as intellectual or epistemological humility. It is concerned with the input side of the task of decision-making, and it is perhaps less likely to prompt instinctive resistance, as evidenced by the fact that both Chief Justice Roberts and Justice Kagan invoked the idea, or something akin to it, during their confirmation hearings. In his opening statement, Roberts said, "Judges have to have the humility to recognize that they operate within a system of precedent shaped by other judges equally striving to live up to the judicial oath. And judges have to have the modesty to be open in the decisional process to the considered views of their colleagues on the bench." Kagan likewise invoked the idea in discussing precedent: "It is a way of current justices saying even if I think these past judges got it wrong, I'm going to be hesitant about saying that. I'm going to doubt myself. I'm going to think that this law that has built up over the years by prior judges has real wisdom to it. Even if I can't quite see that wisdom right now, I'm going to be hesitant about saying that it doesn't exist. So it is a doctrine really of humility, of judicial humility." These depictions capture the idea incompletely, but both gesture toward a core "I might be wrong" that sits at the center of the concept.

One of this book's lessons is that all of us, very much including judges, can unwittingly be led astray. We are susceptible to motivated reasoning and to patterns of thought that are less consistently rational than we imagine. Many of the features of the legal system seem designed to constrain or counteract these forces, but they have weakened. Meanwhile, the profession, along with society more generally, has become more polarized. Judges' salient audiences increasingly consist of ideologically self-segregated slices of the profession rather than the profession as a whole. It is easier, when one confronts an alternative perspective, to avoid engaging with it in a charitable way. Formalistic methodologies, however much they may appeal to our collective taste for the tangible or to an individual judge's desire to depict their decisional process as algorithmic, cannot remove the need for judgment. Practical wisdom is a necessity, and given the complexity of the world and the swirling forces of polarization, intellectual humility is a critical prerequisite to the exercise of practical wisdom.

The claim, then, is that one best performs the judicial role while maintaining a certain intellectual stance, one that involves skepticism about the nature and correctness of one's own knowledge. The merits of intellectual humility have long been explored by philosophers, and more recently by cognitive scientists. As defined by a group of academics, including members from both fields, intellectual humility is a cognitive trait characterized by "recognizing that a particular personal belief may be fallible, accompanied by an appropriate attentiveness to limitations in the evidentiary basis of that belief and to one's own limitations in obtaining and

Handbook of Philosophy of Humility (New York: Routledge, 2020) 451. For an example of an article, coincidentally with the same title as Amaya's, making institutional arguments about institutional humility, see Richard S. Myers, 'The Virtue of Judicial Humility,' (2015) 13 *Ave Maria Law Review* 207.

evaluating relevant information."[59] It should not be confused with the first sense of humility as described earlier, or with traits such as modesty or timidity, any sort of general tendency to undervalue one's self or one's beliefs, or with other related labels that concern how people conceive of or present themselves in a more general way.[60] Nor should it be taken to mean intellectual diffidence. Scharffs captures it well: "Humility does not denote weakness, but rather a proper understanding of the sources of one's strength."[61] It thus entails a situationally appropriate amount of skepticism about what one knows.[62] As Professor Dennis Whitcomb and his colleagues put it, "Proper pride is having the right stance towards one's strengths; humility is having the right stance towards one's limitations. *Intellectual* humility, then, is having the right stance toward one's *intellectual* limitations."[63] It is to be aware that there is always more to learn and to regard one's beliefs as always being, to some greater or lesser degree, tentatively held and subject to updating in light of new information or a deeper understanding. To be an intellectually humble person, or judge, does not mean one should not or does not have strongly held beliefs, but rather that one should do so only when those beliefs have an appropriate grounding. A persistent skepticism about the status of one's knowledge does not preclude reaching confident conclusions so much as it counsels against reaching them too quickly.[64] In Amaya's phrasing, "epistemic humility imposes some constraints on the process of deliberation, but it does not dictate the result of such deliberation."[65] Intellectual humility is a cognitive analog of "measure twice, cut once."

[59] Mark K. Leary, Kate J. Diebels, Erin K. Davisson, Katrina P. Jongman-Sereno, Jennifer C. Isherwood, Kaitlin T. Raimi, Samantha A. Deffler, and Rick H. Hoyle, 'Cognitive and Interpersonal Features of Intellectual Humility,' (2017) 43 *Personality and Social Psychology Bulletin* 793. "This definition was developed by members of an interdisciplinary group that involved philosophers with expertise in intellectual virtues … and social, personality, clinical, counseling, and organizational psychologists with expertise in egotism and humility …." Mark R. Leary, 'The Psychology of Intellectual Humility,' 4 (2018), available at www.templeton.org/wp-content/uploads/2018/11/Intellectual-Humility-Leary-FullLength-Final.pdf. There are, of course, other definitions of the concept. For a general discussion, see Dennis Whitcomb, Heather Battaly, Jason Baehr, and Daniel Howard-Snyder, 'Intellectual Humility: Owning Our Limitations,' (2017) 94 *Philosophy and Phenomenological Research* 509.

[60] Tenelle Porter, Abdo Elnakouri, Ethan A. Meyers, Takuya Shibayama, Eranda Jayawickreme, and Igor Grossman, 'Predictors and Consequences of Intellectual Humility,' (2022) *Nature Reviews: Psychology*, available at www.nature.com/articles/s44159-022-00081-9.

[61] Scharffs, 'Role of Humility', 163.

[62] Id.

[63] Whitcomb, Battaly, Baehr, and Howard-Snyder, 'Owning Our Limitations', 8. "In this connection, notice that the paradigmatically arrogant person is often oblivious to his limitations; they don't show up on his radar. The paradigmatically servile person, however, hardly sees anything else; his radar is perpetually peppered with his limitations. On our view, humility lies in the middle between these extremes. When life calls for one to be mindful of a limitation, then, and only then, will it appear on the ideally humble person's radar. And what goes for humility in general goes for IH in particular." Whitcomb, Battaly, Baehr, and Howard-Snyder, 'Owning Our Limitations', 8–9.

[64] German and Burton speak of "a healthy synthesis of both caution and decisiveness." German and Burton, 'Constitutional Humility', 251.

[65] Amaya, 'Virtue of Judicial Humility', 100.

In operation, intellectual humility is primarily a metacognitive phenomenon, or, in other words, a characteristic that involves thinking about one's own thinking. People who possess intellectual humility are more likely to suspect that their thought processes and beliefs may be wrong, from which it follows that they "are also more attentive to the strength of evidence regarding factual claims and more interested in understanding the reasons that people disagree with them," which may in turn "reflect the fact that people who recognize that their views are fallible are naturally more motivated to think about the accuracy of their beliefs than people who assume that they are right about most things."[66] The intellectually humble tend to invest more effort in gathering and considering information, are more open to others' views, are more empathetic, and display "less rigidity and conceit regarding their beliefs and opinions."[67] Intellectual humility "is associated with motives that reflect a proactive, inquisitive approach to knowledge" and "is also associated with higher need for cognition, the degree to which people enjoy thinking, mulling over issues, and solving intellectual problems,"[68] and may also be a product of an aversion to being wrong. It is also associated with ideological moderation, and those at the political extremes tend to display less of it.

A key component of intellectual humility is acceptance of uncertainty and ambiguity, and acknowledgement that the world is awash in complexity and contingency. Those who tend not to possess it, by contrast, see the world in black and white. They include "people who are high in need for cognitive closure – those who want definitive answers to questions and decisions as opposed to uncertainty or ambiguity."[69] They "have stronger emotional reactions to information that is contrary to their beliefs and to people who disagree with them."[70] The dogmatic, by definition, are not intellectually humble.

I suggested earlier that intellectual humility is a key ingredient of practical wisdom. Effectively mediating among competing interests and principles in resolving concrete cases necessarily entails attentiveness to the nature and strength of the various factors at play. Good outputs – the decisions judges must make – require good inputs. Although work exploring the connection between intellectual humility and decisional quality is in its early stages, the results are encouraging. Shauna Bowes, Anna Ringwood, and Arber Tasini conducted a study examining the relationship among various measures of intellectual humility, overconfidence, and critical thinking.[71] Intellectual humility, they found, "was generally related to more critical

66 Leary, 'Psychology of Intellectual Humility', 8.

67 Id., 10.

68 Id., 9.

69 Id., 9.

70 Id., 10.

71 Shauna M. Bowes, Anna Ringwood, and Arber Tasimi, 'Is Intellectual Humility Related to More Accuracy and Less Overconfidence?,' (2023) *The Journal of Positive Psychology*, DOI: 10.1080/17439760.2023.2208100.

thinking, less overestimation, and less overclaiming." In another study, Bowes and a different set of colleagues found evidence suggesting that intellectual humility "may lessen the influence of partisan cues on decision-making processes."[72] The results of other studies provide further support for the idea that intellectual humility is associated with less partisanship and political hostility more generally.[73]

Other work explores phenomena that have not thus far been conceived of in terms of intellectual humility but that are clearly related. One line of research explores the ameliorating effect of curiosity – which often features in definitions of,[74] and is in any case broadly consistent and correlated with, intellectual humility[75] – on motivated reasoning. For example, Professor Dan Kahan and his collaborators have found evidence suggesting that a characteristic they call "science curiosity" – "a tendency to consume scientific information for the sake of personal interest and pleasure"[76] can counteract the effects of polarization when it comes to the interpretation of evidence bearing on climate change.[77] People who possess that characteristic seem to have a taste for information that runs counter to their existing understanding of the evidence. But not all forms of curiosity are equally efficacious. Claire Zedelius and colleagues draw a distinction between "interest curiosity" and "deprivation curiosity."[78] The former involves a general taste for learning new things for their own sake. The latter "is more specific, and more emotionally ambivalent. It is motivated by the desire to reduce the unpleasant 'itch' of uncertainty and frustration that arises when we are presented with an unanswered question." Those who possess interest curiosity tend to have a "high tolerance for ambiguity and low need for

72 Shauna M. Bowes, Thomas H. Costello, Stacey McElroy-Hetzel, Don E. Davis, and Scott O. Lilienfeld, 'Stepping Outside the Echo Chamber: Is Intellectual Humility Associated with Less Political Myside Bias?,' (2022) 48 *Personality and Social Psychology Bulletin* 150.

73 See Tyrone J. Sgambati and Ozlem N. Ayduk, 'Intellectual Humility and Political Polarization: An Exploration of Social Networks, Attitudes, and Affect,' (2023) 44 *Political Psychology* 807; Glen Smith, 'You Know You're Right: How Intellectual Humility Decreases Political Hostility,' (2023) 44 *Political Psychology* 1319.

74 Scharffs, for example, offers that humility "denotes an attitude of open-mindedness and curiosity, a willingness to learn, reassess, and change. One who is humble can be persuaded that her conclusions are wrong; that her perspectives are limited and should be broadened; that her settled opinions merit reconsideration. One who is humble will possess a quiet confidence that enables learning and reassessment, because she is not defensive or insecure." Scharffs, 'Role of Humility', 164.

75 For an example of work drawing a connection between intellectual humility and curiosity, see Krumrei-Mancuso, Elizabeth J., Haggard, Megan C., LaBouff, Jordan P., and Rowatt, Wade C., 'Links between Intellectual Humility and Acquiring Knowledge,' (2020) 15 *Journal of Positive Psychology* 155.

76 Matthew Motta, Dan Chapman, Kathryn Haglin, and Dan Kahan, 'Reducing the Administrative Demands of the Science Curiosity Scale: A Validation Study,' (2021) 33 *International Journal of Public Opinion Research* 215.

77 Dan M. Kahan, Ashely Landrum, Katie Carpenter, Laura Helft, and Kathleen Hall Jamieson, 'Science Curiosity and Political Information Processing,' (2017) 38 *Advances in Political Psychology* 179.

78 Claire M. Zedelius, Madeleine E. Gross, and Jonathan W. Schooler, 'Inquisitive but not Discerning: Deprivation Curiosity is Associated with Excessive Openness to Inaccurate Information,' (2022) *Journal of Research in Personality* 98, http://doi.org/10.1016/j.jrp.2022.104227.

closure." Those with deprivation curiosity, by contrast, "lack discernment in distinguishing fact from fiction, and the intellectual humility to recognize the limitations of their often faulty knowledge." Error and confusion tend to result.

Consider in a related vein Professor Philip Tetlock's work exploring the nature of expert political judgment.[79] Tetlock asked a group of experts to make predictions about future states of the world and tracked whether those predictions proved accurate over time. The results showed the experts' talent to be varied along what roughly tracked a statistically normal distribution. Some performed well, others performed poorly, and most were close to a collective average only slightly better than chance. Factors including education and experience levels, the field in which that education and experience were earned, and ideology bore no significant relation to variations in performance. What did matter was cognitive style. Tetlock drew on Isaiah Berlin's distinction between the intellectual styles of hedgehogs and foxes[80] in explaining the difference. Those who did poorly "look like hedgehogs: thinkers who 'know one big thing,' aggressively extend the explanatory reach of that one big thing into new domains, display bristly impatience with those who 'do not get it,' and express considerable confidence that they are already pretty proficient forecasters …."[81] Those who did well, by contrast, "look like foxes: thinkers who know many small things (tricks of their trade), are skeptical of grand schemes, see explanation and prediction not as deductive exercises but rather as exercises in flexible 'ad hocery' that require stitching together diverse sources of information, and are rather diffident about their own forecasting prowess …."[82] Foxes, as Tetlock describes them, bear many of the characteristics of intellectual humility. They are self-critical, they are inclined to anticipate objections from others, and they are accordingly more likely to appropriately assess and account for all the information pertinent to a given situation.[83] Even so, foxes have their own weak points and like everyone else would do well to be mindful of the ways in which their epistemic tendencies tend to lead them astray.[84]

All of this is promising, but appropriate caution is in order. As just suggested, intellectual humility is threatened by the same sorts of biases that afflict thought more generally. Confirmation bias, motivated reasoning, and the pressures of social conformity can work to undermine our resistance to reaching easy conclusions. One who values membership in a group, whether social, professional, religious, or otherwise, might reflexively adopt the beliefs, premises, and understandings

79 Philip E. Tetlock, *Expert Political Judgment* (Princeton: Princeton University Press, 2005).

80 Isaiah Berlin, 'The Hedgehog and the Fox: An Essay on Tolstoy's View of History,' reprinted in Isaiah Berlin, *The Proper Study of Mankind: An Anthology of Essays* (New York: Farrar, Straus and Giroux, 2000) (Henry Hardy and Roger Hausheer, eds.) 436.

81 Tetlock, 'Expert Political Judgment', 73–75.

82 Id., 73–75.

83 Id., 82.

84 Robert C. Roberts and Ryan West, 'Natural Epistemic Defects and Corrective Virtues,' (2015) 192 *Synthese* 2557, 2566.

dominant in the group.[85] "The motive to attain status within one's community might also work against intellectual humility. Group members often gain prestige and rank by fervently endorsing the group's ideology."[86]

More generally, the researchers who have investigated intellectual humility and related phenomena consistently emphasize that their work and its conclusions are tentative, that more confirmation and refinement remain necessary. Still, the results are encouraging. And they are consistent with the inherently more speculative, but longstanding, work of epistemologists. Intellectual humility provides no guarantees, but those who practice it consistently consider a wider range of information and perspectives, and they consider that information more carefully. Their thought is more rigorous. This in turn appears to make them comparatively better at both decisions that turn on retrospective inquiry and those that involve predictions about future states of affairs.

Intellectual humility's value for judges accordingly seems self-evident. To the extent that judges are engaged in retrospective inquiry, they will undertake it in a way that is more likely to properly account for all pertinent information. Predictive assessments of the sort often involved in the creation of law will likewise tend toward greater accuracy. As noted earlier, all of this fuels the application of practical wisdom. Law is a device for the moderation of, and in important respects is the product of, social conflict. Our social ends are many, varied, and often in tension with one another. Not all cases present these tensions in stark fashion, but many do. In those cases, taking account of other perspectives is critical.[87] Too readily assuming one's own viewpoint and assumptions are correct runs counter to all of this. "Intellectually humbler people are better able to differentiate between strong and weak arguments, even if those arguments go against their initial beliefs."[88] It can likewise help mediate among the conflicting values at play in any given difficult situation.[89]

It bears noting again that intellectual humility is concerned with inputs, and with the processing of those inputs. It does not require that judges refrain from acting decisively, or even boldly. Indeed, to the extent that the intellectually humble judge

[85] Porter, Elnakouri, Meyers, Shibayama, Jayawickreme, and Grossman, 'Predictors and Consequence of Intellectual Humility'.

[86] Id.

[87] Amaya helps us round this out by emphasizing the other-directedness of humility: "It is one's attitude toward one's place within the community rather than one's attitude toward one's accomplishments that is at the core of the virtue of humility." Amaya, 'Virtue of Judicial Humility', 102. It entails a deeply egalitarian stance, "a profound appreciation of the equality of all human beings," Amaya, 'Virtue of Judicial Humility', 103, among the manifestations of which is a "focus on what brings us together rather than on what tears us apart." Amaya, 'Virtue of Judicial Humility', 105. This, in turn, helps foster legal and political fraternity.

[88] Porter, Elnakouri, Meyers, Shibayama, Jayawickreme, and Grossman, 'Predictors and Consequence of Intellectual Humility'.

[89] Scharffs has made the point that humility facilitates the operation of practical wisdom. Scharffs, 'Role of Humility'.

is more likely to question longstanding assumptions, it may in some situations facilitate the updating of practices that have outlived their usefulness.

Suppose, then, that we agree on the importance of judicial character, that we have concluded that our judges should be practically wise and intellectually humble, and that they should possess some or all of the other characteristics discussed earlier. How do we act on those conclusions? Does character, or at least many of its important components, consist of malleable characteristics that can be nurtured and developed? Aristotle's view was that virtues of character are products of practice and habituation. We are not born with them, "we exercise them first, and that's how we acquire them – just like the way it is with technical skills."[90] Wisdom thus can only be a product of experience. It "requires knowing the details of life, and we only become acquainted with those through experience, and experience is exactly what young people don't have. It's sheer quantity of time that gives you experience."[91] In another translation, using "intelligence" instead of "wisdom": "intelligence is concerned with particulars as well as universals, and particulars become known from experience, but a young person lacks experience."[92]

Educators in a variety of contexts have made efforts to develop wisdom, with some apparent success, suggesting that the task is possible.[93] Professor Mark Leary is optimistic about people's ability to change in terms of their intellectual humility. Still, he cautions, they need a reason to do so, to "believe that approaching the world in a more intellectually humble fashion is beneficial and desirable."[94] Changes at the level of a culture are an important component of this: "fostering intellectual humility calls for societal change in educational, scientific, and business cultures: away from treating intellectual humility as a weakness and towards treating it as a core value that is celebrated and reinforced."[95]

I wish to explore four ways in which we might pursue the enhancement of judicial character, with specific emphasis on how we might foster intellectual humility and practical wisdom. We can adjust existing processes, institutional arrangements, and culture to foster and encourage reliance on desirable characteristics. These are, it bears noting, blunt instruments. I harbor no illusions that we can eradicate human foibles or make dramatic improvements over a short period of time. But we should also not let the perfect be the enemy of the good. Incremental gains in the

90 Aristotle, Nicomachean Ethics, Book II, Ch. 1, 1103a 30–35 (Adam Beresford, ed., 2020).

91 Aristotle, Nicomachean Ethics, Book VI, Ch. 8, 1142a 12–20 (Adam Beresford, ed., 2020).

92 Aristotle, Nicomachean Ethics, Book VI, Ch. 8, 1142a 12–20 (Indianapolis, IN: Hackett Publishing, 1985) (Terence Irwin, ed.).

93 Dunnavant and Levitt, 'Development of Wisdom', 3–4. See also Jason Baehr, 'Is Intellectual Character Growth a Realistic Educational Aim?', (2016) 45 *Journal of Moral Education* 117; Jason Baehr, 'Educating for Intellectual Virtues: From Theory to Practice,' (2013) 47 *Journal of the Philosophy of Education* 248.

94 Dunnavant and Levitt, 'Development of Wisdom', 14.

95 Porter, Elnakouri, Meyers, Shibayama, Jayawickreme, and Grossman, 'Predictors and Consequence of Intellectual Humility'.

exercise and appreciation of appropriate judicial character are better than no gains. Even slight changes to the nature of the conversation can yield benefits, difficult though they may be to quantify.

The first is to adjust existing mechanisms for channeling judicial behavior. There is a large body of literature suggesting various procedural and other tweaks, much of which arose out of concern over the "crisis of volume" in the 1990s. I will touch on only a few here. For example, I argued in Chapter 4 that judges' transition from opinion writers to opinion editors has changed the nature of their engagement with their work. Writing, as I discussed, provides a source of discipline on thought that functions as a catalyst for intellectual humility. The process of attempting to articulate a line of thinking on the page flushes out gaps in an analysis, and in the writer's knowledge. Unpublished, nonprecedential opinions likewise allow for reduced engagement, and some evidence suggests that they enable judges to undermine the force of precedent, either by using such opinions to avoid having to confront contrary precedent or by sidestepping the need to create new law in difficult cases.[96] Modifications designed to increase engagement or otherwise provide checks on the process of decision thus appear to be in order. Some have argued that judges should be required to write all opinions issued under their names,[97] but less significant alterations would be more workable. I have, for example, suggested that the appellate process could be enhanced simply by requiring opinions to include short, party-generated statements of the issues in dispute, which would boost the adversarial process and provide some insurance against a judicial inclination to evade difficult questions.[98]

In multi-member courts, panel composition can matter. Panels of judges who share the same ideology tend toward extremes, while those featuring ideological diversity tend toward moderation.[99] It's possible, of course, that the underlying dynamic is purely ideological, with the former situation serving as an echo chamber and the latter involving a whistleblower. But it may also be that this sort of diversity in the judiciary contributes to the sort of intellectual humility I advocate. At least so long as judges start from a position of openness to the perspectives of others, consistent interaction with those whose views and life experiences are different promises to provide recurring opportunities to have their assumptions tested.[100] But of course that intellectual openness is a seemingly necessary precondition. Someone not inclined to credit alternative perspectives will not be enriched by them and may

96 See, for example, Mitu Gulati and C. M. A. McCauliff, 'On *Not* Making Law,' (1998) 61 *Law and Contemporary Problems* 157 (1998).

97 David MacGowan, 'Judicial Writing and the Ethics of the Judicial Office,' (2001) 14 *Georgetown Journal of Legal Ethics* 509.

98 Chad M. Oldfather, 'Remedying Judicial Inactivism: Opinions as Informational Regulation,' (2006) 58 *Florida Law Review* 743.

99 Cass R. Sunstein, David Schkade, Lisa M. Ellman, and Andres Sawicki, *Are Judges Political?* (Washington, DC: Brookings Institution Press, 2006) 148–49.

100 Michael Nava, 'The Servant of All: Humility, Humanity, and Judicial Diversity,' (2008) 38 *Golden Gate University Law Review* 175.

indeed find exposure to them threatening in a sense that leads to further entrenchment of their views. In addition, demographic and ideological diversity may interact in complex ways.[101] For example, Professors Brittany Solomon and Matthew Hall conclude from a study of decisions of the US Courts of Appeal that demographic diversity is most effective in fostering "integrative complexity—the process of thinking about divergent viewpoints and tradeoffs between adopting one view versus another" when it is present in a context featuring ideological homogeneity, and further that the effect is most pronounced for ideologically conservative groups. This research is suggestive but preliminary, and the precise mechanisms at work require further identification.

Law schools provide a second avenue for fostering judicial character. Judge Edwards opened his critique of legal education, discussed in Chapter 6, with an epigram from Justice Felix Frankfurter: "In the last analysis, the law is what the lawyers are. And the law and the lawyers are what the law schools make them."[102] Law schools have for the most part provided an education that addresses the judicial role only incidentally. Often, as also discussed in Chapter 6, that incidental treatment has tended to depict judges as engaged in the manipulation of doctrine to facilitate reaching their preferred results. Realism's lesson that doctrine does not always constrain gets passed along. The second part of the realist program – that therefore we must look elsewhere, that the lack of complete constraint does not mean the absence of all constraint – tends to be overlooked.

Nearly a century ago, Judge Joseph Hutcheson, in his still-discussed article about the role of hunch in judicial decision-making, wondered:

> Should there not go along with the plain and severely logical study of jural relations study and reflection upon, and an endeavor to discover and develop, those processes of the mind by which such decisions are reached, those processes and faculties which, lifting the mind above the mass of constricting matter whether of confused fact or precedent that stands in the way of just decision, enable it by a kind of apocalyptic vision to "trace the hidden equities of divine reward, and to catch sight through the darkness, of the fateful threats of woven fire which connect error with its retribution?"[103]

More recently, Judge Richard Posner has bemoaned law schools' failure to focus on the judicial role in a way that would provide students with "a realistic

[101] Brittany C. Solomon and Matthew E. K. Hall, 'When (Non)Differences Make a Difference: The Roles of Demographic Diversity and Ideological Homogeneity in Overcoming Ideologically Biased Decision-Making,' (2022) 34 *Organization Science* 1651.

[102] Letter from Felix Frankfurter, Professor, Harvard Law School, to Mr. Rosenwald 3 (May 13, 1927) (Felix Frankfurter papers, Harvard Law School library), quoted in Rand Jack and Dana C. Jack, *Moral Vision and Professional Decisions: The Changing Values of Women and Men Lawyers* (Cambridge: Cambridge University Press, 1989) 156.

[103] Joseph C. Hutcheson, Jr., 'Judgment Intuitive: The Function of the "Hunch" in Judicial Decision,' (1929) 14 *Cornell Law Review* 274, 288.

understanding of the judicial process."[104] Posner's point was that doing so would better equip students to be advocates who understand their audiences. But even Posner's focus on Realism's first strand, undertaken in the right way, could have a salutary effect if it were oriented against an understanding of what we, as a profession, expect from judges, even if we understand that they cannot always deliver. Put differently, we need not resign ourselves to cynicism and can offer an aspirational vision of the role even as we understand that judges are constantly subject to forces pulling away from it.

Some work of this sort is already underway. Many law schools have started to emphasize professional formation as part of the curriculum, including work devoted to the development of practical wisdom.[105] Because wisdom depends on experience, it would be too much to expect law schools to graduate students fully capable of exercising practical wisdom, but they can certainly plant the seeds.[106] This work can be enhanced by including consideration of its implications for the judicial role. A recent line of research conducted by Professor Heidi Levitt and Bridget Dunnavant approaches the topic of judicial wisdom by drawing on the insights of a group of judges assembled via a national effort to identify, via nomination, those who exemplify wisdom,[107] and using those insights to develop ways in which wisdom can be cultivated via education and professionalization. Their conclusions – that lawyers should be trained to avoid viewing the world through a lens of "good versus evil," that they understand that the conditions of judicial service can work against the making of wise decisions, and that judges must bring a fundamental humility and open-mindedness to the endeavor – resonate broadly with the ideas developed earlier.

It's important to remember as well that the exercise of good judgment does not simply refer to the portion of the process that takes place when the rules and other authority run out. It also concerns working with that authority, and doing so in a way that extracts as much law from it as is there to be extracted. Much of this involves working with methodologies, which, to return to Professor Ballantyne's approach to this type of task, entail resorting to principles. Maximizing the value of principles involves embedding them in habit. Put in terms of cognitive science and the material covered in Chapter 3, the goal is to have our intuitive judgments withing System 1 incorporate more reliable rules of thumb. Ballantyne puts it this way: "System 1 underwrites the good character needed to reliably follow rules and System

[104] Richard A. Posner, 'Judicial Opinions and Appellate Advocacy in Federal Courts–One Judge's Views,' (2013) 51 *Duquesne Law Review* 3, 25–36.

[105] Neil W. Hamilton and Louis D. Bilionis, *Law Student Professional Development and Formation: Bridging Law School, Student, and Employer Goals* (Cambridge: Cambridge University Press, 2022).

[106] See, for example, Deborah J. Cantrell and Kenneth Sharpe, 'Practicing Practical Wisdom,' (2016) 67 *Mercer Law Review* 331; Daisy Hurst Floyd, 'Practical Wisdom: Reimagining Legal Education,' (2012) 10 *University of St. Thomas Law Journal* 195.

[107] Dunnavant and Levitt, 'Development of Wisdom'; Heidi M. Levitt and Bridget R. Dunnavant, 'Judicial Wisdom: The Process of Constructing Wise Decisions,' (2015) *Journal of Constructivist Psychology*, http://doi.org/10.1080/10720537.2014.928810.

2 underwrites the practice needed to form such a character. Practice demands consciously reflecting on the rule, but the well-tempered reasoner will follow the rule without being mindful of it."[108] As this suggests, "following principles calls for a type of character."[109] The process is akin to professional acculturation or the development of situation sense: conscious reflection on legal rules, coupled with practice in applying those rules, leads to an internalization of those rules in a way analogous to how speakers of a language internalize its rules of grammar. Having internalized them, those rules become something we incorporate into our intuitive judgments, which might then be better characterized as "quasirational."[110] Law schools must remain mindful of this.

Education might also work to illustrate in a more concrete way what this version of a good judge looks like. One way to do that is to offer examples. The punch line here may be that the kinds of judges who most exhibit desirable judicial character are not the sorts of judges who make a name for themselves. They will tend not to be flashy or inclined toward self-promotion in either their opinion-writing or their extrajudicial activities. Still, we can see some of the characteristics in judges who are acknowledged to have been great. Consider, for example, Justice David Souter's description of Judge Learned Hand's approach: "suspicion of easy cases, skepticism about clear-edged categories, modesty in the face of precedent, candor in pitting one worthy principle against another, and the nerve to do it in concrete circumstances on an open page." Or Judge Michael Boudin's description of Judge Henry Friendly's: "the predicate mastery of precedent and record; a care alike for doctrine and for equity and for social need; the reasoned and candid explanation of the result; and an awareness always of the comparative competencies and limits of judges." Or, for a less-famous example, my own description of Judge Jane Roth, for whom I was a law clerk, and who is among the judges included in the group of wise judges assembled by Dunnavant and Levitt: "As a jurist she was not an originalist, or a textualist, or a subscriber to any other sort of -ism. She had been a lawyer, and she became a judge, in the fullest and best sense of the word." These are not the intellectual habits of technocrats, and they are not descriptions of judges so insecure (or disingenuous) in the exercise of their authority that they feel compelled to press it through the quasi-algorithms of foundationalist methodologies. They depict instead *judges*, in the deepest sense, exercising *judgment*.

Friendly provides a useful example. He served as a judge on the United States Court of Appeals for nearly twenty-seven years, and undoubtedly stands among the most revered judges of the twentieth century. Yet the basis for his fame remains, at least when viewed in light of what makes for judicial fame today, somewhat obscure.

108 Ballantyne, 'Knowing Our Limits', 71.
109 Id., 85.
110 Kenneth R. Hammon, 'Intuition, No! … Quasirationality, Yes!,' (2010) 21 *Psychological Inquiry* 327.

As Professor Adrian Vermeule put it, "it is actually a bit difficult to say what Friendly stood for, or what ideas of general and lasting significance he contributed to law and legal theory."[111] He neither advocated nor adhered to any grand theories of interpretation and was not drawn to theorizing. He instead regarded himself as a craftsman, and his reputation stems from the understanding of those who saw him at work that he was extraordinarily good at his craft.[112]

Much of Friendly's biography is consistent with this book's themes. He spent over three decades in practice doing a variety of work. His primary client was Pan American Airways, for whom he performed both contractual and administrative law work and, eventually, served as general counsel. But his practice covered other areas as well, including a high-profile estate dispute, bankruptcy matters, and government relations. He was deeply involved in bar association work. His personal habits echo Souter's – including a lack of concern with honors and appearance, an innate modesty, and the tendency to eat the same lunch every day – in Friendly's case, "a glass of College Inn tomato juice, cottage cheese, a slice of pumpernickel, and herring from a jar."[113] Although he was gruff and demanding, he was by all accounts interested in and receptive to changing his mind in light of the contrasting viewpoints of his colleagues and clerks.

Friendly was at root a pragmatist. Posner characterized him as a judge who "tempered academic brilliance with massive common sense."[114] "He saw cases not as intellectual puzzles to be solved but as practical disputes to be resolved sensibly and humanely."[115] In the words of his biographer David Dorsen, Friendly "had no agenda," "was not doctrinaire," and "was not attempting to construct a new theoretical framework."[116] "[P]art of his brilliance was recognizing that there were no easy answers to the problems that confronted him." His lack of concern with style extended to his opinions. As his former clerk, Judge Pierre Leval, put it, Friendly was "[n]ot a quotable judge" or "a maker of aphorisms." Leval opined that a reader of the entire corpus of Friendly's opinions would not "find an instance of a rhetorical device used to make an issue seem simpler, or a solution more satisfactory, than in fact it was." Friendly was not engaged in "three-card monte. His efforts to persuade were by painstaking analysis, even when it taxed the limits of the reader's endurance."[117] It was not a recipe for enduring fame or influence, but by most accounts, it did amount to a great judge. And it, rather than (or at least in addition to)

111 Adrian Vermeule, Local Wisdom, *The New Republic*, March 21, 2012, available at newrepublic.com/article/98607/henry-friendly-supreme-court-david-dorsen.

112 David M. Dorsen, *Henry Friendly: Greatest Judge of His Era* (Cambridge: Harvard University Press, 2012) 55–56.

113 Dorsen, 'Henry Friendly', 100.

114 Richard A. Posner, Foreword, in Dorsen, 'Henry Friendly', xiii.

115 Id.

116 Dorsen, 'Henry Friendly', 347.

117 Pierre N. Leval, 'Judicial Opinions as Literature,' in Peter Brooks and Paul Gewirtz, eds., *Law's Stories* (New Haven: Yale University Press, 1996) 206.

the work of the ambitious and rhetorically gifted, can serve as a useful and important model for those being socialized into the profession.

My point ultimately is not to hold Friendly or any other specific judge up as an ideal, but rather simply to suggest that there is considerable room in legal education to highlight and explore conceptions of the judicial ideal that seek to convey a richer and deeper account than can be provided via a decontextualized focus on interpretive theories or depictions of judges as either fully constrained or completely unconstrained. Ideals matter, theory matters, institutional context matters, realism matters, and character matters.

The third avenue for change involves judicial audiences. The available evidence, though not extensive, supports the conclusion that the public continues to want judges who play the triadic role – that is, it prefers judges with strong professional qualifications rather than judges who will decide cases in accordance with their preferred ideology.[118] Yet, as seems often to be the case with elected representatives, there is considerable signal loss that occurs along the way. The public as an audience exerts comparatively little force. As we saw in Chapter 5, judicial selection mechanisms increasingly focus on ideology or its correlates. This suggests that it is the intermediary between the public's preferences and the judiciary's personnel – the bar – that most needs to be addressed.

Re-orienting or reinvigorating norms within the profession provides a promising path to change. As already noted, with very few exceptions, one does not become a judge without having first been a lawyer. Internalizing its norms helps facilitate success within the profession, which in turn helps pave the path to becoming a judge. Making character a core value would send a powerful signal about the importance of the desired characteristics in fulfilling one's duties to clients, courts, and the justice system more generally. In addition, most of the significant players in judicial selection tend as well to be members of the bar, and their conception of ideal judicial characteristics accordingly influences the identity of those selected. If the bar cultivates a strong emphasis on character traits such as integrity, ethical conduct, intellectual humility, and practical wisdom, it increases the likelihood that those elevated to the bench will embody these traits. And, of course, the bar is among the most salient of judges' professional audiences. Formal and informal recognition of those who best embody the desired characteristics, and critique of those who do not, can help to build and sustain the appropriate culture.

As Professor Katharina Stevens points out, there is a community-based aspect to the virtue of humility.[119] In Stevens's conception, "humble judges think of themselves … as servants of their institutional role rather than individuals with the power

[118] Herbert M. Kritzer, *Judicial Selection in the States: Politics and Struggle for Reform* (Cambridge: Cambridge University Press, 2020).

[119] Stevens, 'Humility as a Necessary Virtue', 451–53, 457–59.

to realize their ambitions."[120] In a community that values such an approach, those who lack the requisite humility will find it more difficult to become judges, and may not even want the role. But if they become judges, social forces will push them toward making the same sorts of decisions as their humble colleagues, thus shielding parties and the public "from the non-humble judge's personal power and personal untethered-ness from the law."[121] As I have argued earlier, no connection to virtue ethics is necessary to make this dynamic desirable.

It is easy to say that the profession should embrace a character-based vision of the judicial role. To realize that vision is another matter entirely in a world in which social and political forces pull strongly in the other direction. And there is an inherent tension in the endeavor in that it envisions using acculturation and the power of audiences to produce judges who are comparatively insensitive to the power of audiences, at least in the sense that they do not seek to nurture reputations or celebrity status. It is, no doubt, a tall order. On the other hand, the Federalist Society's success in shifting the nature of the conversation undoubtedly seemed an unlikely result at the outset as well. That change may happen slowly and not to the degree that we might like does not mean striving for it is not worthwhile. There is value in pointing out the fundamental problems and amplifying the view that character matters. And if law schools continue to reinforce these messages in their professional formation work, that, too, will contribute over time to changing the perspective of the larger professional community.

I have already touched on the final mechanism, which is judicial selection. As discussed in Chapter 5, there are strong cases for changing the ways in which judges are selected, but others have already done much of that work. For present purposes, little elaboration is required, because selection procedures would work in tandem with the other three mechanisms for change, especially changes in legal education and legal culture. If the bar shares a sense of the desirable characteristics in judges, then it becomes considerably more likely that people who exemplify those characteristics will be the people selected to be judges even without changes to the mechanisms themselves. Law's dark matter will exert its gravitational pull, and the system's functioning will adjust accordingly.

[120] Id., 457.
[121] Id., 458.

Conclusion

Ours is a world in which the judiciary's legitimacy is under threat.[1] Public confidence in the US Supreme Court has hit historic lows.[2] Something similar holds with respect to the public's perception of state courts.[3] Just over half of respondents in a recent poll said they believe the justices of the Supreme Court decide cases based on their political opinions rather than the law.[4] Little of this is surprising. Media coverage of the output of courts tends to resort to descriptions and explanations that center on ideology rather than doctrine. Partisan commentators cheer or deride decisions based on their short-term political implications rather than any longer-term consideration of their merits. A former president openly accuses jurists who do not rule in his favor of being biased. For politically charged cases, at least, much of the public regards judges as simply another type of political actor.

Troubling though all this may be, these perceptions are not entirely divorced from reality. We have traditionally relied on process to play a substantial role in channeling judicial behavior toward some rough approximation of the standard

1 "Legitimacy," like many of the other concepts explored in this book, is of course something that is multifaceted and contested. For example, Professor Richard Fallon identifies three relevant categories of legitimacy: sociological, moral, and legal. Richard H. Fallon Jr., *Law and Legitimacy in the Supreme Court* (Cambridge: Harvard University Press, 2018). Although my invocation of the term is somewhat informal, what I have in mind is something akin to sociological legitimacy as Fallon conceives of it – how do those outside the legal system regard the courts? Professor Tara Groves' review of Fallon's book catalogs a wide range of instances in which observers have called the Supreme Court's legitimacy into question. Tara Leigh Grove, 'The Supreme Court's Legitimacy Dilemma,' (2019) 132 *Harvard Law Review* 2240.

2 Katy Lin and Carroll Doherty, 'Favorable views of Supreme Court fall to historic low,' *Pew Research Center*, July 21, 2023, available at www.pewresearch.org/short-reads/2023/07/21/favorable-views-of-supreme-court-fall-to-historic-low/; Jeffrey M. Jones, 'Confidence in U.S. Supreme Court Sinks to Historic Low,' *Gallup*, June 23, 2022, available at news.gallup.com/poll/394103/confidence-supreme-court-sinks-historic-low.aspx.

3 National Center for State Courts, 'State of the State Courts: 2022 Poll,' available at www.ncsc.org/__data/assets/pdf_file/0019/85204/SSC_2022_Presentation.pdf.

4 Gary Langer, 'More say politics, not the law, drive Supreme Court decisions: POLL,' *ABC News*, May 9, 2023, available at https://abcnews.go.com/Politics/politics-law-drive-supreme-court-decisions-poll/story?id=99168846.

model's ideal, and in fostering the appropriate accompanying image. But the forces, internal and external, hard and soft, that have historically served to discipline judicial behavior have weakened. Judges' increased delegation of work has diminished internal sources of constraint such as the adversarial process and the expectation that significant decisions will be justified in writing. Judicial selection, in both elective and appointive systems, features greater emphasis on ideology over professional qualification. Both society and the legal profession have become politically polarized such that judges' salient audiences – the groups whose expectations they consciously or unconsciously strive to meet – increasingly consist primarily of the like-minded. Over roughly the same period, our society has become metrics-obsessed, which has facilitated the rise of empirical research into the judiciary that characterizes courts' work as ideologically driven. It has also been conducive to the flourishing of proposed methodological fixes whose algorithmic packaging reflects, if it was not to some more significant degree a product of, these broader intellectual trends. In its theoretical manifestations, that work recognizes the need for nuance and judgment. In its practical application, it often appears to serve as a fig leaf for decisions no less susceptible to motivated reasoning than under the pluralism that preceded them. Indeterminacy (more properly, underdeterminacy) is ineliminable, and professed adherents to textualist and originalist methodologies turn out to be inconsistent in their loyalties when those methods lead down an inhospitable path. What works in theory does not always translate well to practice. Even if those methodologies work well as ideals, they prove to be yet additional examples of unrealizable ideals.

An ideal's being unrealizable of course does not mean it is not worth striving for. But there remain substantial objections to the theory supporting the ideal itself. These methodologies encourage an atomized approach – a "clause-bound" approach to interpretation[5] – that in its focus on trees is apt to lose sight of the forest, and to substitute the realization of a theory meant to be a mechanism for achieving the larger goals of the system for achievement of the goals themselves. More broadly, the nature of the legal system is such that, at least in its best manifestations, practical wisdom must play a role. To follow a recipe that purports to render decision-making mechanical is to deny that there will always be an ineliminable role for judgment. It is further to deny that there is inarticulable knowledge that at least some people acquire over the course of a career, and that can make the necessary application of judgment more effective. None of this is to deny a role for methodological guideposts, but simply to deny the appropriateness of excessive rigidity in following them. (I note again: sophisticated advocates of these methodologies understand this. But the nuanced version of these methodologies are not the ones that get play at the retail level.)

5 John Hart Ely, *Democracy and Distrust: A Theory of Judicial Review* (Cambridge: Harvard University Press, 1980).

As Chapter 1 demonstrated, these problems have always been with us. Disagreement is a persistent feature of any legal system. The limits of language and our collective desire to further values that often conflict in the context of a given dispute ensure that it cannot be otherwise. The scope of the matters about which we disagree will ebb and flow over the course of time and in relation to the scope of dissensus in society more generally. The judiciary's role is to provide an appropriately detached forum for the resolution of these disputes in at least some of the forms in which they arise. And a large part of being that sort of forum is simply appearing to be that sort of forum. As it is often phrased, "justice must satisfy the appearance of justice."[6]

That appearance, and, as I have suggested, the reality beneath it, is threatened. Whether the public, or even the bar, correctly grasps the particulars, there is a sense in which the judiciary is troubled, threatened, and perhaps on the cusp of a crisis of legitimacy. Certainly, the trends are not going in the right direction. To be sure, the specific dimensions of the connection between perception and reality remain somewhat conjectural. It is impossible to point to quantifiable or otherwise tangible evidence establishing that today's judges do in fact act in a less-constrained fashion, or perceive themselves as less constrained, than their predecessors did. I cannot, in other words, point to a statistical analysis of a dataset establishing that today's courts would resolve a given set of cases in some way that is quantifiably distinct from their predecessors of a generation or two ago, or vice versa. There are too many variables to account for to be able to provide the sort of large-scale, empirical evidence that our metrics-oriented society has come to expect. Indeed, another of this book's themes is that any such analysis would inevitably exclude critical but nonquantifiable information from consideration. Much of what is valuable concerns cognitive processes that are likely to be, at best, only loosely correlated with the judicial process's measurable and countable outputs.

And yet it does not seem irresponsible to conclude that not only are judges less constrained by institutional factors and by settled understandings of how to "do law" but also that their behavior, almost inevitably, reflects the resulting freedom. This freedom not only creates more space for the operation of improper factors such as ideology and bias but also facilitates expansion of the range of contested argumentation and the narrowing of the categories of arguments that are, by consensus, both in- and out-of-bounds.

Against this backdrop it is important to remember that courts exist to serve social purposes. Those purposes are contingent on social need, and they will vary both across and within judicial systems. Yet whatever the full range of social functions courts might now serve, their original and still central purpose is to provide a forum for the peaceful resolution of disputes. Two parties, unable to resolve a dispute on their own, turn to a third, thereby engaging the logic of Shapiro's triad. The third party's ability to provide a satisfactory resolution depends on the disputants' perceiving

6 *In re Murchison*, 349 US 133, 136 (1955), citing *Offutt* v. *United States*, 348 US 11, 14 (1948).

them as a truly disinterested third – depends, in Shapiro's phrasing, on preventing the triad from breaking down into two-against-one, and on doing so until as late in the process as possible. Those who find themselves as losers must, in general, nonetheless accept the legitimacy of the results the system generates. If potential litigants do not think the judicial system likely to provide what they seek, they will look elsewhere.

The alternatives they seek can take a variety of forms. They might resort to non-judicial decision-makers, including private dispute resolution mechanisms. These often incorporate triadic features, but they can also bring their own pathologies. Systematic inequities in bargaining power can result in a situation in which parties with greater resources are able to resort to private mechanisms that benefit their interests. For example, the inclusion of mandatory arbitration provisions in employment contracts may enable employers to prevent employees from making use of otherwise-available rights.[7] Other alternatives are even less palatable. Some disputes may not be pursued at all, based on a perception that the nature of the system makes it unlikely that claims will be resolved in a satisfactory manner.[8] In other words, some rights will effectively go unvindicated. In extreme cases, those who feel themselves unable to get an appropriate resolution through the courts will take matters into their own hands, and a sufficiently widespread sense that the judicial system is "rigged" could contribute to revolution in some more- or less-dramatic form.

There are no magic, one-size-fits-all solutions to these problems. To refer in some general sense to "judges" is to elide a vast variety of actors. Different courts have different functions, and they have different resources both in terms of law clerks and other forms of institutional support and the quality of the advocacy that provides them with the raw materials of disputes. Judges share the same basic legal training but bring a range of different types of experience and expertise to the role. They differ as well in characteristics such as diligence, motivation, and intellectual horsepower. Theories of judging often fail to account for these differences and tend to be more a reflection of the capacities and worldview of the theorists than an attempt to account for the limitations or capabilities of those who would put the theories to work.[9]

Any remedy will be partial, and some will be more appropriate to some parts of the judiciary than will others. Past commentators have advocated in favor of changes

[7] Jean R. Sternlight, 'Disarming Employees: How American Employers Are Using Mandatory Arbitration to Deprive Workers of Legal Protection,' (2015) 80 *Brooklyn Law Review* 1309, 1310.

[8] The notion that parties' incentives to pursue claims are shaped by the perceived likelihood of success and the magnitude of anticipated recovery is uncontroversial. For example, Stephen Daniels & Joanne Martin, '"It is no longer viable from a practical and business standpoint": Damage Caps, "hidden victims", and the Declining Interest in Medical Malpractice Cases,' (2010) 17 *International Journal of the Legal Profession* 59.

[9] Judge Richard Posner's prescriptions for judging, for example, seem in some respect to reflect his inability to perceive the extent to which other judges lack his prodigious ability to absorb and process information. Chad M. Oldfather, 'Limitations (A Response to Judge Posner),' (2013) 51 *Duquesne Law Review* 67.

targeted toward some of the developments noted earlier. Many, for example, have called for an expansion in the size of the judiciary to enable judges to be able to spend more time on each case.[10] Others maintain that judges should write their own opinions.[11] Still others contend that judges on courts of last resort should serve only a single, relatively lengthy term.[12] Each of these suggestions contains more than a kernel of merit. And each addresses one aspect of a complex and developing problem.

As I hope to have established, a renewed emphasis on norms and character is also appropriate. If rules alone aren't enough, and if institutional and procedural constraints have weakened, then it becomes even more important to identify judges who we can trust to administer and develop the law in an appropriate way. To suggest that, I recognize, is to swim up the intellectual stream. An emphasis on finding judges with good judgment, who are practically wise and intellectually humble, strikes the modern ear as too diffuse. However appealing the ideas may be in the abstract, they are impossible to pin down, invisible to metrics and thus to the sorts of large-scale empirical study craved by residents of the current historical moment. Nor do they lead to concrete implications for judges confronting individual cases. They are not signposts marking out an established, easy-to-follow path, but instead offering the general injunction to proceed with caution. This may be uncomfortable, but it is not new. As Holmes observed in *The Path of the Law*: "The language of judicial decision is mainly the language of logic. And the logical method and form flatter that longing for certainty and for repose which is in every human mind. But certainty generally is illusion, and repose is not the destiny of man."[13] The prescriptions are negative in nature: Do not be so sure of yourself.

This, too, is a partial solution. Judges are human, and even Homer nods. And it is a solution I have strived to offer in a manner consistent with the intellectual spirit of this book: with appropriate care and precision, and mindful of limitations and qualifications. Nonetheless, portions of the analysis are necessarily speculative. As I write, they make deep logical and intuitive sense to me. But I have lived long enough to appreciate that the "end of history" illusion – the tendency to believe that the conclusions we have reached at a given point in our lives will remain stable for the rest of our lives – is truly an illusion. At a fundamental level, then, my views are tentatively held and subject to revision, as I believe should be a core feature of all people's (but especially judges') beliefs. But I could, of course, be wrong.

[10] William M. Richman and William L. Reynolds, 'Elitism, Expediency and the New Certiorari: Requiem for the Learned Hand Tradition,' (1996) 81 *Cornell Law Review* 273.

[11] David MacGowan, 'Judicial Writing and the Ethics of the Judicial Office,' (2001) 14 *Georgetown Journal of Legal Ethics* 509.

[12] For example, Philip D. Oliver, 'Systematic Justice: A Proposed Constitutional Amendment to Establish Fixed, Staggered Terms for Members of the United States Supreme Court,' (1986) 47 *Ohio State Law Journal* 799.

[13] Oliver Wendell Holmes, Jr., 'The Path of the Law,' (1897) 10 *Harvard Law Review* 457, 466.

Index

For EU product safety concerns, contact us at Calle de José Abascal, 56–1°,
28003 Madrid, Spain or eugpsr@cambridge.org.

www.ingramcontent.com/pod-product-compliance
Lightning Source LLC
LaVergne TN
LVHW011813200926
848484LV00005B/1179

* 9 7 8 1 0 0 9 3 5 4 5 8 5 *